MEDITERRANEAN CRUISE

With The Cruise Addict's Wife

Deb Graham

MEDITERRANEAN CRUISE

With the Cruise Addict's Wife

Deb Graham

Copyright 2015 All Rights Reserved

Other Books By Deb Graham:

Tips From The Cruise Addict's Wife

Whether you are an experienced cruiser, or in the dreaming-about-it stage, you'll enjoy ***Tips From The Cruise Addict's Wife****. Besides being crammed with more tips and hints than you'll find anywhere else, including how to save money, be the smartest passenger on any ship, and plan a great vacation, this acclaimed book is loaded with tips and stories that will have you laughing aloud.*

How To Write Your Story record your personal history in 30 minutes a day

. No one can tell your life's story as clearly or as accurately as you can! Now's the time, before it's too late. In only thirty short minutes a day, you can begin to tell your own personal history, drawn from your own memories, using these easy prompts.

How To Complain...and get what you deserve

A customer's guide to complaining effectively in this day and age when customers feel like the low man on the totem pole.

Kid Food On A Stick

From breakfast to midnight snack, kids love food on a stick. This book contains recipes easy enough for a child, yet fancy enough for a party, all on a stick!

Quick and Clever Kids' Crafts

Loaded with easy, classy crafts for children and adults. A must for parents, teachers, scout leaders and anyone else who'd rather see a creative child than a bored one

Awesome Science Experiments for Kids

Simple, oh-wow! science experiments; a fun teaching tool for adults to share with kids, one on one or in group settings

Savory Mug Cooking

Easy-yet-impressive lunch recipes made with fresh ingredients, cooked right in your favorite mug! Expensive Take Out lunches—not anymore!

Uncommon Household Tips

Use ordinary items in extraordinary ways! Dozens of new uses for twenty ordinary household items you don't think twice about. From using golf tees to hang your hammer to dental floss for scrapbooking, you'll be inspired to look around the house before you run back to the store.

Contents
MEDITERRANEAN CRUISE 1
Deb Graham 1
MEDITERRANEAN CRUISE 2
Deb Graham 2
Why Cruise Europe? 13
   The Cruise Addict 14
Part One, Two, and Three 17
   I'm Not Telling About… 18
   Packing Considerations 19
PART ONE: 21
   Seemingly Endless Planning 21
   Who Are We? 22
   Getting There 24
   Concerns 26
   Cell Phones, Electronics, and Electricity 29
   All Charged Up 31
   Currency Conversion 32
   Planning the Flights 33
   To See and Not to See 34
   Planning Time in Port 37
   Who's Going Where? 41
   Historic Zones 43
   What If We Miss The Ship? 44

    Decide, Already! 45
    Cruise Lines and Itineraries 46
    So, Where Are We Going? 47
    Consider Itineraries 50
    The Itinerary: 52
Planning Details 55
    Cabin Decisions 55
    A Travel Agent, or Book On Our Own? 55
    Shots and Medical Obstacles 58
    Petty Crime and Purses 64
    Restrooms and Language 67
    A Quest 68
    Gelato, a Quest of its Own 71
    To Avoid... 72
    Blending In 73
    Jet Lag 75
    Locals 76
    Meet and Greet 77
    Telling Time and Cameras 78
    Prepurchasing Entry Tickets 80
Planned Itinerary 81
    Sweden 81
    Venice 83
    Getting Around Venice 84
    Gondola Or Not? 87
    Hotel in Venice 89

Sites to See in Venice 90
　　Athens, Greece 94
　　Kusadasi, Turkey 95
　　Istanbul, Turkey 98
　　Mykonos, Greece 103
　　Naples, Italy 104
　　Rome, Italy 106
　　Florence and Pisa, Italy 107
　　Toulon, France 107
　　Barcelona, Spain 108
PART TWO 112
　　The Planning is Over: The Trip Begins! 112
　　Water 112
　　Restrooms 115
　　On Our Way! 118
　　A Product Plug 121
　　Long Flight, Made Longer 122
　　Unexpected Hurricane 124
Stockholm, Sweden 129
　　First Impressions 129
　　Where's Dinner? 132
　　A Palace 134
　　A Warship 139
　　On Our Way To Venice 142
Venice, Italy 144
　　Cisterns 146

San Gallo Hotel	147
Bring On Venice	149
Gondolas	151
Dinner	153
Venice at Night	155
Venice in the Morning	156
San Marco	159
Rialto Bridge	161
On to the Museums!	162
To the Ship	167
Checking In—and a big surprise	168
First Impressions of the Spirit	172
The Norwegian Spirit	175
Behind the Scenes Ship Tour	182
Provisions	182
A Shopping List	187
Food Prep	189
Water	192
Crew Only Areas and Theatre	193
Laundry	194
Day One: On Board	196
Meet and Greet	196
Lucky Friends	198
Dinner For Twelve	199
Day Two: Sea Day	201
Day Three: Athens, Greece	204

The Tour Begins	204
Acropolis	205
Temple of Zeus and Mars Hill	209
Changing of the Guard	210
Authentic Greek Food	213
Agora	215
Marathon and Stadium	216
Acropolis Museum	217
Successful Tour	219
Wrap Up The Day	220
Day Four: Kusadasi, Turkey	**222**
Ephesus and the Terrace Houses	222
Turkish Rugs	228
Wrap Up The Day	232
Day Five: Istanbul, Turkey	**237**
Meeting the Tour	237
Ancient Hippodrome	238
The Blue Mosque	241
Basilica Cistern	243
Topkapi Palace	244
The Grand Bazaar	246
Wrap Up The Day	249
Day Six: Mykonos, Greece	**251**
Tender Tickets	252
A Greek Philosopher	255
Where Pirates Walked	258

Wrap Up the Day	260
Day Seven: Sea Day	262
Day Eight: Naples, Italy	266
To the Tour	266
Pompeii	269
Ancient Toilets	272
Herculaneum	275
Pizza	279
Archaeological Museum	280
Wrap Up the Day	281
Day Nine: Rome, Italy	284
Saint Paul's Basilica	286
Seven Hills of Rome	287
Coliseum or Colosseo	288
Back on the Road	290
The Pantheon	292
Spanish Steps	294
The Vatican	295
Vatican Museum	296
The Sistine Chapel	298
Wrap Up The Day	299
Day Ten: Florence/ Pisa, Italy	302
First Impressions	302
Pisa and the Leaning Tower	304
Overlooking Florence	306
Angels of the Mud	307

    Santa Croce Basilica 308

    The Duomo 311

    Tuscany Awaits 312

    Wrap Up the Day 314

Day Eleven: Toulon, France 316

    Le Petit Train 317

    Maritime Museum 319

    A French Éclair! 321

    Wrap Up the Day 323

Day 12, Disembarkation Day: Barcelona, Spain 325

    Hop On Hop Off 326

    Los Ramblas 327

    Is It Time To Panic Yet? 331

    Leaving Barcelona, Heading Home? 333

    Copenhagen, at High Speed 334

    Oh, Not the South Koreans! 336

    Only One Flight Per Day 337

    Icelandic Perspective 340

What We Learned 344

    …and might have done differently: Some Final Thoughts on a Marvelous Journey 344

    The Amazing Race 349

PART THREE 352

    Potential Cruise Itineraries: 352

    Shore Excursions Versus Private Tours 354

        Websites and Comparisons 354

Advantages of Private Tours 356
Disadvantages of Private Tours 360
Criteria in Choosing Tours: 361
Comparing Tours: 363
Shore excursions 366
Tours Research 374
The Debate about Travel Insurance: 380

Why Cruise Europe?

Husband and I always thought we might go to Europe, eventually, and probably on a cruise. A cruise is the best, least expensive, and easiest way to see a lot of ports in one trip. However, it was not in our short-term plans. Maybe after we retire in another few years. For now, we were content to cruise around North America, more or less. It's always been a dream of ours; this cruise just came on earlier than we expected.

Brett had always dreamed of going to Europe. He and Melissa, his wife, had sailed to the southern Caribbean with us several years ago, and we had a great trip. They are good people, and fun traveling companions. When they began thinking seriously about Europe, they naturally included us. Before long, word had spread. By the time we sailed, our group had grown to a dozen of us, ranging in age from 17 to 69, including one very last minute addition --- the week before sailing! Age wise, The Cruise Addict and I fall somewhere in the middle. Okay, more towards the upper middle.

I am always up for traveling anywhere, especially if it involves a passport. I'm happy traveling by ourselves, but for something as big and life-changing as going to Europe for the very first time, going with our friends just sounds a little safer. And I think it'll be more fun. If nothing else, it's always good to have a witness, someone to back up our story! I, frankly, don't believe half of our travel stories, and I was *there* at the time.

The Cruise Addict

If you have read my book, ***Tips From The Cruise Addict's Wife***, you already know that I'm married to a guy with ...well, let's politely call it a cruise obsession, because that is what it is, and you can't go wrong starting a book with honesty.

Some years ago I created a monster; inadvertently, of course. Our 20th wedding anniversary was coming up, and I wanted to really celebrate, to do something we had never done before. I knew I could never talk Husband into an African safari, or a month-long vacation in Peru. After all, I could not even talk him into going camping for our honeymoon all those years ago! Okay, we did get married in January, in the Rockies, so I guess he had a defense. *But still*-!

For this momentous anniversary, I wanted to do something romantic. I wanted an adventure, to go to a place we had never been before. As I considered this, a cruise to Alaska came to mind. We live halfway between Vancouver and Seattle, so it'd be an easy drive to either port. I dreamed about this cruise for months. I began leaving hints, and then I began leaving brochures of different cruise lines with gorgeous pictures of Alaska. The glaciers, the bears, the wildlife, the scenery! When the broad hints failed, I flat out told Husband, "I want to go to Alaska on a cruise for our 20th anniversary."

He promptly said "no way." He is usually an agreeable soul, but I had hit a nerve. While I was picturing romance, elegance, wonderful food on a beautiful ship with exciting ports of call to explore, with beautiful scenery, open seas, time to really celebrate and step off the world, Husband was envisioning being stuck on a smelly, stinky, overcrowded boat, bored crazy for days on end, trapped with annoying strangers. The discussion went on for several weeks. And it felt pretty fruitless, from my point of view.

Then one day, Husband complained to his buddy that his wife, that's me, had a ridiculous idea. He started to say, "My wife wants to go on a cruise for our upcoming anniversary--" Before he could finish his sentence with "-- but I don't want to go--" his buddy turned to his wife, who reached for the phone, and the plan was in motion, that fast.

Turns out friend's wife had an uncle who was a VP of Holland America cruise line, and he had been encouraging them to go on a cruise for some time. Uncle was delighted to offer a steep discount and even threw in a shore excursion. There we were; the four of us suddenly had tickets to go on the cruise of a lifetime, a romantic, wonderful vacation. And Husband was stunned, hung by his own complaining, so to speak.

To his credit, Husband fought valiantly. *He did not want to go on a cruise.* Even as we drove to the port, he complained nonstop. It was a two hour drive, and I'm telling you, he barely stopped to draw breath. He complained mightily, using words like 'kidnapped,' 'railroaded,' and 'shanghaied,' as he dug his heels in verbally. But Husband loves me, and he was frankly outnumbered. He reluctantly boarded the ship, and within a matter of hours he had a new name; The Cruise Addict.

Husband happily settled in the very front of the ship with the floor-to-ceiling windows with his high-powered binoculars, enthralled by the ever-changing scenery. Fueled by diet 7-Up and warm bar food delivered by uniformed waiters, he morphed into a molten puddle of relaxation. Obsession was not far behind. He is on every cruise line's mailing list, has our travel agent on speed dial, and he has become the Go To Guy for finding great deals for friends and family members.

I had no idea that I had created a monster until I noticed Husband started most days by asking, "Can we book a cruise today? If I find a good deal, *then* can we?"

We have cruised all over North America, but this book is about Europe. I've written it in three parts; planning and anticipation, the actual trip (as if you were right there with us!) and the follow up with websites so you can plan your own marvelous Mediterranean cruise!

All the information you could ever want on a ship is available online, or in the cruise line's brochures...stats, weights, where the ship was built, all those dry facts and figures. When we began dreaming about taking on the Mediterranean, my mind leaped right past all that. What I *really* wanted to know was how real people actually did the cruise planning. I wanted to know where did they go, and what did they do, and what did they like, what did they wish that they had done differently? What did they learn along the way, what did they enjoy the most, what do they wish they had not wasted time on?

What I really wanted was to have a conversation with a whole bunch of people. That's it, I wanted a think tank of other cruisers, and I couldn't find one. I studied tour books and cruise books and multiple websites, I read hundreds of reviews, I learned about each city, and each port. And I feel like we were very well prepared. I felt like I had a good idea of what we're getting into, but I pretty much did all the work myself, with a lot of help from The Cruise Addict.

Right in your hands, I'm saving you hours of legwork!. Part travel guide, part story, come along on this journey, our first to Europe!

Part One, Two, and Three

This book is divided into three sections. **Part One** is all the pre-cruise planning, tour comparisons, decisions on which cruise line and itinerary to take, expectations, hopes and dreams, from the comfort of my nice familiar American home.

Part Two was written on the journey, day by day. It includes the actual trip, starting at our home airport, flying across the pond, each hotel, each port, every tour, the ship itself, what I learned, and what I wished we had done differently. In other words, you'll get to see the cruise through my eyes. I'll describe my impressions of each city, the places we explored, the tours we took, the history we experienced. I'll give a good overview of the ship, including a behind-the-scenes tour. All along the way, I learned tidbits and tricks that will make your planning smoother than ours, and give you a point of reference, should you follow in my footsteps. Ah, footsteps—I developed a warm spot in my heart for footsteps on this cruise!

I'll include helpful websites in the back, in **Part Three**. If you are planning to take this same ---or a similar one –cruise, you'll be way ahead. If you just enjoy reading and dreaming about cruises, here you go. Read on. I think you're going to enjoy it!

Bottom line: Would I go again on a Mediterranean cruise, such as this? In a heartbeat!

I have a terrible fear of missing something. How awful would it be to come home and learn about that great and wonderful thing *right there* and I didn't get to see it because I wasn't prepared or planning ahead? Especially on a trip this size, over 16,000 miles from home, round trip, I want to hit the highlights, the things that are important to see. Meeting locals and tasting local food is also important. All told, I wanted to see and do as much as we possibly could. We succeeded in spectacular fashion, and that's what this book is about.

I'm Not Telling About...

You will find that I do not describe a lot of things that other people might partake of on a cruise. For example, I think a spa day on a cruise ship is a wasted day. I could get a massage at home. I would not, but I *could*. Spa days do not agree with me. The last time I had a massage, I raised a bruise the size of a turkey platter on my hip. I had a hot rock treatment that ached for 2 days. A "sample" exfoliation on my arm left that area feeling sand blasted; I prefer to keep all layers of skin in place and intact. I tried a wonderful eye serum that made my skin so tight, I think I sprained an eyebrow. For other people, the spa is the main point of going on a cruise. They should write their own book. You may tell them so.

I don't describe the food on the ship, because we all know food preferences vary. The menu would likely be different anyway, by the time you book your own cruise, so don't get your hopes up. Really, do you care what somebody else ate, anyway? However, if you care about food, or how a ship runs, you're going to enjoy the detailed behind-the-scenes tour in Part Two.

We didn't spend a lot of time at the pool on the ship. I had things to do and places to explore. And I'm not going to be giving you a comparison of the bars on the ship, either. For one thing, I don't drink at home; why would I do that on the ship? And for another thing with this being my first trip to Europe, I darn well wanted to *remember* every bit of it. I'm not going to tell you about the casino – except to tell you we traveled with some *really* lucky people – or about some of the assorted amenities available on the ship. We had no children with us, so I have nothing to say about the kids' programs, except that the kids' pool looked like great fun.

Packing Considerations

I will not detail packing lists. There are some fine ones all over the internet, along with some so ludicrous you'd need a steamer trunk and two Sherpa to haul it all. My packing advice: figure out what you need for the day, and pack it. Add in a light wrap or jacket for cool evenings, and a wide-brimmed hat to protect your head from the sun. Remember that Europe is less casual than America. On the ship we chose, the dress code was Resort Casual, with a couple of very optional dressy nights. It's up to you how to plan for that. I did just fine with embellished cotton tops, capris, a reversible skirt, and linen slacks, with dressier tops for evenings. Husband wore collared shirts and khakis to dinner every night. He did pack a tie, but it spent the week in the suitcase, never to see the light of day.

I won't list my packing, beyond telling you that condensing was a challenge. At home, I often wear three to five shirts a day. I get bored, or a grandchild wipes his dinky nose on my shoulder, I get too warm, or need to add layers; like that. On this trip, to pack enough for nearly three weeks in one suitcase while being mindful of weight (and leaving space in case of shopping) was a serious trial!

 Because we will have to be hauling our luggage around through airports, with all the changes we're making, packing will require more thought than usual. I'm trying to make sure that everything I bring will have at least dual or triple duty. For example, I'm not going to bring any jeans because denim weighs way more than khaki or light cotton slacks or capris.   I will not bring anything warmer than an unlined nylon jacket; no bulk there.

I like wraps and scarves, so I will bring some and buy more. Those are perfect for blocking the sun, and protecting from aggressive air conditioning and wind gusts, plus they jazz up the most casual attire. They also are respectful for churches; if we go somewhere where I need to have my head covered, flip out my scarf and I'll look good. I will also bring some nice breezy shirts. I will expect the temperatures to be like home in August; hot, unless Summer's canceled. Sometimes in western Washington, calendar pages flip without delivering any summer weather at all! I need to remember to bring tops that are not too tight because I have to wear my money belt under it and I don't need to be bulging any more than I currently am.

Good walking shoes are critical. A lot of the areas we're going to be walking through are hundreds, even thousands, of years old. Add in cobblestones, ancient steps, and broken bricks... I don't want to wear wobbly shoes that invite a turned ankle. I will wear walking shoes with good soles; nonskid, cushy, and versatile. This is definitely not a time for heels or flip flops. I want to be free to explore, without blisters.

PART ONE:

Seemingly Endless Planning

My Husband and I like to cruise. We go on at least a few every year, since his cruise addiction began some years ago. I believe five is our record in one year. You know how the fireworks shows are on Independence Day? They shoot off a few glorious fireworks at a time, then they add more and more and then the finale is dozens of fireworks all going off at once! I hate that. I cannot appreciate them at that speed; they blur together. Too many cruises too close together leaves me asking "Now, which ship had the giraffe sculptures in the pool area? Which one had the delicious orange cookies? "

For us to be planning a new cruise isn't anything new. I live with The Cruise Addict, and it seems we've always got several in various planning stages. My friends tease me about my Gypsy Gene. I love to travel, and I can break a land speed record for packing. However, *I'm* open to traveling by any method; let's keep it straight here, I am not The Cruise Addict!

I have a file folder for each upcoming trip. Currently, there is one for a Caribbean cruise, and a summer beach house family reunion, and details on the Panama Canal trip next summer. In each upcoming folder, I put tickets, receipts, reservations, tour confirmations, car rentals, hotel details, maps, etc. This folder, labeled 'Mediterranean Cruise', feels different; bigger, a little daunting.

I added important data on sticky notes, as the weeks passed, with essential info such as "mosquito repellent for Venice" and "granola bars for plane." Husband teased me for having so many; mind you, he looks to me for information, but teases mercilessly anyway. Even I admit that perhaps 167 sticky notes could be weeded out. I narrowed it down to just 22 by the time we left. Husband would be grateful later when he asked "do we have any—" repeatedly on the ship, and I handed it to him. Well, maybe not *visibly* grateful.

We've been on a several dozen cruises, on quite a few different cruise lines. I have been to Canada, Mexico, and all fifty states, plus all over the Caribbean, multiple times. Alaska is my favorite place to cruise. I love the wild aspect, the not-quite-civilized atmosphere, the wild nature and untamed places. This is our first time to Europe, however. I suspect visiting cities in Europe that have been inhabited for 3000 years or longer will be a change!

I'll detail the tours and such that we considered in Part Three.

Who Are We?

Since you're reading this book as if you were with us, you should know our friends. There will be approximately 2300 people on the ship, including our group. Our group includes myself and Husband, plus ten friends. Todd and Julie are going with us. They are retired and they are a lot of fun. Julie, however, has mobility issues, including a brand-new knee. They are seasoned travelers, and have been to Europe several times. Todd is also a historian, and a story teller, and can pull interesting facts out of his head for any occasion. On cruises, they have taken ship shore excursions exclusively. Todd and Julie are easy-going people who don't really like to plan; they're content to rely on our research and happy to go wherever we decide.

Brett and Melissa have been our friends for years. Our kids are about the same age. We been really busy over the years, but our families have been remained good friends. Our interests are different; Melissa teaches dance, and daily runs miles and miles, on purpose, without even being chased. I'm more of an audience; a very good audience, I may point out. I'm appreciative, polite, and great at cheering people on, but I see no reason to run, unless being pursued by a bear. Or in Copenhagen, but let's not get ahead of the story. We traveled on a nine-day cruise to the Caribbean with Brett and Melissa several years ago, and we had a blast! You look at people differently when you travel on a cruise with them. In fact, I think catching the flu, and traveling with people, is the best way to get to really know them. When you're together for days on end, you just can't keep your façade up that long.

Brett and Melissa's youngest daughter is a freshman at the local college. She's also coming along with us on this cruise. It's Brett, Melissa, and Kim's first time on the European continent and we are excited to explore new places with them. Melissa is quite happy to go wherever she's put. Her philosophy is, "I've never seen it before. It's all new, and I'm happy to be here." She's a lot of fun to travel with. Brett and I get along very well, because we're both compulsive planners. Brett and I both have the same philosophy: "I may never get here again; I'd better see it all while I'm here." Wouldn't it be awful to realize that there was that wonderful thing *right there* and you missed it, just because you didn't do any research ahead of time?

Brett and Melissa's eldest daughter, Sarah, and her husband, Cue, are also coming with us on the cruise. We've known Sarah since she was four. We have only met Cue at their wedding; we're looking forward to getting to know him better. He seems pleasant, and has a wicked sense of humor. This is their first trip to Europe too; in fact they're going a few days early, with Kim, just to make sure they don't miss anything. It's Sarah and Cue's first anniversary that week. Somehow, the idea of a romantic anniversary in Paris, just the two of them, loses its appeal when I add the younger sister into the plan, but who asked me?

Husband happened to mention to a friend at work that we were going on this cruise months ago. Clint asked for some details; the name of the ship, the dates – he didn't really seem all that interested – yet an hour later he came back and announced that he and his wife, Mary, had just booked the cruise and they're going with us! I'm a big fan of spontaneity. It will be fun getting to know them, too.

Speaking of spontaneity, nine days before the cruise, Brett and Melissa suddenly added Cade to the trip. Cade is their son, early 20's, between semesters, an easy going sort. This last-minute addition made my stomach hurt, thinking of the logistics... the tours, last minute airfare, lodging, cabin space, and all. I quickly remembered "this is not my problem." They made it work, somehow, with a whole lot of phone calls!

Getting There

If we all get there. The way we're arriving is going to be pretty amazing! Kim, Sarah, and Cue are going to fly in a few days ahead of time. They're going to Paris and to Rome, and then they will take a train to Venice. Melissa, Brett, Todd, and Julie are going to have a day in Amsterdam before the cruise. Brett and Melissa wanted extra an day in Venice, so they'll make their way there the day before the ship sails. Cade's last minute flight plans put him on the same flights as Todd and Julie. The three of them will fly into Venice early on disembarkation day. Clint and Mary are going Paris for two days, then will fly directly to Venice, the night before the cruise. They want to meet Husband and me for dinner in Venice. The idea of having *dinner in Venice*-- it's on my calendar—doesn't sound real. This whole thing is quite overwhelming. I can't wait. I just can't wait!

As if going on a European cruise isn't big enough, Husband and I are going to spend a pre-cruise weekend in Sweden! The ship leaves out of Venice, Italy, and for us to fly directly from our home airport in Seattle to Venice is very expensive. My frugal heart balked at the cost. We began looking around for other options.

Is there a cheaper way to get from Seattle to Europe? In my research, there seem to be several main hubs across Europe that will save all kinds of cash. Barcelona, Venice, Rome, and Naples are very expensive to fly into. However if we had a layover in Frankfurt, Paris, London, Copenhagen, Amsterdam, or Stockholm, the price drops by almost a third, and then to get a flight to the smaller cities in Europe costs only about $100. Wait-- *Stockholm?* Stockholm is an option?

We figured since we need to have a layover, we may as well take advantage, and extend the trip. We're on vacation, right? Husband lived in Sweden for two years, long ago, right before we got married. He always talked about going back, and somehow we just never have. Well, I admit one of the reasons we never have was because of the cost. It's expensive to travel that far! However, we never really looked into it, so we didn't know how expensive would be.

We did little bit of shopping around. And we found that for us to fly to Venice directly from Seattle would cost approximately $2700 for the two of us. If we flew into Stockholm, instead, we could save close to $1600 total on airfare! I admit we are good at researching online. I found a hotel-- a 4.5-star hotel, mind you – and including the flight from Seattle to Stockholm and then flying to Venice and the Hop On Hop Off tour in Stockholm and money for food, we still came out saving money over the cost of flying from Seattle directly into Venice. Our excitement kept growing, as pieces fell into place.

Another advantage is the passport stamps. I've traveled quite a bit. I've been to all fifty states, all over the Caribbean, Canada, and Mexico, and nary a passport stamp among them. This time the cruise goes to five different countries, plus we will be having layovers in Iceland, England, and the stay in Sweden. Surely, dealing with the customs officials in all those places is bound to net me at least a few passport stamps!

Concerns

I have a few concerns. We're away quite often, but usually under ten days at a time. The cruise itself is twelve days, and then with flights over, flights back, and our weekend in Stockholm, it's going to be close to three weeks away from home! There are always a few niggly worries. We have a newborn grandson, who is doing just fine at the ripe old age of eleven days as I write this, but will he stay Just Fine? We're expecting another grandson, due two months after we get back, and I hope that everything will go well while we're away. To cancel a cruise can be quite expensive, especially close to sailing, and after the final payment has been made.

Okay, I admit it, I'm a skilled worrier. We all have talents, and I worry better than anybody I know. To assuage my fears, this time we decided to get travel insurance. We don't often do that for cruises, but this is a long one. And the trip is a major expense, more than I wish to lose should Something Happen. Although Husband and I are pretty healthy for the condition our condition is in, thinking about unforeseeable medical bills can be daunting. I've heard horror stories of people on cruises or vacations in in faraway places that needed to be airlifted home or needed sudden medical care. To be airlifted off the ship, or to be life-flighted back to the States can cost between $50,000 and $175,000, which is significantly more than we're paying for this or any other cruise!

That's more than my credit card needs to have on it, so we went ahead and bought travel insurance. For only 6% of the cruise cost, it's barely noticeable. We have a discussion before we go on any cruise. It includes people with whom we will not associate on the vacation, such as security on the ship, which is basically the police force, and the medical staff, and sometimes the family listens. I think the only times we've had any medical problems were when I had a severe infection in my thumb in Alaska, and my Husband turned his knee dancing with our daughter in the Caribbean. Both times we found the medical staff on board to be quite effective. I know that they can handle minor things such as cuts, sprains, bug bites, and bruises. But for something like a heart attack or stroke, an evacuation would be necessary and very expensive. And you can bet, if something dire occurs, I'm going to want to be treated somewhere fairly civilized.

On several cruises we have witnessed an evacuation helicopter or Coast Guard ship; a heart attack, kidney stones, a stroke, a production cast member severely injured, a cook burned. It can happen, and when it happens thousands of miles from a modern medical facility, it can be scary. At least, we can take away the fear of financial ruin.

Travel insurance can also cover things such as trip interruption. And since this itinerary takes us pretty close to a war zone, that's a concern. Actually, if you're watching the evening news, anywhere in the world can be a danger zone without much warning at all. Sometimes I think a cruise ship looks like a great big target full of presumably wealthy mostly North Americans. Why take chances?

Within a couple of weeks of our booking the cruise, we had an email from the cruise line, saying that Izmir, Turkey, had been canceled due to civil unrest. They replaced the port of Izmir with Kusadasi. I was looking forward to going to Ephesus out of Izmir. We can still do that out of Kusadasi; no problem. However, in the back of my mind there is a little naggy unease, as it were, about civil unrest... Can anyone predict that almost a year in advance? What else might happen?

If we lose our luggage, our homeowners insurance will cover part of the replacement cost, and travel insurance would pick up the rest of the reimbursement. If we miss a port-- for example, if a private tour gets us back after the ship has sailed – travel insurance will cover getting us to the next ports where we would meet up again with the ship. Good to know, but I'm not worried about this---I know that tour operators make great effort to not let passengers miss their ship!

Cruise lines go to great lengths to stay off of the evening news. However, in the unlikely event that the ship would break down, trip insurance would also cover incidentals, such as the cost of the cruise, hotels, and flights back to the states; whatever the cruise line didn't pick up.

Husband and I both have an elderly parent, and there's a risk of ... well, they're in their mid-eighties; who knows what there's a risk of? They have lived over 85 years; you'd think they could go another few weeks. If one of them suddenly decides to go to

The Great Beach In The Sky, mid- cruise, that's a problem. Because we like them, we would have to fly back suddenly in the middle of the trip, from wherever we were when we get word. Travel insurance would cover that; death or illness in the family is covered.

I will, of course, email my usual disclaimer to my young adult kids, and our elderly parents, as well. We always warn them to avoid crises, mishaps, adventure, calamity, injury, illness, disaster, catastrophe, problems, and adversity while we're away on any trip. We also used to warn our children to avoid associating with medical personnel; now that we have a daughter in law who is a registered nurse and one who is a medical assistant, we no longer include that disclaimer. It sometimes works.

There was that time when our daughter had a car accident just after dropping us off at the pier, in my car. We had a frantic call from same daughter who said she could not meet us at the train station after a cruise because she was at the Emergency Room with her husband, and another time she ...*Wait.* I see a pattern here. Does Daughter need a stronger email?

Cell Phones, Electronics, and Electricity

We use our cell phones extensively at home, but on vacation, I love the idea of just putting aside my cell phone and not dealing with it for three weeks. When we travel, I like to step off the world. One of the things I enjoy doing—it marks the beginning of a vacation for me --is to put my cell phone in the cabin safe and not touch it until we reach the end of the cruise. Actually, that never happens, but I start out every trip with that intention. In reality, what usually happens is that I put it in the cabin safe, and I don't take it out until the first port. I carry my cell phone in port and I utterly ignore it while we are on the ship. It's a reasonable compromise.

And it usually works. A few cruises ago, when I turned my phone on after three sea days, I had a message from a grandkid's school, saying she had fallen, broken her collarbone, her parents were not answering their phones, and since I was her emergency contact, could I come get my grandchild? From 2190 miles away...not realistically! A few quick phone calls sent help to rescue the child, and to track down her parents.

Ditching the cell phone may not be practical on this trip. Sigh. We will be traveling with friends. We're going to need to keep communication open with them. We have private tours booked, and they each require a cell phone contact. I guess that's in case we get distracted shopping and forget to go back to the van; that way the tour guide can get a hold of us.

Foreign phone fees are quite expensive, though. One of our tours in Turkey required us to fax in a form. I was shocked when the phone bill came ---$15 for one fax!? Husband looked into our cell phone coverage in Europe and found that we can buy an international plan, for 30 days, making each call to the States cost $2.75 per minute. Without the international plan, phone calls will cost $2.50 per minute. Wait-- not really much of a savings! In fact, it'll cost more to use the international plan.

Of course we need to be reachable in the event of an emergency at home, but I think I will suggest to my kids that unless it's a truly dire emergency they use text messaging instead of calling. Texts cost $.50. Unless they go into a long-winded text story, that will save us a significant amount of money. I'm not sure how texting will work between tour guides. But even if it's $2.50 a minute for a call, we can keep the calls short; it's all we can do. In the back of my mind, I'm secretly hoping the cell phones will just not work in Europe. Remember that long ago time, when people traveled and went about their business without being tethered to a device at all times, you know, like ten years ago? Aaah...

All Charged Up

Keeping things charged is going to be a concern. Dead electronics are just more weight to haul around. We plan to bring cell phones, two tablets, e-readers, cameras, and may or may not bring a small laptop. I bought an outlet adapter / power converter on Ebay. It only cost five dollars and it might make my life easier. The one I purchased has three connectors so we can charge three items at a time. The cruise ship will have a standard outlet, but probably just one or two in the cabin. Once we are on the ship, we can recharge everything overnight. We don't want to do it during the day because there can be up to five or seven people in a cabin every day, coming in for one reason or another; room steward, maintenance, bar staff, etc. We will charge things overnight and then pack them away out of sight during the day. I just don't need to be leaving temptation in full view.

When we are in Venice, Stockholm, and again in Barcelona, we will need to be aware of Europe's electrical system, which is different than what we're used to. American appliances run on 110 volts, while European appliances are 220 volts. Newer travel accessories and electronic gadgets are "dual voltage," which means they work on both American and European current. I see a range of voltages printed on our electronics, or their plugs ("110–220"), so I think we'll be okay in Europe. At least we won't worry about melting our e-reader, but we still need to find a way to plug it into the wall.

The plugs and outlets in Europe take two round prongs. In America, we're used to the standard two flat prongs. Never being skilled at fitting square pegs into round holes, it's best just to have what I need in the first place. In Europe, the voltage of the current and the shape of the plug both differ. We will not be able to simply walk up to an outlet in the wall and plug our equipment in, as we do at home. The plugs are recessed into the walls in a fist size alcove-- anything too big simply won't reach the outlet, even if it has the right size prongs. I figure if worse comes to worst we can always ask at the hotel. If we brought the wrong kind of adapter, maybe they'd have something at hand. I know in America, the most commonly left behind items in hotels are cell phone chargers. Maybe in Europe, it's power adapters.

Currency Conversion

In America, we pretty much use four kinds of currency. We have cash, personal checks, debit cards, and credit cards. Personal checks are not worth the hassle, away from our hometown. Travelers' checks used to be the thing to use; now they are a chore to find and not everywhere accepts them. They're out. In Sweden, the currency is krona, and in Turkey, it's the Turkish lira. Everywhere else will accept euros, and every place we go will accept credit cards.

We're planning on using our ATM card to replenish our cash stash if we run low---ATMs should be easy to find. In fact, I decided that will be our main source of money as we go. We don't want to carry thousands of dollars with us, either on our person or tucked in our luggage. We plan on getting about $1000 in euros before we go, along with some Swedish kronar. The bank charges a rather high exchange-rate, but I don't want to regret not having any cash in hand when we arrive in Europe.

We will use the ATM machine in Venice, which I've read is in the baggage claim area at the Marco Polo airport. We can do that while waiting for our luggage to appear. In Sweden, we will have maybe a couple hundred dollars converted into kronar. It's inconvenient to break out a credit card for a small purchase, such as breakfast. We also don't want to be carrying around a lot of leftover kronar that we cannot use anywhere else in the world. Unusable currency becomes an expensive souvenir.

We're not going to worry about Turkish lira. I've heard that Turkish vendors and merchants will take just about any form of currency from anywhere in the world. If I need to buy something while I'm in Turkey, I will use euros and just do a math problem in my head.

Planning the Flights

Unless you count Canada, I've never been on an international flight and I am looking forward to it… Well, except for the distance. On a flight that long, I need to do whatever I can to be comfortable. Choosing seats on a plane is always an adventure when Husband and I travel anywhere together. He prefers to sit by me, because he likes me after all these years. The problem is, he prefers to sit near the window to accommodate his broad shoulders. Seriously, his shoulders are so broad that when he needed a MRI scan on a sore shoulder, he visited the Seattle Seahawks' team doctor and still didn't fit in the MRI machine---- they sent him elsewhere. Who has shoulders broader than professional football players'? Sitting beside him in the middle seat makes for a miserable, cramped flight.

I prefer the aisle on planes. I can see farther, I feel less closed in, plus it's easy to get out in case I need to stand, rather than climbing over some guy's cords and wires and computer and interrupting his video...oh, wait, he's asleep, too. An aisle seat gives me the illusion of freedom of mobility. It kind of takes my mind off the fact that I'm in a very large aluminum and composite tube soaring through the sky at several hundred miles per hour crammed full of overweight people and their overweight luggage.

I *understand* the principles of flight – I could diagram it for you. I understand about lift and velocity and curvature of the wing. I get all that. I know also know that gravity is a true and nonnegotiable principle, and that if I throw even a light a potato chip across the room, it will not go very far at all. I understand flight, but deep down, I do not trust it. Sitting on the aisle probably makes me not one bit safer, but it makes me feel more in control. And after all, control is all about illusion, isn't it? Husband and I booked an aisle and a window seat. Hoping with an aisle and window booked, we may actually luck out and have the middle seat empty. Slim chance, but what is life without hope?

To See and Not to See

The planning, researching, talking about, negotiating, and actually booking private tours in each port took weeks. How did people plan grand trips without the internet's resources?

On large ship sponsored shore excursions, the passengers will go where they are put, with no say in the plan for the day. On this particular cruise, there are places I long to see, and others I distinctly do not wish to visit. We don't drink wine, so we can avoid wineries across France and Italy. Look at all the time we'll save! I'm not fond of olive oil, so we don't need to tour any olive oil processors, either.

Not fond...now, there's an understatement! I have a full feathered aversion to olive oil. I have Sunday morning breakfast childhood memories, swimming in olive oil. My Dad traveled all week, and on Saturdays and Sundays, he loved to make breakfast. I would lie awake early on Sunday mornings, listening to Dad singing at the top of his lungs. O Sole Mio, or Deck the Halls, depending on the season; very off key, but exuberant.

Dad would be cooking, and there would be visible olive oil fumes three feet down from the kitchen ceiling. He fried everything in a couple of inches of olive oil, the expensive dark green imported stuff. Onions and peppers, sausages, kusa; all cooked on high heat and scorched almost black, served with runny, nearly raw eggs. Dad's family was Syrian and kusa was a form of Syrian summer squash. Kusa was very good served for dinner; hollowed out and salted, then my aunts would put rice and lamb inside. It was delicious! However, on Sunday mornings, the stench of olive oil was enough to make me put the covers over my head. Yes, I'm no fan of olive oil.

I particularly do not want to go to a Turkish rug factory! I don't want a rug. I respect the art form. I recognize that it takes many many months to produce one, and I'm sure the process is fascinating, but my time is so limited in each of these ports. I don't want to spend it watching how something is made that I don't ever want in my house.

Okay, I admit – the main reason I want to avoid Turkish rug merchants is that they are legendary for high pressure sales. The tour books all recommend, "just say NO firmly and repeatedly," but I have a soft heart, and I can be a pushover. My father's people were Syrians, as I said, and I have childhood memories of their negotiation skills. My relatives would follow a person around the house and yard and neighborhood, hollering, wheedling, pleading, manipulating, shouting, until they made their point ---or wore the victim down, whichever came first-- and it tires me out. I'm not interested in dealing with that skill set on a vacation.

Plus, I'm a lousy negotiator. I prefer to buy things with price tags on them. I like being able to walk into a store and look at a blouse and say, "oh, $39.95," and decide on the spot if it's worth it to me.

For example, there was a folk art doll that I wanted for my granddaughter in Barbados, and Brett happened to be near me at the time. The seller was asking $10 for the handmade doll. Well worth it, I thought! My thought process went like this: 'I know how to sew, I recognize the quality and hours of work in it, I would not make it for that price, I can afford the $10, and the extra dollar or two I might save will not change my life...but may change hers; it may be the difference between providing dinner that night, and not, and I really like the doll!'

Brett's thought process was "these people are not used to much money, and they see us tourists as a vending machine. I can talk her down." He pulled me aside, and asked if he could buy the doll, as well as whatever else I wanted all week, since he enjoys bargaining, and I decidedly do not. I gave Brett my $10 and walked away. Three minutes later, I owned the doll, and had $3 in my hand. I still feel a little guilty. With regard to rug sales, I am not interested in enduring a high pressure sales pitch for something I don't even want---and you can bet $10 wouldn't buy a handful of scraps there!

Planning Time in Port

As the planning began to flesh out, we had to decide what we wished to do in each port, and how to do it best. Husband and I quickly dismissed using public transportation. I know it is easy to use and goes just about everywhere in Europe, but wrangling with train schedules in a foreign language sounded risky. It's also not the best use of time; a car can zip along, without making stops at every station. We even faster discarded the very idea of renting a car in each city. Driving is tough enough when you know where you are going! Not knowing the roads, laws, and routes would make us on edge the whole time.

We did talk about a **Hop On Hop Off tour** in each port. They tend to be open-top busses that make a circuit, and as the name indicate, passengers can hop on and off at any stop, then rejoin the tour later on. We have done this in several US cities, and it worked well. It's an easy way to get an overview of a place, while learning some facts and history.

In San Francisco, on a previous cruise, we had a great narrator on a Hop On Hop Off tour. Chris was a master story teller, and he had us laughing so hard tears streamed. I still remember vividly some of the facts he laid on us. He called pigeons "sky rats" and told us why the state house's gold dome has no pigeon poop to mar the surface. Peregrine falcons! Brilliant idea---baby falcons love pigeons for dinner, so when the city installed a nest, the pigeons were either eaten or smart enough to move to a new, falcon-less home. We learned that Tony Bennett's song, "I Left My Heart In San Francisco" was so appreciated for the tourism it brought in, they gave him a giant heart sculpture to paint on Union Square. The paint is called "Golden Gate Bridge Red," and the heart and bridge are the only places in the world that paint is used. Who else knows that?

Chris told us of an enterprising young sail maker, named Levi Straus, who moved to San Francisco during the Gold Rush. At that time, adventurers smitten with gold fever would sail into the San Francisco Bay, and abandon their ships right there, as they rushed inland to seek their fortunes. Levi simply boarded the ships and cut down the sails. With the good sturdy material, he fashioned pants for gold miners, and sold them for highly inflated prices. You gotta honor entrepreneurial spirit---and how many pairs of Levi Straus' legacy do *you* own?

A Hop On Hop Off tour was a definite option in Europe, but I also read a lot of reviews that were not positive, especially in Rome and Florence. They complained about being stranded for hours on a corner, as one overfull HOHO after another drove past. Not for me---we do not have time to waste like that! Yes, if we felt stuck we could always hail a taxi...but why pay for a taxi *and* HOHO tour?

Next option was **ship's shore excursions**. These are the tours offered by the cruise lines. We avoid these when we travel, with very rare exceptions. I hate the idea of not being able to plan my own time, and being with crowds isn't an efficient way to see a place. Now, I admit it worked well in Boston where we took a ship-to-airport tour the last day of the cruise. Besides giving us more opportunity to explore Boston, we did not have to find a place to stash our luggage. We also enjoyed a transfer that detoured two hours at Johnson Space Center, on the way to Houston's airport from Galveston. There is just no convenient way to get to and from Galveston. No bus, or train service, no rental cars, and a taxi costs $140. In both of these cases, it actually cost less money than a plain airport transfer, and it beat waiting an extra three hours at the airport, bored silly. But in most cases, a ship shore excursion is not for us.

Think about it; even stopping for a restroom break with 60 people on a bus is going to take at least a half an hour. With just a few of us, we can cover a lot more turf and see a lot more. And since I've never been to Europe before, that is the goal. Being with a small, intimate group of friends, in our case, is going to be much more flexible.

The Cruise Addict and I have traveled enough to know that we don't need to do shore excursions offered by the ship. We're going with **private tours** instead. This will give us more flexibility as we can determine where we will go and not go. We can also avoid the large buses, which is basically taking your own crowd with you. On ship sponsored excursions, participants wear little numbered stickers on their chests all day. To me this looks like you're labeling yourself as a very inexperienced traveler, a prime target for crime, pickpockets, and disreputable merchants. Of course, being Americans, we will stand out, anyway; there's no way to disguise one's nationality, but at least we don't have to tag ourselves with a little gold sticker, like kindergartners.

Private tours are usually booked by the vehicle, not by the number of passengers. While a tour may seem expensive initially, look closer. Say a tour is $300 for four hours. $300 for one person is a lot, but $ 300 split by twelve people is only $25. For four hours, that comes out to only $6.25 per person per hour! You can't beat that.

Cruise line shore excursions are usually priced per person---and they add up fast! The cruise lines make a lot of money with selling shore excursions, along with drinks, bingo, and the casino; those are their top money makers. On this cruise, in particular, we estimate that we can save between 30% and 70% by booking our own private tours. That's one of the main things I want to focus on in this book; to let you know you can see a lot more at your own pace, while having the element of control with a private tour.

If there's more than one person in your group---by definition, there is, or you are not a group at all--you can also save a significant amount of money. If you are traveling alone, you can often link up with others easily to reach the minimum required for some private tours. This has great advantages! You could make new friends, you'll have someone to take pictures of you with your camera, (enough with the selfies already!), and it's just more fun having someone to share the experiences with. Just let it be known on the cruise's online roll call, or on the tour company's website, that you're looking for shared shore excursions. You could also ask the tour company to link you with a partial group. There are many that you can add onto. For example, a private excursion may have room for ten people, but only have six on it. They can take four other people. You could easily be one of them, thus saving as much money as everyone else, meeting new people, and seeing more than you possibly could on a shore excursion sponsored by the cruise line. Be a smart traveler!

Many people feel that "I'm on vacation! I don't want to do any thinking." If that's you, well, go for a ship excursion, but in most places the spirit of adventure will serve you well. If you can operate a clock, and hail a cab, you're much better off avoiding shore excursions through the ship. You've never heard of anyone really being permanently lost. Have you?

Who's Going Where?

Our group is a varied bunch, with a range of ages, interests, and even athletic ability. We are friends, but do not have to stick together like glue the whole trip. In some ports, we'll all be on tour together. In others, there will be a few of us, and in two ports, the group will scatter, each on our own. This guarantees everyone will see and do what they most desire, and hopefully, we'll all still like one another at the end of the cruise. Planning who goes where is a challenge. In fact, it required a color-coded spreadsheet to figure it all out! Don't worry; Part Three details the companies we looked at and ultimately booked.

In the two ports in Turkey, we decided that all of us want to be together. We found a company, Eklo Tours, that has a deal where you get two tours with the same company, and it is one reasonable cost. In our day in Livorno, we'll go to Florence and Pisa. Half of us wanted to climb the Leaning Tower of Pisa. Half of us would sooner try to repaint the Mona Lisa in the dark than hike up a leaning tower that requires seasickness pills. Did you know that? With the steep spiral staircase and the tilt of the tower, many people actually get sick; thus, motion sickness meds are strongly suggested. I'd like to *see* the Leaning Tower of Pisa, but I do not have to climb it to enjoy being there. Others in the group want bragging rights.

Five of us are going to hire a private tour that will take us to Florence, and then stop in Pisa to look at the Baptistery area and the Leaning Tower of Pisa. The other seven, the more athletic, plan to catch a local train to Pisa, climb the Leaning Tower of Pisa and then make their way to Florence. We'll meet back for dinner.

Sarah and Cue and Kimi are flying in early to Rome. They were afraid they would not be able to see everything they wish to explore in the one day we have in Rome. They're going to be there a couple of days early. On the day the ship is in port, the three of them will go off on their own, having already seen the major sites, while the rest of us enjoy a tour around and through Rome. The spreadsheet is giving me a migraine, but it's going to be an intense cruise and we're going to love it!

We find also the shore excursions sponsored by the cruise lines tend to be very expensive, considering what they cover. With this in mind, we set about shopping around and comparing prices and figuring out how to personalize our experience in Europe.

Let me tell you about our trip to the Canadian Maritimes. Peggy's Cove is a popular tourist spot in Nova Scotia. It's a charming town, population thirty-five on a good day, with Canada's most photographed lighthouse. I wonder how they count that. We took a private tour, two town cars with eight friends, and drivers who had grown up in the area and were full of stories. It was a highlight of the cruise. Our group toured a maple processing plant (with tastings), spent an hour with the author of the Peggy's Cove book series in his home, stopped as desired for photos of gorgeous fall colors, saw a beaver dam, explored Peggy's Cove and the scenery, took scads of photos and admired the lighthouse, stood in awe as our driver told personal stories at the Titanic cemetery, and best of all, had two pound lobsters for lunch at picnic tables on a bay so pretty it rivaled postcards. Our drivers knew the proprietor, and those giant fresh lobsters cost less than market price. I felt sorry for the hordes of tourists in Peggy's Cove, herded with whistles on and off six big busses. Several fellow cruisers told us the tour went straight from the ship to the Cove, and back, with no stops. They paid more than double what we paid for our tour.

Historic Zones

In Europe, most of the places we will go have Historic Zones where vehicles over twelve passengers are not permitted. We lucked out in that there are exactly twelve of us, so the private tours will be able to take us to the door of whatever site we're aiming after. The larger buses will have to park way out there in the coach parking area, and then people will have to walk in a distance, before they even arrive at the sights they wish to see. A 45 minute walk before I even arrive where I want to be does not appeal!

Another plus of a private tour is that each will give us an opportunity to meet at least one local resident in every port. Our driver will be from the city which we are visiting. We will be able to communicate with them and ask personal questions, like what is it like living here, education, economy, and other questions that make people more three-dimensional. On a bus, the driver is pretty much invisible, an anonymous part of the machinery.

Plus – face it – we are Americans, and we come with American attitudes. We are used to the freedom of having our own car. In Europe, most people use public transportation, and so for them, it's familiar. For us, figuring out timetables in a foreign language sounds stressful. If, as we drive in our van, we see a place that we wish to stop, to take a picture or find a restroom, we can simply ask the driver to pull over, and they will do so. When you're on your own, you can do that. I think it will be a lot more fun. There's also a privacy issue. I don't really want to be on a bus with 65 people I don't know. Being on our own, with people we already know and love, and a local driver who knows where they're going, is the best way for us.

What If We Miss The Ship?

One concern that people have expressed to us, over and over, when we tell them that we take private tours when we travel, or go off on our own, is "the ship will not wait for you if you are late!" A couple things you need to know about this. First: It's true if you are on a ship sponsored shore excursion, the cruise line does promise to get you back to the ship. However, this does not mean the ship will necessarily wait for you. The cruise lines pay astronomical fees for their time in port. They're not going to pay extra berthing fines for staying overtime, just because one little bus is late. They promise to get you back to them, but that may mean putting passengers on a train or even a plane to get to the next port, if the cruise tour is significantly late. It's up to the captain to make this call; in cheaper ports, they may choose to wait.

It's also true that if a private tour makes you miss the ship, you're on your own, responsible for getting to the next port. This simply doesn't happen. For one thing, in our day and age, tour guides in ports that cruise ships frequent are painfully aware of the cruise ship schedules. This is how they make their livelihood. They know that with so many reviews online, that one bad review, just one person saying "they made me miss my ship!!" can cost significantly in future lost business. They make a great effort to get you back to the ships on time! Their job depends on it

The tours we found all end at least an hour before the ship is to sail away. I'm not worried at all about missing the ship. I know that they will do everything they can to get us back to the ship on time. Oh, about that extra hour. No problem --there are always little shops near the port and I don't mind taking advantage of shopping at all.

We, of course, *could* just get off the ship, and hope for the best. This works well in some places. In Halifax, for example, it's an easy walk to the huge Citadel on the hill. In Juneau, people are lined up in kiosks on the port, anxious to sell a tour to a dogsled camp or a ride to Mendenhall Glacier. In a foreign city, were we willing to count on that being available? Not much.

Decide, Already!

Finding a taxi might be an option, in most ports, but there were some drawbacks. For one thing, there are twelve of us on this trip, and we wanted to be together at least some of the days. Twelve people finding a cab is tricky. A cabbie may be able to drive, but there is no guarantee that they could speak to us, or be knowledgeable enough to tell us what we were seeing. A cab is fine for getting from here to there and back, but it's not the best way to get a brief, in depth, overview of a place. And several ports are actually pretty far from the sites we wish to see. It's tough to determine the cost of a cab before you arrive.

After much thought, we came back around to our first choice: private tours. Next, did we want to buy a package, with a tour in each city through the same tour company, or find different ones in each port? A package could be wonderful, but we needed to remember that ultimately, it depends on local operators. One day in Rome might be amazing with a knowledgeable and friendly driver, but Naples might have a grumpy grouch with her own agenda, who cannot be convinced that we are really serious when we said we'd prefer a panini and gelato over a three hour trattoria lunch, so we'd have time to see that other museum right there!

Cost is always a point near and dear to my frugal little heart. If I can save money, why not? It seemed that the packaged-together tours would end up costing more than tours hired individually. Plus, they seemed to be more set-in-stone, with regards to scheduling. We finally decided to book separate tour companies in each port, except in Turkey. Eklo Tours seemed best for both Istanbul and Kusadasi.

We waded through many companies, comparing and comparing. I've included my notes in Part Three of this book. Some well-known names kept coming up again and again; others were obscure, but perfect for our needs.

My friends don't call me Information Booth for nothing. I have a fear of missing something wonderful, so I make sure I am very well informed beforehand. I do a lot of research anywhere we travel, far more than anyone I know. I call and email companies to compare, I read local websites, I compare prices and options, I study reviews, I make charts, I put a lot of effort in making sure we have the best deal in seeing what we really do not want to miss in the most cost-effective, personalized, relaxed, yet efficient way possible. And then once I'm shutting the house door behind me, passport in hand, I can finally relax.

Cruise Lines and Itineraries

Out of our bunch -- the twelve of us- only four had ever been to Europe at all. We're Americans. We live in a very young country. I've been to some of the oldest sites on the American continent; Saint Augustine, Florida, Santa Fe, New Mexico, the missions in California. I've seen very old buildings. I've seen a lot of history. Our family's big on history---our daughter in law marvels at our son, who probably knows as many facts as most guides when they visit a museum. My family traveled a lot when I was a kid, too, focusing on Revolutionary War, Civil War, and colonization sites, plus visiting just about every National Park in America. I've been all over the continent. I admit that I am awestruck at the idea of going to somewhere where buildings are 2000+ years old- way older than my own country. It just amazes me, and I'm looking forward to this so *so* much.

I'll show some of the itineraries we considered, in Part Three. This is the general discussion.

So, Where Are We Going?

Once we decided we were going to Europe, we had a group meeting with our friends to decide what dates, itinerary, and cruise line we were going to choose. Of course the meeting involved dinner. After dessert, it also included a lot of maps, and cruise brochures spread all over the table, along with four laptops open to different websites.

We had to consider the dynamics of our group with whom we're traveling. If it was just us two, we would book as we pleased, but because there are twelve of us going together , of course we took into consideration everyone else's opinions as well. Well, nearly everyone's opinion... Cade suddenly decided to add on just a week before the cruise began, so he was not consulted at all.

I take great pride in being frugal. Okay, cheap… And scheduling promptly became a minor bump in the road. Had we been able to take the same cruise, same itinerary, same ship, a month later, it would've been about $400 less for each of us. However, had we done that, our friends could not have gone along with us. Husband and I can be very flexible. Husband is not called The Cruise Addict for nothing! I've seen him bend schedules into full on pretzel --shaped contortions to make a cruise possible. Brett and Melissa are self-employed, and able to juggle, although on this trip, Brett was still working on his computer at the airport gate right up until final boarding call, and Melissa was up until dawn, finishing up one last set of choreography! Sarah finished a 22 day business trip sixteen hours before their flight took off.

This itinerary is only offered a few sailings each year, Spring and Fall. Kim, the youngest, is a college freshman and had to be back before her school starts, mid-September. Todd works seasonally, a tax guy. His schedule would not work for the Spring, his busy season. So we are going in September, right after Labor Day. This part of the world is known for being very hot in the summer and crowded with many tourists during high season. Extra cost aside, maybe we will be better off. I'm hoping that maybe after Labor Day, it will be just a touch cooler and maybe not quite as crowded. Hope needs no basis in reality, does it?

Husband and I have been on quite a few different cruise lines, and all have good and bad points. Some are fancier, a little more upscale, and we like that. Some are a lot more laid-back and more casual, and we like that, too. This time we're going more for the itinerary than the ship. It is our first trip to Europe. We want to see as much as we possibly can in the time we have. We want a decent cruise line, but with this being so port-intensive, a very upscale cruise line is not required.

Size of ship was another consideration. I really am not in favor of the giant mega ships. The idea of dealing with crowds and all that extra walking onboard and the vast Central Park atmosphere does not appeal to me at all. I don't want a dinky ship, either. We took a Princess ship some years ago. It was so small, it had no theatre . The shows were held in the bar, and I very nearly got hit in the head by a feathered dancer's foot mid-performance. That's too small. We all agreed on a moderate size ship.

Each cruise line has its own personality . Of course, cost is a factor – the more we save on any cruise, the more cruises we can go on – but we also want to have a quality experience. We have friends who have traveled on Carnival, for instance, and tell us that its main draw is as a party ship. Since we don't drink or party, we've rejected Carnival outright. Watching drunken guests throwing up in the hallways is not my idea of a fun cruise activity. We also rejected the super high-class expensive ones, such as Azamara and Regency. The goal is to see as much as possible; the ship is not the destination. We'll have enough adventures on this trip---it's not the time to choose regional ships, where we could have unexpected issues with language onboard. We felt more comfortable with a well-known, mainstream cruise line for this trip.

We know people who have sailed on Costa, and had a miserable time, not to even think about the occasional erratic captain joyriding off the Italian coastline! Our friends hated the food on Costa so much; they even lost weight, and skipped meals to avoid the same menu with overcooked food. One would expect an Italian flagged ship to know how to properly cook pasta. Again, the ship is not the destination, but a decent dinner at the end of a full day is important.

Holland America has pretty good itineraries, but I have a problem with the lighting on some of the ships. I'm just not willing to risk that for such a long time. We have been on several HAL cruises, and I was okay, but there was that one time... we were on the Volendam for just a one-day cruise from Seattle to Vancouver and I was completely miserable due to the lighting. We pretty well covered the whole ship, all the public areas at least; dining areas, atrium, library, lounges, and there was not a location that was bright enough to read-- it seems every light bulb was just dim, no brighter than 25 watts! Now I know that Holland America has many ships, and many light bulbs, and I would probably do just fine, had we taken the Holland America ship to the Mediterranean, but I'm just not willing to chance it. Plus, HAL tends to roll up the carpets at 9pm. Not that we're going for the night life, but I would enjoy more activity after dinner, other than beddy-bye at dusk.

Princess is one of my favorite cruise lines, and we have elite status with them as well as on several other lines. But their itinerary for the Mediterranean is just not that good. It doesn't cover the ports that we were most interested in seeing. Royal Caribbean Cruise Line is a good fit, but their itineraries to the Mediterranean just don't go all the places we want to go, either. There wasn't an itinerary that suits our needs, and if we are going that far we want to be able to see as much as we possibly can. We may never get back again!

Consider Itineraries

Brett and Melissa are heart set on going to Venice and the Greek Isles. That's important to them. Todd and Julie have been to Italy and Greece, on a land tour. The place they really want to go to is Turkey; Istanbul especially. Clint and Mary took a similar cruise last year on NCL's Epic. They had a good time in each port, but did not book any tours at all. They are anxious to see as much as possible, having heard The Cruise Addict's wife's reputation for seeing more and doing more than pretty much anybody on board any ship. I am more flexible, although Turkey is not high on my list of places to see. So long as we can explore new places, we're good! The Cruise Addict, of course, is just happy to be going on any cruise, any place, any time.

After much debate about cruise lines, we settled on Norwegian Cruise Line. NCL is perhaps the most casual cruise line, without being totally classless. We chose it because it has the best itinerary. We will be able to see the most possible places in the least amount of days, hitting all the high points our group desires. We have traveled on NCL extensively along with Holland America, Princess, Celebrity and Royal Caribbean. All have good points and bad points. NCL is not our favorite but for itinerary, they had the others beat! another selling point: Norwegian's dress code is resort casual every day. There is a dress-up- or -not night, but formal wear will not be required, which is a plus when going to Europe where we really will be limited with our luggage weight. I do love elegant dress, but we don't want to be bringing sequined gowns and tuxedos if we can avoid it this time.

We decided on a Grand Mediterranean cruise on the Norwegian Spirit, on Norwegian Cruise line. The original itinerary that we agreed upon begins in Venice and goes to Athens, Greece, Izmir, Turkey, Istanbul, Turkey, Mykonos, Greece, Naples, Rome and Florence, Italy, Toulon, France, and it ends in Barcelona, Spain. This itinerary looks ideal! Everyone's happy, everyone gets to go where they wanted to most. It's going to be a port-intensive cruise. There are only two sea days built-in. I have no desire to start running with Melissa, but I will try to get more in shape before we go. We have so much walking ahead of us!

The Itinerary:

We will board the ship in Venice, and that's Day One. It looks like we have that whole day and the next whole day in Venice, but actually the ship departs at 1 AM on Day Two. We can check in any time before 7pm, and must be back onboard by 11:30pm, for a 1:30am sailaway. Day Two lists Venice, but it's an effectual sea day because you can't get off. Day Three is at sea and Day Four we arrive at Piraeus, Greece. That's the port to Athens. The ship will be in Athens from 7 AM to 5 PM.

Day Five was to be Izmir, Turkey, but it was changed to Kusadasi, Turkey, instead. It probably doesn't matter to me a whole lot one way or the other – except for the part about being cancelled for civil unrest – because the main thing I want to see in Izmir is Ephesus and it's actually closer from Kusadasi to Ephesus. Kusadasi's port time is 7 AM to 2:30 PM. Day Six is Istanbul, Turkey, and we'll be there 8 AM to 7 PM. Istanbul is one of those places so exotic-sounding to me, it sounds a lot like going to the bottom of the Marianas Trench or maybe to Mars. I have been assured that Istanbul is a very modern, very clean, very safe city. Yeah, I'm not sure I believe that. Day Seven, if we survive Istanbul on Day Six, is Mykonos, Greece.

I'm going to like Mykonos, I could tell from here, by the pictures. Oh my goodness, it looks so beautiful! In Mykonos we have only from 1 PM until 9 PM, which should be enough time for wandering. I read an interesting fact about Mykonos. It was designed to confuse marauding pirates fleeing from the city. Getting lost there is actually one of the activities. With my sense of the direction, I would've gotten lost anyway. However, I've read that it's often windy there. Sometimes this port is even canceled for wind. The trick is, if the wind is at my back then I'm heading back to the shore, where I should be able to see the ship, once I can see the water... It's a big big ship. Plus, it's an island; not likely we can be lost forever. Misplaced, perhaps, but not *lost.*

Day Eight is at sea and I would think after four intense port days I'm going to be grateful for that! Day Nine is Naples, from 8 AM to 7 PM. Naples is going to be fun—we're going to go to Pompeii, Herculaneum, and even climb Mount Vesuvius! Day Nine is the second at-sea day, probably a recovery day after hiking to the volcanos' caldera.

Day Ten is Citiavecchia, which is the port for Rome. We will be there from 8 AM until 7PM; a long day, but we've much to do, including Rome's main sights and the Vatican. The Vatican is a separate country. America is so large; we don't just zip through tiny countries at home, part of a day trip! Rome is actually a bit over an hour from the port. It's going to be a full and exhausting day.

Day Eleven is the port of Livorno, Italy. The ship will be there from 8 AM until 7 PM. From there we'll go to Florence and Pisa, an hour or so from the port. I should be pretty well walked out by then. I think I'll be grateful for the private tour of Florence.

Day Twelve is in Provence, France, the port of Toulon. The ship is supposed to be there from 9 AM to 5 PM. This will be a lazy day for Husband and me; the group decided not to plan anything together. Toulon is a jump off point for tours to Marseilles, but we plan to just enjoy the port itself.

Day Thirteen, we will disembark in Barcelona, sometime in the morning. Our group will scatter at that point. Some plan to fly directly home. We plan to stay an extra night in Barcelona, as do Brett, Melissa, and Todd and Julie.

We discovered that Barcelona is another very expensive port to fly directly in and out of, as was Venice. Obviously, with the cruise beginning and ending in different cities—different countries!—a round trip flight doesn't work for us. To fly directly to Seattle from Barcelona would cost about $1600 per person. If we fly from Barcelona to Frankfurt, Copenhagen, London, or Paris, first and then take a direct flight to SeaTac, we can save around $800 per person! After much research, we determined that the least expensive way for us to fly home would be to go from Barcelona to Copenhagen, Denmark, to Reykjavik and on to Seattle. The only drawback I see to this is that we will have to deal with wrangling our luggage through Customs in Copenhagen, but we have a couple of hours to do it. And since we don't plan on leaving the airport in Denmark, we should be just fine. Hey, will I get another passport stamp for being in Copenhagen?

Planning Details

Cabin Decisions

Todd and Julie wanted a balcony cabin. Melissa, Brett, and their daughter wanted an inside cabin for frugality's sake. They later added Cade, their son, to their cabin. (I heard later that it was a tight fit, but they like him well enough.) Sarah gets seasick, so she and Cue chose a lower deck, near Clint and Mary, who also feared mal de mer. Husband and I are big fans of saving money and often cruise in inside cabins or oceanviews or balconies. We decided a balcony on this itinerary would be a waste of money, since most of the sailing will be at night, and we will be in port during the days.

This time I decided that the little extra expense of an oceanview cabin was very much worth it to me, to be able to have natural light in the mornings. It doesn't matter on a two or three day cruise; but for twelve days onboard, a window makes a difference to me. With the ship arriving in a new port almost every day, I'm looking forward to bouncing out of bed to greet the day--- it's an awesome way to start the morning, to get a glimpse of a new place before I even have my clothes on!

After some wrangling, the twelve of us ended up in five cabins on four decks – good enough! So long as everyone is good about showing up at the designated meeting spot on time, it won't matter one bit.

A Travel Agent, or Book On Our Own?

In the beginning, we all decided to book the cruise together on Travelocity.com. I had some hesitation. We have a cruise travel agent that we have worked with for years. We met him in Alaska when he and his family were traveling, on a special radio- listener- only cruise deal. As the story goes, our family, along with several of Husband's extended family members, had a cruise booked to Alaska in late August. It was probably springtime when I had the radio on in the car. I heard a commercial by a travel agent I had never heard of, offering the exact same cruise, the exact same itinerary, the exact same ship, only a week later, for significantly less than we paid. Since there were so many of us going--we had most of our kids with us, cousins, nephews and aunts, uncles, and Husband's parents-- the savings would be dramatic.

I called a sister-in-law, the one with the most kids going, the one who paid the most for her cabin, and asked if we could move our trip back another week. She promptly listed a chart of why they could not possibly work. I immediately backed down. "Oh, well," I said, "it would've saved you about $850, but we'll go with what we have-" I could hear her backpedaling at high speed over the phone, brakes squealing and all! We ended up canceling the cruise and booking through this cruise travel agent, a week later.

Since then we have booked quite a few cruises with him, and gone on cruises with his family at least a couple more times. The Cruise Addict actually has him on speed dial. We called our travel agent, and explained our wishes, and told him the prices we had found online. He listened, did some research, then called us back. He said he could not get close to the price we had found online---and suggested we *not* book through him! I value that kind of honesty. We booked through Travelocity.com. I immediately regretted it. The nice thing about having a travel agent is that, in case of any snag, they can help sort it out.

Booking through a faceless online agency lacked any hint of a personal touch. Turns out, I was right, and you may quote me.

Over the next couple of weeks, we endured several run-ins with the online travel agency, Travelocity.com, including price hikes, unauthorized credit card charges, unexplained cabin changes, and weird emails regarding cruises we were not even going on, followed quickly by other emails apologizing for having sent the erroneous one in the first place. It just did not seem like they were on top of things! For a cruise this big, with this much money being spent, I really needed my own travel agent, a human one. I needed to be able to ask questions and not have to wrestle with the internet, which has a mind of its own. You know it does.

I finally told Husband I was uneasy, and he agreed. He looked online to see what cabins were available before calling our travel agent to make a switch. We knew we wanted an oceanview cabin. We're not that picky. Nevertheless, we still wanted a good cabin in a good location.

We found *a great* cabin on the Spirit! There are only two this size on the whole ship. It's an oceanview category, with a large picture window, same price as the other oceanviews, but almost twice the size. 8500 is in a good location, right where the hull bends in the straight part on the side of the ship, on deck 8. And it looked to be available! How could that be?

Husband quickly called our beloved travel agent and said, "I want you to book this cabin, 8500, for us, *fast,* I'll explain later." Our travel agent got on the computer instantly. He saw real-time available cabins and said, "oh, I'm sorry, it's not available. Too bad, that would've been a good one—" and then he said, "Hey, wait it just opened up! You really lucked out. Primo, somebody must have just canceled! I'll book it right now." We must've caught a cancellation right then, which, in the scheme of the way the universe works, looks like serendipity to me! A much larger cabin for $150 less per person? ---I can live with that, and happily. Bye, bye, Travelocity.

Shots and Medical Obstacles

Seems to me that no matter where we go, we have a few pre-trip speedbumps to hurdle. This was no exception!

One of the things that I found very daunting about planning this trip to Europe is the fact that I'm going to need shots. I have traveled quite extensively and I've never needed shots before! I have a medical phobia. Without reviewing my interesting medical history, let me just tell you I earned it! In particular, I'm afraid of needles. Yes, I know that that it's no big deal, I've hurt myself worse sewing, but it IS a big deal, and I really, really hate needles. I had a nurse explain to me one time, as she was planning to impale yet another bodily part, that the diameter of the needle is directly proportionate to the end of the needle upon which you find yourself. In other words, if it's incoming, the needle's HUGE. I'm not so good being on the receiving end.

When I heard a rumor that I might need shots to go on this trip, I immediately looked up the government's Center for Disease Control website. If you travel pretty much anywhere somewhat exotic, I recommend you look at it. It is loaded with facts about stuff you had never considered. Detailed scary place, that website. I'm creative enough to write my own nightmare scripts, but if you need a bad dream, spend some time casually reading the CDC website.

Now, on our trip, including layovers and the weekend in Stockholm, we're going to have time in Sweden, Spain, Greece,

France, Italy and Turkey. Iceland, Denmark, and London do not count; they are just layovers, and we do not even plan to leave the airport. According to the CDC, the only shots that are required for most of the trip are your basic, standard, routine, most –Americans-already –have them-kind of shots. Those places are considered pretty civilized and I should be just fine already. Then we get to the big, glaring CDC concern: Turkey. The cruise goes to two Turkish ports. It's going to be probably the most foreign place I've ever seen!

One of the things I enjoy doing in new places is seeking out street food. I like to have local fare wherever I am, unlike Husband, who loves Tex-Mex food, familiar things, and is a big fan of Veal Parmesan. I like to eat right, and right where I am. Crab in Alaska, saimin and garlic shrimp in Hawaii, conch chowder in the Keys, lobster in New England. Husband is known for eating odd things in odd places, like tacos in Boston and enchiladas in Honolulu and chili in Alabama. Culinary speaking, he's not real brave. I, however, am. So the idea of going to Europe got me thinking about interesting local food --- gyros, skewers, pastries, baklava, pasta, gelato, Turkish Delight, Swedish meatballs!

The nice thing about food is that it can be a good memory. It doesn't break, it doesn't require packing, doesn't add to your luggage weight, nor do you need to find place for it at home. You could even take a picture of it, if you want to. Do not post it, however, on Facebook, or anywhere else. No one is interested in your dinner.

Back to Turkey, back to the CDC webpage, back to the idea of shots. How can I go to Turkey and *not* taste the food? How can I *not* have baklava and kebabs and falafel? Yes, I could just eat the predictable, safe food right on the ship, but where's the fun in that? The shots looked unavoidable, unless I wanted to risk a dire disease, which is not a great souvenir. There is a significant risk of food-borne illnesses, including hepatitis and typhoid, and that's a bad way to end a trip. I called my doctor, who informed me that they don't do exotic shots. Oh, *exotic* --now there's a word I don't like in regards to my health! The doctor sent us to the county health nurse down at the courthouse.

The Cruise Addict and I went in together. The travel nurse was very nice, although I knew she was armed with hidden weaponry; needles and such. She reviewed our itinerary and commented that it's probably the most thorough she'd ever seen, covering the most turf in the smallest period of time. I was already having second thoughts, however—I've never needed shots anywhere I've ever gone before! The nurse pulled up the CDC website; thus she had the same information I had read at home. She agreed that Sweden, Iceland, Spain, Greece, France, and Italy were all fairly civilized and I could get by with just the routine up-to-date immunizations. However, Turkey...

The CDC recommends that people who are going to Turkey have the routine shots, and also hepatitis A, hepatitis B, typhoid, tetanus, plus malaria and rabies, if you're going to be handling bats. Handling bats on a cruise never crossed my mind, so that was easy to ignore. I decided to opt out of the hepatitis B shot, too. The nurse agreed with that, as long as I avoid prostitutes, tattoos, and piercings. I should be okay-- prostitutes, tattoos, and piercings are not part of my everyday life at home. There is no reason to act like that in Turkey.

I also decided to skip the malaria shots. Malaria is spread by mosquitoes, infected mosquitoes in particular. I think it's unlikely that I would encounter *any* mosquitoes in Turkey, much less infected ones. We will be in the heat of the day in the desert in Turkey, and by nightfall we will be back on the ship. I think I'm safe. Besides, malaria medicine has side effects I really didn't want to deal with.

That left hepatitis A, typhoid, and tetanus. Mercifully, I was current on my tetanus shots, because those hurt and I didn't want to get another one. I was assured that the hepatitis A and the typhoid shots were really no big deal, and I probably would not even notice them. Ha. Nevertheless, when I heard that there was an option for typhoid that I could take orally, I was all over that --one less needle in my life! The nurse carefully explained I would have to take pills twice a day exactly on time for a week, and it might cause , shall we say, digestive side effects. No problem; I'll just set a timer, and I can deal with unhappy guts, if it means I can avoid another needle. The oral route even costs less! Did I tell you I'm very frugal? I opted for the pills.

We're not going to say that Husband was less than compassionate, but he just does not understand my phobia. He thought that I was being a bit of a chicken. He may have mentioned it right out loud. "Just get it over with. Don't be a wimp," were his exact words, as I recall. Oh, all right, I'll go ahead and get shots, hepatitis A and typhoid, so long as he went first. No big deal for him. One shot in the arm, one shot in the other arm – took him under a minute.

Meanwhile, I was thinking about the dentist. My dentist thinks I'm terribly courageous. When I need dental care, I refuse to have Novocain or other pain killers. My reason for not having Novocain is that I'm *not* very brave and there is no way I'm going to let anyone stick a needle in my *mouth*. I don't even have much padding in there, as opposed to my rear, for instance, which is quite well padded. If I was <u>actually</u> brave, I would have the needle and the dental work and go about my day. Instead, it takes all the courage I have to get through a filling or whatever torture the dentist devises; the important thing is that I manage to avoid a needle. I sometimes think that dentistry without anything to numb the pain could be useful in prisoner interrogation, but I digress.

There is, however, no way to avoid shots this time, if I intended to get off the ship in Turkey, and I'm not going on a cruise to a new place and staying on the ship. It was my turn with the nurse, who was looking less friendly by the minute. The first shot was not that bad; left arm, no problem. When I was birthing my children (delivered with no drugs, no epidural, nothing; not that I'm courageous, mind you, but the only available pain relief involved stab wounds), I needed a focal point to concentrate on during labor to lessen the pain. I use the same strategy at the dentist, and at the doctor's office. Wherever I need to concentrate on not screaming, I just find a focal point.

In this case, I used the bulletin board at the travel nurse's office. It was not an interesting bulletin board, but as focal points go, it was just fine. The nurse put the second needle into my arm. I mentioned that the bulletin board was getting blurry. The room tipped counterclockwise. Suddenly the nurse and The Cruise Addict were all up in arms. Ice packs on my neck, ice packs on my forehead. In my defense, and I guess I need one, I did not actually faint. Husband asked as we walked to the car a few minutes later, "why didn't you just take the pills?"

As we were leaving, the nurse handed me a packet and smiled, "See you in six months, for your hepatitis booster shots." The deal is, if we get the shots now, we are good for six months; if we get a booster, we're good for life. Am I going back in six months? We will see! This cruise had better be worth it.

We, meaning The Cruise Addict, had a couple of medical obstacles as we prepared for this journey. Just a week before we were to fly out, he had an abscessed tooth treated by a dentist, who assured him it'd be Just Fine the following day. Not so.

Husband was in great pain, even with high-power pain pills. Good thing he has a compassionate wife. You should remind him of that fact. He forgets.

He had a routine doctor visit two days later. I drove him to the doctor's office, since letting him drive while that drugged sounded unwise. The nurse who checked his vital signs was immediately concerned. She said, "I don't like the way you look." Husband took umbrage at that, for some reason. The nurse continued, " you are sweaty, and your blood pressure is pretty high. I'm ordering an EKG. I think you're having a heart attack."

I don't know about Husband's heart, but mine sunk. This was not a good time for a medical drama. Husband protested, saying that of course he was sweaty, it's 88 degrees today, and the exam room had no air conditioning or windows. He insisted the elevated blood pressure was from the pain he had from his tooth, or the pain pills, or anything but a heart attack. He was ignored.

The EKG machine was wheeled in, and over his protests, various stickers were placed on his legs and chest. It looked to me like they aimed for hairy parts, but what do I know. Uh, oh, he was dead—nothing registered at all! No, it was the machine that was dead. The nurse yanked off the stickers, and called for a different machine. It also required electrode stickers...why didn't they use the same ones? More stickers were applied, on nearby hairy spots. By now the doctor had moseyed in. She glanced at Husband, who looked like he was prepped for electrocution.

She greeted me with, "Hi, what's new?" I mentioned we were going to Europe later this week. She rolled her eyes, then stared at the calendar on the wall for a long minute. "But we don't leave until Friday," I assured her.

"I hope you have travel insurance-" the doctor began, just as the paper tape scrolled out of the EKG machine. She glanced at it. "Oh, never mind; you're fine. Toothache, you said?" I resumed breathing while she calmly went about Husband's routine exam. Whew—that could have been bad!

Petty Crime and Purses

Throughout the crowded cities in Europe, minor crime is a concern. Face it; it's an issue in America, too. We will just take precautions against pickpockets. Being very aware of our surroundings and not making ourselves an easy target are key. Even at home, I refuse to carry a purse. I like having my hands free. You never know what I might need to haul grocery bags, pick up a grandchild, or grab the railing to prevent stumbling. Besides, handbags are heavy! I've actually weighed my mother's purse. It was close to 9 pounds! If I'm going to carry around something that weighs 9 pounds and doesn't even speak, it had better be looking up at me with a little face of a dimpled grandchild, not some inanimate object into which things get mindlessly dumped.

That's actually why I stopped carrying a purse decades ago. I had small children and I found that whenever we went anywhere, one child or another, or even Husband, would often hand me something and say, "here, will you please put this in your purse?" I ended up carrying the detritus of the whole day, while they had their hands free. One day I drew a line. I said "no, today I have no purse. That item you handed me, I would have to put in my pocket. You have pockets, too; put it in there."

I realized that I did just fine without carrying a purse at all. I have a rubber banded stack of cards, my Costco card, my driver's license, a couple of credit cards and some cash that goes in my pocket along with my car keys. My cell phone goes in my other pocket.

Reading glasses are an annoyance. I've only recently started to need them. They either go on my head or I stuff them in a pocket. I also have a pin, like a brooch, a silver circle, and I put one arm of the glasses in the circle, and the rest hangs down. It's kind of stylish and not in my way. I did buy one of those little chain necklace type glasses holders. I tried it on, looked in a mirror, and frightened myself. I aged about 40 years right then and there! That obviously is not for me. About the only thing I ever wish I had with me is a pen, and anyone in America has access to a pen. They have a purse. They have a desk somewhere. It's very easy to borrow a pen. I quit hauling a purse around years ago and never looked back.

Italy and Spain, well, all of Europe, but those places, in particular, are legendary for pickpockets. Have you heard of Susie, the pickpocket? Susie the pickpocket lives in Barcelona and she is so thorough and so quick that many tourists have filmed her at work, just to catch the art form. You can see her on YouTube. I'm taking precautions against pickpockets.

I have purchased low-profile very comfortable money belts for Husband and me to wear in Europe. Our plan is, we will just have enough money for the day in our front pockets, and then extra cash and credit cards in the money belt under our shirts. I will have a money belt in which I will carry my passport, along with extra cash. If I suddenly need to buy something wonderful that's fairly expensive, I will simply duck around somewhere where I can discreetly reach my money belt, get more money out, and go back and purchase the item that I have in mind. A pickpocket may be able to snatch a purse, but no one is going to be able to swipe a money belt from under my shirt without me noticing! I'm already a middle-aged grandmother, so I'm not terribly concerned about my money belt making me look any more pudgy.

A tip I picked up is just brilliant. A large safety pin on all outer zippers! The tallywhacker, or zipper pull, can be easily opened, but it might be just enough to deter a pickpocket with speed on his mind. When we traveled to Samana, in the Dominican Republic, we encountered swarms of little five and eight year old children, pulling at us, pulling at our clothing, trying to get into our pockets, and unzipping our friend's backpack. It was unnerving to say the least! I'm not expecting a repeat in Europe, but a safety pin is a quick fix. It's cheap, easy, and since pickpockets need to hurry, I hope it'll slow them down enough to choose another target.

Even without a purse, I realize that I will need access to some sort of a bag every day. On the tours, there are things that I will have to have. I will want my wrap to protect against air-conditioning or sunburn. I will need a water bottle, sunblock, my big floppy hat that folds down to nothing, the camera, and the Bathroom Bag.

Restrooms and Language

Oh, yes, I'm concerned about bathrooms. Did you know there's even a website on how to use bathrooms around the world? My daughter came in one day and saw me looking on the Bathrooms Of The World website. "Mom! You know how to use those!" I do *here;* I know how to use the facilities in North America. They may occasionally have a different button or knob for flushing, or even a pull chain, but I can figure it out. They may have different names. For instance, in United States we call it a bathroom or restroom. In Canada, it's called a washroom. In England, it's called the 'WC, 'which is totally confusing because what does needing to powder my nose have to do with the Wesleyan Church? I have also heard them called 'loo,' 'powder room,' 'facilities', 'the john," 'little room', and of course 'toilet.' I may just stick with 'toilet', although it does sound crass.

I'm just concerned about this whole topic in foreign places. And I've heard horror stories about hole in the ground toilets that one might encounter in Greece, or Italy, or Turkey. Those are even scarier. I know in the times we've been camping or hiking, and I've needed to avail myself without facilities at hand, when I've sought the privacy of a tree, I invariably fill my shoe. And what if soap and water is not available? Or paper??

In my little drawstring bag, I will have a third of a roll of toilet paper with the core taken out, and squished flat—that's a camping trick. It takes up a lot less space. I will have hand wipes in there, too. I guess if I need to find a bush or use a hole in the ground, or worse, well, I'll be prepared.

Speaking of cleanliness, we must discuss bidets and their usage. You just don't see them in America. I know of some Americans living abroad who were unsure what to do with the extra porcelain item in their bathrooms...so they put it to use, holding goldfish, potted plants, or magazines. I understand the basic philosophy; I even agree washing one's nether parts is a good idea, especially in countries where daily showering is not the norm. However, my behind does not need a drinking fountain.

Another concern is bathroom attendants. We rarely find those in America. I would prefer to be alone, if you please. And how does one tip them? Is it a tip, or a fee? I guess I'll just make sure to have some small coins with me at all times in the local currency, because if I need to Go, money should not be my first thought. I'm just uneasy about this whole topic in foreign places, and it's unlikely I'll go a whole three weeks without some issue or another arising.

Language!! Americans deep down believe that if we speak English loudly enough wherever we are, the locals will understand us. If that fails, we can always pantomime. I think for this occasion, being so far from home, I'm going to learn a few words in each of the languages we're going to encounter. For Greece, Italy, Sweden, Turkey, France, and Spain, I will need to learn how to say: please, thank you, hello, goodbye, and where's the bathroom. Well, no, not bathroom; people might be puzzled as to why I would like to bathe during dinner. That, and a dazzling smile with some patience, should get me by.

A Quest

Sometimes when we travel, we have A Quest. A Quest is where we're after one thing in particular. It's often a local item that is exclusive to particular place, such as the caribou horn buttons in Alaska, or the lobster-shaped cookie cutters in Maine. I collect metal cookie cutters as souvenirs. They're inexpensive, lightweight, and look really cheerful on my wall over the bay window. I often buy a spiral-bound photo calendar of the place where we are visiting for the next year. That way, I can smile at happy memories every time I have to book another doctor appointment or get the car tires rotated.

Although I love my family dearly, kids, grandchildren and all, I have made it a point never to bring souvenirs or presents home for any of them. The problem is... my family is growing. I was looking at our family portrait on the wall the other day and realizing that it's under a year old, and already outdated, twice. I have to think of the precedent; it's no big deal to bring home a present for each of them now, but what do I do when there are so many more of them in years to come? If I need to bring home a gift for all of them, my vacation is no longer a vacation. It's a shopping spree! I may, however, break that this time, and bring home some scarves for my daughters. I can afford the space in my suitcase and they certainly don't weigh very much.

On this particular trip the Quests are: an authentic Swedish cheese plane – I will get that in Stockholm – marbled paper from Florence, nougat candy in rice paper from Venice, a scarf (or eight) from Turkey and a small Nativity set , maybe wooden. I do not know where the Nativity set will come from or what it looks like, but I know I will recognize it when I see it.

One thing I absolutely do not want to bring home as a souvenir is surströmming. Surströmming is a traditional fish in Sweden and my Husband has memories of it from when he lived in Sweden, decades ago. The basic recipe is: put whitefish and yeast in a can, seal it and put it on a shelf for a couple of years. When the can is bulging, it's ready to serve. The stuff is so incredibly rank that the best way to open it, I understand, is underwater. I've heard that if you open it outdoors, people can smell it for blocks around.

 Husband tells a story about a woman he knew who opened it in her apartment in Sweden. The next day she found bags of groceries donated by her neighbors on the front step, because they thought things were so bad in her house that she had to eat rotten food. There is a YouTube video online that shows big, tough gangster type people, opening a can of surströmming outdoors. They're all big and brash. Oh, yeah, too cool--until the can is opened... then they're retching in the bushes.

 Husband says they would often buy surströmming just as a joke for newcomers to the country. He thinks our sons would get a laugh out of it. I have been very clear in my directions that we will not purchase, open, buy, partake of, or get anywhere near the stuff while we are in Sweden. There is no reason to ruin a perfectly good vacation. Do I trust him? I do not. I probably will go through the suitcase just to make sure we're not taking any on the ship after our stay in Stockholm. Surströmming is *not* a Quest.

Speaking of food, the edible kind, I do have a couple of Quests for food while we're on this vacation. I enjoy trying local foods, wherever we go. In Sweden, of course, we need to have Swedish meatballs, and lingonberries. In Naples, we must seek pizza; it was invented there. We will have gelato and cannoli in Italy. Gyro in Greece is a must, and those tender herb-coated kebabs. In Turkey, we'll seek Turkish Delight and baklava.

Gelato, a Quest of its Own

I love frozen treats. I love frozen lemonade. I love frozen virgin peach daiquiris. I love slushes and ices and ice cream and sherbet, and particularly I love gelato. Gelato is a frozen confection, ice cream's cousin. It contains more sugar and less cream than ice cream. The freezing process makes very small crystals, so it's smoother than regular ice cream. The best gelato flavors, in my opinion, are fruity. The best gelato by far I've ever had was in Antigua. It was mango, and to this day I do not know how they got so much mango flavor into the gelato. It was a hot, sweltering day in the Caribbean, and this gelato was the most magnificent explosion of frozen glacial mango-ness imaginable! It was exquisite! That mango gelato that angels serve in heaven? That's not this good. Nevertheless, I will seek gelato in Italy, especially in Florence, where gelato was invented. I can't wait.

I will certainly seek gelato out in Florence, but what's stopping me from enjoying another in Naples, or Rome, or elsewhere? Face it; I'd rather have a cold fruity gelato than lunch, most days! And with as much walking as our agenda calls for, I can ignore that inner voice, the one that nags about calorie intake. Gelato has less fat than ice cream, making it nearly virtuous.

I've learned several things about gelato. I've learned that we do not want the brightly colored gelato. They are designed to attract children, not adults with broader palates. I want the real deal; I can get artificially flavored gelato at home. Lemon is pale, not yellow, off-white is peach, tan is pistachio, not the bilious neon green that we have here in America! I'm also interested in sampling gelato made on-site. The signs will indicate 'Atigianale', or 'produzione propia,' meaning it was made right there. Not that imported from across town is bad, mind you, but having it made on site adds to the experience. One more Italian phrase I need to learn: "Un assaggia, per favor?" (a taste, please?)

To Avoid...

In each place, there are places and things I can't wait to see! With rare exception, I want to see as much as possible. And then we come to the Sultan Ahmet Mosque in Istanbul, where my heels are firmly dug in. I do not want to go inside the Mosque.

The Blue Mosque is a world famous tourist site and the pictures I've seen are gorgeous. I have decided that, for myself, those pictures will be just fine. The only reason I would like to go there is to see the old building itself, and the beautiful mosaic on the tiered domes. We're going to be in Rome and Florence, Venice and Athens---we're going to see old churches and basilicas, starting even before we can get on the ship. I'm so looking forward to going to Saint Mark's Square and seeing the gold cathedral and the museum there. We will see many mosaics, many domes, many old buildings on this cruise. I'm choosing to miss out on the Blue Mosque and I'm doing it for a very political reason.

Normally I recognize that the whole point of being in new places is that it is different than my home at home. I understand that when I travel, that I'm a guest, and I must be respectful. I'm fine with that. I'm also quite conservative in my everyday dress. I figure if the Good Lord meant for me to flaunt very short skirts, He'd have given me better legs. I know that traveling across Europe, we will be going through a lot of cathedrals and churches and I have every intention of keeping my shoulders and my knees and the parts in between covered out of respect. However...

The restrictions at the Blue Mosque are more than I can bear. I'm fine with modesty, but I'm really uncomfortable butting up against the strict, almost sharia law, standards required of women at the Blue Mosque. The dress code for visiting the Blue Mosque is that men must have their knees covered. Women must have their ankles to wrists to neck covered and they must not have hair exposed. The official website says "clothing is provided for those who do not meet the standards of modesty to conceal hair, arms, legs, wrists, ankles, and the female form." I, being a female, happen to have a female form, and I know that from a distance, you cannot disguise a woman even in a flour sack, which is pretty much the requirement. I'm big on modesty, but I'm not going to be covered from the top of my head to my ankles in a bag. I'm a woman, an American, and that makes me incredibly uncomfortable in Istanbul to begin with. The Mosque isn't for me.

All twelve of us will be on the same tour that day, and I've already let the others know that if they would like to see the Blue Mosque, they had better do so; it may be the one opportunity they have to visit it. I, however, cannot go against my personal convictions as an American, as a woman, and I will content myself wandering around the gardens outside. I'm not going to regret missing out.

Blending In

Melissa is concerned about looking like an American. She thinks that we must be careful to blend in. There are some things we can do. For instance, wearing flashy name brand athletic shoes is going to mark us as wealthy North Americans, as will wearing running shoes or track shoes or exercise shoes around cities. Especially white ones; white shoes are for nurses in Europe. Athletic shoes are for working out, and for exercising in Europe. No matter what we do, we are still going to look and act like Americans.

There will be many differences in on this trip. I'm looking forward to this! In Sweden, for example, in all restaurants want you to feel satisfied. With every meal, all second helpings of potatoes in any restaurant across the country are free. They want to make sure you don't leave hungry.

In Europe, ice in cold drinks is something not done... your drink is already cold, so why would you put ice in it? In many of the places we wish to go, we'll need to factor in that they have a siesta midday, a rest period for a few hours every afternoon. Stores close, and the museums shut down for a few hours. We don't do that at home. We need to plan outdoor activities during those times.

We also need to adapt our schedule a little bit, jet lag aside, because Europeans start their days later than I do, and tend to go far in the night. I'm pretty much home by ten o'clock most every night. This is when a lot of cities are just coming alive! People are just heading out for dinner when I'm winding down.

We're factoring in closing times as we plan. Museums across Europe are often closed on Monday, except for a few places where they're closed on Tuesday, and a few places where it looks like they randomly close whenever they darn well feel like it. Again, I need to member that we are the guests. The only place I see this being a minor obstacle is in Istanbul, where Hagai Sophia is closed on Monday, the day we will be there. We will exchange the underground Basilica Cistern on that tour.

There are norms and mores that we are simply not going to get. For example, in France, smiling at people you do not know is considered odd. Why are you smiling? you don't even know one another! To ask for directions with a standard big broad American smile would be off-putting. The main thing we need to remember is that we are in *their* country. When in Rome, do as the Romans, and that'll apply in every other place we visit.

Jet Lag

No way around it, is there? (yes, there is! I'll do a product plug in Part Two)

I do not want to spend my limited time feeling like I have been run over by teams of grumpy horses. Yawning in museums and falling asleep during performances would make me sad. I'm not really sure how we're going to adapt to a place that's a good 8 to 12 hours ahead of home.

All told, it'll be 17 hours from home to Stockholm, including a layover in Iceland. The longest flight I've ever been on was 11 hours, and I don't remember it being a lot of fun. My mother, who has traveled farther than I have, suggested that we take a sleeping pill, maybe a Tylenol PM or something, when last boarding call is called for the flight. It might help with the nerves, too. Being American, we're used to domestic air flight conditions, which is basically being packed in a flying tube like sardines. I'm not very tall, and I've been on flights were *my* knees hit the seat in front of me. Heaven help my six foot four Husband, who often has to sit diagonally! I think the planes will be the same flying from here to Europe but I hope that service will be better. I am going to bring my e-reader, keyboard, a couple of magazines, a sketchpad, my maps and folders to go over midflight. Still thinking about Mom's sleeping pill.

Locals

When I was a child, we traveled a lot. My family traveled all summer, from school's out till Labor Day weekend. I remember these road trips, very, very well. They've increased my respect for America as well as improving my geography grades as a child. My parents had a plan for each day when we traveled. My father would work in the morning, calling on accounts in the area, and we would act like tourists in the afternoon, seeing as much of the place as we could fit in. Drive to the next city, and a swim in the hotel pool rounded out the day.

My father was legendary. He was just a little guy, but he didn't know that he was size-deprived. He was outgoing and gregarious and loud, the light of any room he entered. Dad explained to me once that he did not like strangers, and so he made sure there were none around him. He talked to *everybody*, asking questions, and consequently, he knew a lot more than most travelers. He would talk to the hotel valet and ask him the best place for dinner. He would talk to the woman in the gas station and ask him where to buy his wife some flowers. He would ask what should we not miss; "show us your city—we have never been here before." He often found restaurant suggestions for out-of-the-way places which were a little, frankly, scary, but had phenomenal local fare. He steered clear of the major tourist places and chain restaurants, especially.

I learned a lot from my Dad. One of the things I learned is that local residents always know more than I do. Think about it; who knows more about your hometown than you do? If someone passing through asked you to recommend a restaurant, you would know where to send them, right? It's the same when we travel. Wherever we go, we talk to people who actually live there, as Dad did. This will hold us in good stead all over the Mediterranean, I'm sure!

Meet and Greet

In our preparation for this cruise, we signed up on CruiseCritic.com, for the ship's Meet and Greet party. CruiseCritic is a great resource; I highly recommend wandering through its pages! You can't read it all, so hone in on the parts that apply to you. And join the Meet and Greet for your particular sailing dates. It's made of other passengers on the same cruise. In the past, we have arranged private tours with Cruise Critic people, and made some long-term friends. It's a great way to compare notes, long before the cruise sails!

NCL does a fine Meet and Greet. Refreshments are provided, along with a venue, and senior officers attend, often from every department onboard. It's a small group, and you won't get a better opportunity to actually meet and talk to the officers, all in one place. They really do want to make you feel welcome. They are keenly aware that, simply by being a member of CruiseCritic, you are internet- savvy, and you have the power to spread your experience far and wide, just by writing a review. It seems to me that they go out of their way to make Cruise Critic members, particularly happy.

They will also give out a "magic card" with the direct phone numbers to the head of each onboard department. This is a godsend if you have a problem onboard; going directly to the source will save the hassle of wading through the maze that is

Guest Services. A Meet and Greet is also a good chance to meet up with other passengers on the "roll call" with whom you've been chatting online, putting face to name at last.

Often surprises occur at Meet and Greets. We have had free bowling tickets handed out, bridge tours, invitations to private cocktail parties, and free specialty dining vouchers, just for attending! It's well worth the 45 minutes or so. Actually, on this Mediterranean cruise, the host ended up canceling his cruise a month before it sailed. The Cruise Addict and I took over the Meet and Greet host position, which greatly enhanced our cruise in a big way---but let's not jump the story, shall we?

Telling Time and Cameras

I wear a wrist watch about as often as I wear my fingernails. Time is important to me. Telling time in Europe is different than in America, and I foresee some adjustments. In America, we are used to a twelve hour clock with AM and PM attached; 4pm, 3:15am, like that. In Europe, it's a 24 hour clock, the same as our military uses. I'm not military, so I'll need to think differently. For example, midafternoon would be two o'clock or 2 PM, at home. In Europe, it's going to be 14:00. I'm not used to thinking in terms of fourteen hundred hours. I may need to do some quick mental math in order to figure out what time we need to be wherever it is we are going.

It's really not that difficult. As I understand, the clock starts at midnight, with 100 hours, 200, 400, and so forth, until you hit 1200 hours, which is noon. Anything after that requires adding on to the twelve hours already acquired. For example, four o'clock in the afternoon in the USA would be 1600 hours in

Europe, because 1200 (which is noon) plus four more hours. The minutes just complicate things! Half past 5pm is 17:30 hours.

Mercifully, I think the only time we are going to need to keep track of this dramatically is with our tour guides. Our friends know that we talk in terms of five o'clocks. The tour guides will be very aware of getting us back to ship on time, no matter how they read their clocks!

We have a perfectly good camera; actually it's a remarkably good one, but The Cruise Addict insisted that he have his own. I'm in favor of this. I tend to do most of the photography in our family and I must say, we have had some rather wonderful pictures. However, because I'm the one taking the pictures, I don't tend to *be in* the pictures. If Husband has his own, I'm more likely to show up in some of them. This also gives us the opportunity to catch that great shot in case Husband and I are separated, or he sees something that I miss, or I want to take a picture of something that he considers completely irrelevant. If the only camera is in his pocket, he may not give it over fast enough. We'll take a stack of fresh SD cards, probably at least one per day, each. Gone are the days of carefully weighing whether or not to take a photo, for fear of wasting film.

Prepurchasing Entry Tickets

Many of the most popular sites in Europe are known for having significant wait times, up to two or three hours, just to get tickets! With our time being so limited, we are going to buy as many tickets to as many sites as we possibly can ahead of time. That way, we can bypass the long line; just show our printed receipt or voucher and go on in. Several of the tours we chose included tickets—even easier!

It's a good idea to wade through the ticket process at home. Several sites are complicated, not to mention the language barrier. The Vatican requires pre purchased tickets, but the process is so complex, it requires an online video! That's not something I want to mess with, last minute. I've read that in some places, entrance prices can suddenly vary due to the perceived nationality of the customer. I'm nicely anonymous online.

Planned Itinerary

Let's look at our plans for each city. Part Two will detail what we actually end up doing in each place, day by day. How close do we get to what we planned from our dining room table at home?

Sweden

Once we determined that by flying from Seattle to anywhere else, pretty much, and then flying into Venice, rather than a direct flight from SeaTac to Venice, we could save a significant amount of money--- hundreds of dollars-- we began to look into extending our vacation. Husband lived in Sweden, years ago, and has always wanted to return.

Now's his chance. So with our two days in Stockholm booked, we began planning. The first thing we found was a 4.5 star hotel. We booked this through Travelocity after doing some research on hotel.com and trip advisor. Marina Elite Tower in Stockholm was having a deal; it ended up costing very little surprisingly little, like Holiday Inn price. Nothing wrong with having little elegance in my life. Especially after a long flight, I'm going to want some pampering!

Online hotels almost always have a website. Almost always they have pictures of the site, of the venue, of the restaurants nearby, of the rooms, designed to make it look terribly appealing. This hotel is so classy it had a full on video instead! As we were looking at the video, deciding whether or not to book it, I was struck by the beauty. I exclaimed, "Oh, look, it has Scandinavian furniture, all throughout! It's beautiful!" Husband shot me a look. Oh, yeah, wait... Scandinavian furniture... Sweden obviously is in Scandinavia. They probably bought the furniture down the street at IKEA. Regardless, it looked pretty.

We decided that our best use of time in Stockholm would be to take a Hop On Hop Off tour, since the reviews for that city looked good. I did not know that Stockholm was made of a series of fourteen islands-- looks like we're going to be seeing a lot of islands on this particular vacation. I'm excited about this! Instead of having a Hop On Hop Off *bus* tour, as in other cities, Stockholm has a Hop On Hop Off *boat* tour. It includes eight stops in the archipelago. This will allow us to get on and off when we come to interesting things. I think I would like just to get an overview, maybe go a complete circuit and then go back to look at those stops that look most interesting.

The tour takes us around the city, to museums, including the Wasa that sank right there in the harbor hundreds of years ago and was perfectly preserved in the icy cold Scandinavian water. We will be able to see Old Town and the newer architecture, old churches, even an amusement park, which I think we will probably skip. This seems like a good price and the best way to able to get a good overview of Stockholm. With 24 hour tickets, we can get on and off as often as we choose. The price for this Hop On Hop Off tour is 160 Swedish krona, which comes out to be about $24 US. Very reasonable. It will save us a lot of walking, especially over Stockholm's big arcing bridges.

I hope I will be feeling good enough to enjoy it. I've never had an 11 hour flight before, and I believe that there at least nine time zones to go through! The flight has a one hour and 40 minute layover in Iceland. Hopefully I'll be able to get out and jog around the airport a couple times and get my body back on speaking terms with me!

Venice

Our flight out of Stockholm leaves in the early morning. We will arrive in Venice just after noon. Venice has been described as a 'mysterious city amid elegant decay.' In its day, it was the religious and political center of Italy and the remnants are going to be great fun to explore. When I think of Venice, I think of romance and vibrancy and glitter. It's a small island, and we will have to plan on a slower pace and a lot of tourists.

Tourists tend to congregate in main areas, no matter where they are on a map. I'm not big on crowds. Everything I've read says that 80% of tourists only venture into 15% of Venice. Silly--- why go so far just to be with more tourists like yourselves? The area between Saint Marco and Rialto Bridge is the most touristy area. However, if we take a ten minute walk in any direction, that will get us away from tourists and into the more authentic Venice. That's our goal; we will wander. Wandering should be easy. It's an island. We may not find our way directly, but we cannot get permanently lost. Temporarily misplaced, perhaps, but probably not permanently.

I am a big fan of serendipity, and that's seldom found in crowded places with hordes of tourists. I think heading off the main streets will make me happier.

Of course, we are also tourists! Reminds me of walking along a crowded San Francisco street, holding my little granddaughter's hand, so as not to lose her. She was annoyed at all the people, and finally burst out "Stupid tourists! They should all stay home!" I had to pull her aside and issue a reality check. She, too, was a visitor to that city, and as a guest, she needed to Be Nice, same as anyone else!

Our planned flight from Stockholm goes to Marco Polo airport in Venice. Marco Polo is known as a small airport. I hear that, on embarkation day, cruises that leave from elsewhere and end up in Venice really clog up the airport! We'll be incoming and we are coming a day before the cruise sails. I think we should be fine. I *hope* we will be fine!

Getting Around Venice

Husband and I decided to stay by Saint Marco Square. It's farther from the cruise terminal, but it's closer to the town center. When we leave the center of Venice and head to the cruise, we are going to have to take public transportation anyway. What's an extra mile across the lagoon? By staying at Saint Marco, we will be in a central area, which will make it easier for exploring. It will also consolidate walking, starting out near the center. We have never been to Venice and we have only a day and a half to have to see the place. Venice is made of a few more than 100 islands, approximately 400 bridges, and about 2000 narrow streets and alleys. My main goal in Venice is to get into the history, and soak up some of the atmosphere. Whatever I see will be new to me!

The first problem will be how to get to our hotel in Venice. Marco Polo airport is on the mainland, and our hotel is by San Marco Square, out in the lagoon. Water taxi looks to be the most expensive, and also the most direct route between the airport and the hotel. It should take about 30 minutes, but it's going to cost at least €210 for up to five people. Ouch! If we could find some people going to Saint Marco Square at the same time, that might be an option.

Another choice would be the airport shuttle. That should only cost about €18 per person, but it takes an hour and a half, and the buses only leave every 30 to 60 minutes. They go from the airport down the coast and across the long bridge onto the main island that makes up Venice. From there, we'd still have a goodly hike, or we could catch a passing Alilaguna at that point. The Alilaguno is a public bus, of sorts, only on water. It looks to be the most inexpensive way to get to San Marco, although we'd have to think about its extra stops. It would cost the least. Time versus money; the age old conundrum!

Regardless of which route we take, the hotel is still a few blocks from any water, and there are no motor vehicles on the islands of Venice. Wherever we get off of whichever boat we choose, we'll still have to schlepp our luggage through San Marco Square to the hotel. Then, the day will be ours! The following day, probably late in the afternoon when it's time for us to board the cruise ship, we will have to figure out how we're going to get to the cruise ship itself.

We could take a boat to the Piazzale Roma and take an Alilaguna to the people mover, hauling our luggage all the way. That should take about 20 minutes. We could also splurge and take a water taxi, which would get us directly to the ship. The advantage of that would be that we could skip the people mover, plus we could skip hauling our suitcases on and off two more boats and a bus. With a water taxi, we'd be left off right at the pier, where we could just hand off our bags to NCL employees. That sounds like an awfully good expenditure; I'm frugal, but smart, and I expect we will be tired after walking so much all day! I think we are probably going to go that way.

Venice is known for being expensive. That makes sense. At home, every item in every store arrived in the store by truck. In Venice, there are no trucks or delivery vans. Everything that gets into any store was delivered via a guy on foot with a hand truck or a small wagon after he offloaded it by hand from a boat. I'm used to dodging wild UPS and FedEx delivery drivers and giant trucks daily at home. Just walking in a car-free place sounds very appealing! A day in a new place is worth a little expense.

I'm very frugal in my day-to-day life, contrary to what Husband may report, but it's okay to splurge occasionally, reasonably. I'm okay with spending €80 for a fabulous dinner in Venice. Spending €800 on a beautiful Venetian mask that I will never take out of the box once I get home is not frugal nor wise. I plan on doing a lot of window shopping in Venice, and probably on the rest of our trip as well. Memories and photos are great!

One of the ways we can save money is by using a Vaporetto in Venice. It's like a city bus or like our own Hop On Hop Off tour. We can get a one hour pass, which allows us to go anywhere within 60 minutes, or a 12 hour pass for slightly more, or 24 hour pass. The 24 hour pass looks most reasonable. It'll be cost effective if we take at least three trips, and I would expect will be taking at least three trips in the two days available. For our purposes, we need to be aware of Vaporetto routes One and Two. One and Two go up and down the Grand Canal approximately every 10 minutes, one way or the other. One is the more direct route. It's faster and stops in fewer places, whereas Two stops at every stop along the way. I think we'll probably end up doing both. In the mornings and afternoon, the vaporetto, which is like a city bus, experiences rush-hour as people take it to get to work in the shops of Venice . It may be too crowded for us even to ride at those times. However, at night, after about 6 PM, the Vaporetto is nearly empty. It becomes like a private gondola ride from which we can admire scenery and the glittering lights of the city for much less cost than a private gondola and it covers more area, too. Like a harbor tour, without narration.

Gondola Or Not?

Our group is flying in from five different cities and we plan on meeting on the ship. However, Husband has made arrangements with Clint and Mary to meet the night before the cruise in Venice on Saint Marco square. I have not met them. They want to go out for dinner together and share a gondola ride. Were we on our own, I would seek out a place where the locals eat, and have a fabulous meal and an experience I cannot get at home, and probably spend less than any tourist spot.

I'm not very interested in a gondola ride. Yes, I know, it's tradition, but I also think it's touristy and hokey, and a needless expense. In my frugal mind, money equals stuff or experiences. I have to enjoy the item I bought, or the experience, enough to make it worth its cost. To me, a gondola just simply does not appeal. I would like to *see* one, but I'm not excited about riding one.

A gondola ride costs between 90 – €120 for a 45 minute ride. If we wish to add an accordion player and a singer, it's an extra €120. Prices are per gondola, not per-person, up to five people. Gondolas are not motorized. They are propelled by gondoliers with poles. I'm thinking about the time when we hired a rickshaw in Victoria. I felt terribly guilty as that driver hauled us around, although I'm sure he skipped the gym that night. I think it would be fun to lean over a bridge in the evening and watch some romantics down below in gondolas, but I really don't want to ride in one. Husband, however, does. He said that he cannot imagine going to Venice and not riding in a gondola, like in all the movies. Sometimes compromises must be made!

One of the first things we will do is buy a map of Venice. A map of any local area is a cheap souvenir. If we can spend a couple of euros and save a lot of extra walking and aimless wandering, it will be well worth the cost. Also, every shop has a business card, with a You Are Here map on the back. I don't have much of a sense of direction, but I read maps very well.

Husband, on the other hand, has an excellent, built-in, innate sense of direction that works even when he's asleep. It's kind of spooky. That time in Nebraska comes to mind. Have you seen Nebraska? The first five miles are flat, with tall grain growing, as far as the eye can see. The rest of the state looks pretty much just like that. It's so boring that the state painted random white lines across the highways every so often, just to jar a driver's eyes enough to break the inevitable dozing off. I was driving across Nebraska some years ago, while Husband slept. He had been asleep a good three hours, and the sun was straight overhead. I was bored silly---you can't even get a radio station way out there! At last I saw a sign: Historic Marker Next Left. Who cares what it led to...anything was better than admiring cornstalks without end. I turned at the next left. I assumed the marker would be nearby, but I guessed wrong. I had gone about three miles, when Husband abruptly woke up. Eyes still half shut, he asked, "why are we going north?" *North*--- with not a single landmark, not even a leaning shadow! How did he do that?

Hotel in Venice

The hotel we have chosen is the Hotel San Gallo. My mother's parents are from Italy and Mom grew up speaking Italian. She laughed when I told her what hotel we were staying in. She said "Gallo" means chicken; basically, we're staying in the house of the chicken...or the chicken coop. However, the website looks very nice. It looks elegant and clean and Old World. Not like a Holiday Inn or a Marriott, but again this is why we're going; to explore new places and see things that are different from home. We booked a good price on the hotel, a seasonal rate, after comparing websites and reading reviews. We lucked out because 'low season' starts the very day that we arrive!

 The hotel is back-to-back with Saint Mark's Square, and about a 10 or 15 minute walk to the Rialto Bridge. How did they measure that time? Surely it did not account for admiring the place on the way! The hotel comes with some unexpected perks. It comes with free Wi-Fi, a coupon book for discounts on authentic Venetian restaurants – the only kind available - a free one-way boat ride to the island of Murano where traditional glassblowers ply their arts, an on-the-rooftop breakfast, and puzzlingly, free parking! Venice is made of little islands and it is a car free area. What would I park? Nevertheless, I appreciate the sentiment.

Breakfast sounds great—imagine, breakfast on a roof top in Venice! I'm happy about it being a typical Italian breakfast. Those are not like American breakfasts, which is good because I don't like traditional American breakfast food. Soggy cereal, greasy sausage and hash browns, springy pancakes shiny with oozy butter.... eeww... don't forget slimy eggs! Personally, if I have to face greasy mushy food first thing in the morning, I'd really rather sleep in the extra 20 minutes. I usually do. In Italy, breakfasts are crusty rolls, fresh pastries, fruit, yogurt, mortadella, salami, fish, both cold and warm. This is my kind of food! I'm all in favor of Old World breakfast foods, along with Old World charm!

Sites to See in Venice

We plan to meet a couple of our friends for dinner that first evening, but we also have things to explore on our own in Venice. The main touristy things we need to see: San Marco Square, and the Rialto bridge area. Then I want to venture into the less explored areas. Saint Mark's was originally the religious and political center of Venice.

At night San Marco turns into *the place to be.* Music, food, elegance; it sounds wonderful! The cafés, from what I understand, have three pricing tiers, depending on whether a patron sits, stands, or grabs-and-goes. Least expensive is to get some food and stand; if you sit, it costs about double. At San Marco's Square in the evening, the cafés have competing musicians and you can walk around and listen to all of it for free. However, if we sit down it'll cost us a drink or food plus a cover charge. The cover charge is probably a good price for music and a drink, but in my case, I think we'll keep moving. I just want to absorb the atmosphere. We can do that better by not staying in one spot.

During the day, Saint Mark's Square is known for history and culture, and all sorts of people watching. I'm going to enjoy it! Elegantly dressed people from Paris and Dubai, rubbing shoulders with British teenagers with their Mohawks in all the colors of a snow cone, and quite likely that guy with the beer T-shirt from Boston… I like to people watch. To be surrounded with history and beautiful architecture---oooh!

The four main things I wish to see in Saint Mark's Square take up the four corners. I want to see the Campanile bell tower, Saint Mark's Basilica, the Corror Museum, and Doge's Palace. Many of the places in Europe are going to be opulent with fabulous architecture, beautiful art and a lot of gold to enjoy--- Saint Mark's Square is a fine place to start.

A Basilica is a church, and the one at San Marco is one of the oldest in Europe, with a wonderful jumble of different architectural styles, all blended together. I understand that we should go early or late in the day, to avoid crowds. It's probably best explored our first day, before the cruise ships disgorge their passengers the next morning. The Basilica is known for being crowded, even under the best conditions!

It has no entrance fee, but modesty is encouraged. Men, women, and even babies must have knees and shoulders covered in every church in Europe, and I'm fine with that. It's only respectful. The exterior architecture alone should be amazing. I'm American. America is just a baby country. We don't have anything dating back hundreds and hundreds of years. Our country's been around less than 300 years. I'm looking forward to seeing the architecture, and the art, especially the sculptures and mosaics. I was not gifted with a great pile of patience; I have great awe for meticulous art.

The other places that I wish to visit on Saint Mark's Square have a modest fee, but we're going to get a combo ticket. A fellow passenger on a previous cruise told us that the best way to get one is at the Correr Museum at the opposite end of the Square from the Basilica. This will save waiting in line. Our time is limited. I want to avoid lines as best I can, everywhere! The combo ticket will get us into Doge's Palace, Correr Museum, and four other museums. It even comes with a bonus entry into one of the other city -run museums in Venice.

I don't think I want to climb to the top of the bell tower, the Campanile in Saint Mark's Square, but we will definitely admire it. The main reason to climb the bell tower would be to get an overview of Venice. It's one of the higher points in the city. I think I'd better conserve my energy for places I really want to climb. I would prefer to spend my stamina walking to places instead of walking up stairs. Venice is only our second city on this epic journey. I still have to climb all around Pompeii, the Coliseum, assorted ruins, Athens and Rome, and quite likely Mount Vesuvius as well!

Doge's Palace interests me. This was the seat of the original Venetian government and the home of its ruling leader, the Duke, or Doge. He pretty much had his finger on the whole of Europe at the time. The Doge's Palace included living quarters for his family, as well as the Senate Hall, the Armory, and the Hall of the Great High Council. The largest oil painting in the world is over the Doge's throne. It is *The Paradise* by Tintoretto---and I'll see it with my own eyes! The Bridge of Sighs is where the prisoners were taken to prison below the Palace, glimpsing their last sight of Venice, and freedom. They knew that once they crossed over that slim bridge, that their life was functionally over. Very few prisoners were released.

The Correr Museum is known for being uncrowded and overlooked. I think this'll be a good break for us. After being jostled at the Basilica and the Palace, we'll be ready for some calm. Correr Museum is known for presenting a good overview of Venetian art and history.

I'm not big on Typical Touristy Places, but we cannot go to Venice and miss Rialto Bridge. This area is lined with little shops, both elegant, upscale, and touristy. On most of the days of the week, there is a fine market. I do love a good market. Maybe we could have lunch there. A produce stand, some local cheese, and crusty bread...mmmm. Not on the bridge itself, though: getting stepped on by tourists isn't the ambiance I seek for any meal!

I think once we explore Saint Mark's Square and Rialto Bridge, we will be pretty well done with Venice's tourist areas. Next, I would like to venture off the beaten path, where few sightseers go. If we go five or ten minutes in any direction, we will be in the more authentic Venice, and away from crowds. In particular, I want a nice restaurant for dinner; not a touristy restaurant, not an expensive, put –on-airs kind of a restaurant, but an authentic Venetian restaurant where the locals would take their families. I looked up Venice on Google Earth's satellite view. I easily located restaurants, many restaurants with menus posted in their window. Some of them even had pictures of the foods they offer. They looked wonderful to me!

On our second day in Venice, we will have the whole day to explore. Our ship leaves at 1:30 AM the following morning and we don't have to be on board until 12:30 AM. We'll probably wake up early ---if jetlag allows-- enjoy the rooftop breakfast, check out, and leave our suitcases in the hotel and then we'll explore Saint Mark's Square again. I find cities are very different at different times of the day; to see San Marco with fewer crowds sounds nice. We plan to wander the narrow streets of Venice to get a feel for people who live there.

Later, we will make our way to the NCL Spirit. We will check in with hours to spare, in case there is any hitch. Makes sense to me to have a buffer in case a credit card jams or a paperwork issue rears its ugly head, to leave time to deal with it before sailaway. Once we jettison our luggage and backpacks, we will be free to return to Venice.

Athens, Greece

Ancient Greece, long known as the cradle of civilization, as well as the bane of middle school history students. Early medicine, literature, theatre, astronomy, government, and Greek mythology all originated here! Imagine Alexander the Great, Plato, Socrates... the wonderful discussions that took place on the very same steps where we will be walking! Greece was the center of civilization in its day, setting the pace for all of Western civilization to follow.

Unfortunately, modern Athens has a sad reputation for being run down and dingy. Unemployment rates stand at about 23%, even higher among young people, and of course that affects the city's morale. Any city whose populace is discouraged will often turn to crime, and then you have opportunistic things such as gangs, pickpockets, and so forth. It's tough to care about things like sweeping the streets and picking up trash when they're worrying about money. General travel advice is to get through Athens, into the historical district as quick as possible. I guess that's what we're going to do as well. In our limited time in this port, we are going to focus on history. Sorry, Athens, maybe someday we will come back and explore the more modern aspects of your city.

Athens is approximately seven miles from the port of Piraeus. With traffic, that translates into about a 30 minute drive! I'm grateful that we booked an all-day private tour here; I don't have to worry about driving at all. Several of the places we aim to visit are known for massive crowds. Our guide assures us he can sidestep much of that. The local perspective will be a big advantage, I'm sure!

The Acropolis is going to be a highlight of the day. Democracy itself grew from the heated discussions on the complex of the Acropolis. The architectural features still influence architecture to this day, including ante-bellum mansions across the South. The most famous structure is the Parthenon (built in 438 BC). Socrates' old stomping grounds still stand, albeit stripped of much of its former glory. The passing of time isn't always kind.

The Plaka is the old town area of Athens, also on our agenda. Located close to the Acropolis, it has kept much of its original character and seems a world away from the urban sprawl that occurred to the rest of the city. The Plaka consists of many shops and cafes, and is also a good area to find something to eat as many of its restaurants have outdoor seating and some pretty awesome Greek food. We'll ask our guide to recommend a place. I love Greek food in America---it's bound to be even better in Greece!

North of the city center is the world's best collection of ancient Greek art, the National Archaeological Museum. I enjoy history, and this will be awesome. Imagine, actually seeing artifacts that were in my textbooks, in person!

Kusadasi, Turkey

Turkey is the only country on the planet that straddles two continents. This day, we will be in Asia; Istanbul is in Europe.

Izmir was originally scheduled as our first port in Turkey. NCL canceled the port eight months before sailing "due to civil unrest." Not sure how civil unrest can be forecast eight months out, but I'm in favor of reasonable precautions being taken, as needed. Izmir is an ancient city, formerly known as Smyrna. It's now the third largest city in Turkey. The port was replaced with Kusadasi, a small sleepy coastal town. Might not have been our first choice, but Kusadasi it is!

Kusadasi is best known as a jumping off point to Ephesus, which is our main goal for this port. Most cruise ship passengers race right through it on their way to ancient Ephesus, and then hurry back to the ship without even stopping to explore the town. There is a very nice market right at the port. Who knows, I may find a beautiful scarf that I would like to buy! I need to be careful to read the tags, though, because from what I've heard, even in Turkey, 'made in China' labels are ubiquitous. I'll check to make sure that it's authentic and not imported from somewhere else. I don't have to go all the way to Turkey to buy Made In China items.

Our entire group of friends opted to book tours together, both in Kusadasi and Istanbul, through the same company. Of course we want to go to the Ephesus ruins. The tour usually goes to The House of the Virgin Mary, where Mary may or may not have spent her last days. The Pope long ago decreed that the House of the Virgin Mary is a sacred place, whether or not the mother of the Savior actually lived there. It has become a shrine of sorts for Catholics. The tour books describe it as "non-descript," not a word I wish to seek on vacation! We agreed as a group that we are not interested. We arranged by email to tour the Terraced Houses in Ephesus instead. It costs a little more, but sounds more worthwhile.

Ephesus may be a highlight of the cruise. It's a giant open air museum, ruins of a fabulous ancient city. In its heyday, the city had one million residents. It was influenced over the years by Christians Romans, Persians, and Greeks, along with the Ottoman Empire. This is where the goddess Artemis, the daughter of Zeus and Apollo's twin sister, was worshiped, and had a major shrine. Saint Paul, the missionary apostle, preached there—in fact, he was imprisoned after speaking in Ephesus. His crime? Turning the hearts of the people to Christianity, which in turn cut into the sales of Artemis/Diana statues. The metallurgists in the city protested when it began to cut into their income stream.

Saint John may have also come to Ephesus, after being exiled for teaching Christianity in the Roman province of Asia. To walk these ancient streets, where so many people went about their daily lives, speaks to me. Ephesus contains the largest collection of Roman ruins in the eastern Mediterranean.

I love history. Not the dry dates-and-places memorization of those painful history classes, but the real kind. I love the idea of people living ordinary lives, courageous lives, plain daily lives, raising their children, doing their work, following their passions, providing for their families, worshiping, living, leaving evidence behind. Places pick up the energy of those who inhabit them. I love the idea of walking in their footsteps.

Ephesus was surprisingly advanced for its age. It even had plumbing! Early engineers arranged it so the runoff from the surrounding hills streamed into four aqueducts and then was funneled into the city through clay pipes and a filtration system. To think of there being plumbing 2000 years ago-! Many places in the modern world still have not reached that level, still washing clothing in buckets and using trench toilets. Amazing.

The Temple of Artemis, one of the Seven Wonders of the Ancient World, is represented only by one inconspicuous column, was unearthed during an archaeological excavation by the British Museum in the 1870s. The swoosh symbol the Nike company uses in its logo was designed after this frieze

The theatre, Library of Celsius, the Temple of Hadrian, public baths, shops, and the two Agoras (one for commercial business, the other for state affairs) are visible, and waiting for my footsteps to join centuries of others. There's even a large graveyard of gladiators, which we just don't have at home.

Istanbul, Turkey

Istanbul! This port will be the most exotic place I've ever visited. Think of sultans and harem and sheiks, desert wanderers, conquerors, elegant jewels and turbans, mosaics, incredible art, palaces, minarets, all ancient history in very early civilization! Sounds glorious – so why am I so uneasy? Well, part of it is that Istanbul from my home is about 6100 miles, as the proverbial crow flies, and that's the farthest I've ever been from home. There's no way I can hide my tourist persona. You can tell at a glance I'm an American! Will it make me a target for crime? Or, worse yet, merchants wishing to barter and bargain with me? -- that is not where my talents lie! Another reason I'm nervous is the hepatitis, typhoid, and tetanus shots required. I've never been to a place before where I've had to get inoculations just to visit!

Istanbul itself intimidates me a little. Part of my unease is that it's a huge city. Estimates run between 20 and 22 million people, all of them on the Golden Horn. That's seven times larger than the population of Los Angeles! The city straddles Asia and Europe, across the Bosphorus Strait. In the beginning, Husband and the others guys in our group wanted to not to book a tour, to just 'wing it' on our own. In *Turkey!* Cooler heads (namely, mine) quickly prevailed.

Seriously, am I the only one who feels uneasy alone in such a foreign country? I suspect I'm the only one to admit it, that's all.

We have eleven hours in port, and the tour is eight and a half hours long. This sounds ideal, because at the end of the tour, I would like to have time left over for a small cruise. What's one more boat at this point? The cruise I would like to take is a local one that goes up the Bosphorus Strait, from the Galata Bridge. It has no stops, no narration, and boats depart seemingly randomly, but it sounds like it would be fun. The tickets costs 15 Turkish lira per person, for ninety minutes. Not a bad price at all – that's only about seven dollars US.

The tour will take us to the first Hippodrome, built in the fourth century A.D., which is too far back for me to even think about. Imagine—Constantinople's friends ran chariot races there! The Hippodrome in its heyday could seat 100,000 spectators. It has since been taken apart by different conquerors, as well as common people who lacked a quarry. The very idea of builders scavenging precut stones from a mark of history jars my American psyche, but I guess it beat cutting fresh ones without power tools. The Sultan Ahmet Mosque—also known as the Blue Mosque—was constructed from a lot of the Hippodrome's blocks.

Oh, the Blue Mosque. I have no desire to go in the Mosque, but I will enjoy meandering through the gardens, while our friends who don't feel their gender is a threat go in. It's their vacation, too. The main attraction of the Blue Mosque is the architecture, five huge domes with no inner support columns. The opulent interior with famous mosaic is probably stunning. I'm content to miss it.

Five times a day, the mosque is closed for prayer; all mosques are. The call for prayer is amplified by loudspeakers at the top of the minaret, a modern improvement over an imam climbing to the top of the minaret to shout. I'm all in favor of prayer, but I admit that this makes me feel a little uneasy. It reminds me of our son's wedding day brunch a few years ago in Seattle.

We had a brunch for just the immediate families before the wedding. It was a time for us to get together, to relax, and to visit. Our son and nearly- daughter-in-law had assigned each parent to have a little opportunity to speak, a pep talk of sorts, because the rest of the day, of course, would be about the bride and the groom.

The brunch was at a private venue, and on a very hot day in July in Washington we had flung open the sliding glass doors onto the patio. Very warm days in Washington are pretty rare, and so's air conditioning. I stood to give a little speech on how proud I was of them and how much fun my son had been to raise from a little fluffy headed baby to a fine young man. Suddenly my words were drowned out by a very loud amplified sound, almost singsong, streaming in from outdoors. My first immediate thought was 'that sounds like the Muslim call to prayer!' But how could that be?

Two guests discreetly moved to close the sliding doors, so the sound no longer echoed through the room. The brunch continued. Turned out there was a mosque right behind the venue, back to back, which we had not seen when we parked in front. It made me chuckle. Where else could you hear a Muslim call to prayer on your way to a Mormon wedding? Only in America!

Topkapi Palace looks like it will be awesome. It's where the original Ottoman sultans lived. We'll see religious artifacts, jewels, ceremonial robes, and I think it will be wonderful. Hagai Sophia is a typical stop on a tour. This is Constantinople's great church, later converted to a mosque. Now it's converted to a Museum. The Hagai Sophia closes on Mondays, the day we will be in Istanbul. We arranged with the tour company to substitute the underground Basilica Cistern. The pictures look amazing online! I'm thinking on a hot day in Turkey, we're going to appreciate being underground for a while. Plus, I think it will be beautiful. It even has Medusa heads, complete with snakes, between the pillars. Not something we have in the USA!

After the cistern, the tour will take us on an obligatory stop at the Grand Bazaar. The Grand Bazaar houses over 4000 shops under one roof. It started out being a little country market and it just got bigger and bigger and bigger and was finally completed around 1701AD. Over 4000 merchants sell everything from spices to furniture to souvenirs to knock off high-quality purses, furniture to clothing to spices to fish, pewter, and horsemeat, along with a lot of gold, porcelain, pottery, leather, and of course Turkish rugs, things from all over the world. I'm hoping to find some Turkish scarves. I like scarves and pashmina. I probably only own about thirty. Certainly some from Turkey would be nice thing to add to my collection.

Oh, street food! Somewhere during that day, we are going to have to have lunch. I'm going to insist on local food, maybe something on a skewer. After all, I had a tough time getting my hepatitis and tetanus shots, just for this occasion. I'm not going to go through all that pain and almost fainting, and not even eat anything, after all!

At the very least, we must find a Turkish candy shop. There is a world famous sweet called Turkish Delight. It's basically a dense fruit gel candy, with or without nuts, rolled in powdered sugar. It's really quite wonderful. Turkish Delight is rather humorous, because it's a local delicacy here at home, too.

 Long ago, maybe a hundred years ago, there were some Turkish immigrants who settled in central Washington, in the Cashmere area. Central Washington, of course, is where apples and cherries and pears and a lot of other fruits are grown. When people immigrate to a new home, they need a career or job, and they often do what they've done before, in the Old Country. These particular Turks brought along their candy making skills. They quickly began making an entire livelihood out of Turkish Delights, using the fruits at hand. For us, it's a common treat that we get in candy stores and grocery stores, familiarly called Applets and Cotlets. Nevertheless, to have Turkish Delight in Turkey... Well, that's a whole different thing.

The tour we chose looks like a good one. It includes all entrance fees and museums, and it comes with an English speaking tour guide, too. I like the idea of our group being all in one vehicle. The 15 passenger van will be easier to maneuver and to park than a big old bus and will be able to get to the doorstep of areas, thereby saving a few steps. It looks to be a tiring full wonderful day.

Mykonos, Greece

The Greek island of Mykonos looks like the picture postcards of stereotypical Greece. Its city is Hora or Hcherra or Chora---as if the language isn't already confusing enough, the Greeks like to give multiple names to each place. Have you ever heard anyone say "It's all Japanese to me"? No, but "it's Greek to me" is a common idiom. Anyway, however Mykonos' town is pronounced, I can't wait to see it.

It's a small coastal town with glaring white stucco houses with bright red and blue contrasts, pastel flowers, flowing down the steep hills. Add in a sea breeze...this sounds perfect! Remember the movie, *Mama Mia*? Like that, only with tourists. This will be a rest day for us. The other ports are very intensive with a tour scheduled in pretty much all of them. By the time we reach Mykonos, we will have seen museums, mosques, art, basilicas, sculptures, scenery, and will have been hustled from one place to another by informative tour guides. Mykonos is a designated down day, with no tour scheduled.

The main activity, according to the cruise line, is its beautiful beaches. If the Good Lord intended me to be a beach bum, he would have blessed me with a long, lithe body that looks great in a swimsuit. Instead, I have a comfortable, shall we say, grandmotherly body, and I avoid being seen in public in a swimsuit even at the best of times. Did I mention we also be traveling with Melissa, who runs long distances on purpose, teaches Zumba and dance, and could pass for one of her teenage daughters easily? No, no beaches for me. Instead I will be content to wander. And take a lot of photographs. If we feel energetic, we may make our way up to the five iconic windmills on the highest point. I definitely need to seek out a Greek feast, probably involving gyros, baklava and something on a skewer. Oh, yum!

Naples, Italy

We can't possibly see as much as I'd like to on this trip, but I'm excited about the attempt. We'll consider this just a taste, and plan to return someday. Due to the fact that there is absolutely no way we can see everything, we've decided our time in Naples will be spent exploring Pompeii, Herculaneum, and Mount Vesuvius. I'm hoping to have a *little* time in the Archaeological Museum in Naples. The run down museum in town is where a lot of the pillaged artifacts from Pompeii ended up. Our guide politely assured me by email, "you can add in the museum, but you will miss your ship." We will see how flexible the actual day is!

The public train system to Pompeii and Herculaneum is reputed to be easy, but a private tour will allow us to walk less, wait less, and hopefully beat the crowds. Either way, the day is going to be very hot. We will need bottled water and sunscreen for sure. Oddly, even a hat won't help block enough, as the marble ruins reflect sunlight up to burn skin from below! Being from Seattle, too much sun sounds great, but I'll have water, sunscreen, and my big floppy hat at hand. Pompeii is expected to be hot and dry and dusty. If we are going to get a sunburn, this is probably the place.

Pompeii alone is going to be too big to see completely. We will spend hours there, but we will still not be able to see it all; just get a taste of it. I think we're probably going to hire a walking guide, once we arrive there. I've heard that they are just available there at the entrance and not very expensive. Greece and Italy have a law that says people can either be a driver or a guide, but not both; so our guide cannot even enter the site with us. I'd prefer a specialist in such a place anyway.

When I started college, I majored in archaeology. It went well, until I found that I nearly fainted every time I walked into the archaeological lab, as if there was simply not enough oxygen in the air. It was rather a setback in my career choice. Nevertheless, I've always been fascinated by the way people lived before our generation, before our time. We know what we know because this is what we know, but to learn from those who have gone before is amazing to me. Remnants of everyday life were preserved by the volcano, frozen in time, and the archeological exploration is ongoing in Pompeii and Herculaneum.

I've heard of Pompeii my whole life. However, I think that I will probably enjoy Herculaneum just as much as Pompeii; perhaps more. Herculaneum was a more upscale elite community at the time of the Vesuvius eruption, and it's better preserved. One thing we think of as Americans when we look at ruins is colorlessness. Think about it --when you think of any ruins of any kind, don't you think of them in terms of being sun-bleached gray? This area of Pompeii, Herculaneum, and the other nearby communities at the time of Vesuvius' eruption were not like that at all. They were bright and bold and vibrant, and at Herculaneum a lot of the colors have been preserved. I can't wait to go!

Rome, Italy

Rome! Romance, deep history, corruption, and terrible traffic. Everyone I've ever talked to who's visited Rome has complained about the traffic, about the Vespers zooming in and out, wild drivers, honking cars, traffic rules being largely optional. Think about all the romantic movies set in Rome you've ever seen. They all have crazy traffic in the background! We are not planning on renting any cars on this cruise vacation. But even if we were going to, Rome is one place where I would not choose to rent a car! We're going to be grateful for our tour; I can tell already. Our tour will be guided by someone who's from Rome and knows how to navigate. I will just sit back and shut my eyes as needed. Not too often, I hope---I don't want to miss anything!

To save time, our guide asked us to buy tickets ahead of time to the Vatican. Husband is heart set on seeing the Vatican and the Sistine Chapel. I am less so. I know that the artwork will be incredible, along with the history. Just to say 'we were there' is something I must do. I expect I will love it when we are there; not so much from my home far away.

My extended family is has a lapsed Catholic background. Sadly, I know too much of the history of how the amazing artwork was built, the oppression of the church towards the 'little people,' the poverty while the priests and popes ruled in unrighteousness and opulence, and controlled the political and the social environment. I'm American. We don't have clear social classes in our society. The early Catholic Church did, and to some extent it still does, have classes. It grates on my nerves. I am not comfortable with that at all, although I credit the current pope with trying to turn that atmosphere around to some extent. Husband says that we can't possibly go to Rome and not to the Vatican and the Sistine Chapel, and he's probably right. The artwork and the history will be amazing and I am looking forward to that. Michelangelo, Raphael~!

Florence and Pisa, Italy

This will be our smallest tour, with just four of us going together. The rest are heart set on climbing the Leaning Tower of Pisa, so they'll make their way there on public transport. The four of us hired a tour that will show us Pisa, then all around Florence; museums, the David, and immerse us in history.

Italy's a very old place, but a relatively young country. Florence's history is rich with and the coming together of Italy, less than 160 years ago. Before the unification, the area was made up of small city states, each walled off from its neighbors. This area is marked by many walls, made of beautiful rock work and arches and towers, boundaries of the former city-states. As I have read about this area, I came upon a fact that made me smile. Nearly every town has a Saint Niccolo or Saint Nicholas church or guard tower or square or something. Yes, yes, that same Saint Nicholas *–Santa Claus!*

I hope we will have time to drive up in the countryside. This is *Tuscany*, after all!

Toulon, France

The south of France...ahhh! Toulon is frequently considered a waystation on the journey to nearby Marseille or Cassis. There is much to do from this port, but we plan on just staying in town. Toulon is the last port of the cruise. I suspect by this time, we will be pretty well exhausted. Just wandering around in an unstructured day sounds very pleasant. Toulon was severely hit in World War II. It's not known for old world charm; much of the city was rebuilt in more modern styles, the hasty, boxy variety.

Husband dearly loves Naval Museums, as much as I enjoy clambering around ruins. Since Toulon has a 600 years history as a leading French naval port, the National Naval Museum might be worth looking into. It's small, but they do have an audio guide in English, which I would appreciate, since my French is about as good as my Martian. France's one and only aircraft carrier, the *Charles de Gaulle,* is based there. The little train, appropriately named "Le Petit Train," would give an easy overview of Toulon; that's an option. There's also a cable car that goes up 540 feet to the top of Mont Faron. This is not a high priority; we may come to that, but mostly wandering around the town with the market and the Museum sounds like a nice way to spend most of the day.

Barcelona, Spain

The cruise disembarks in Barcelona, in the Catalunya region of Spain. We will only be in Barcelona about 30 hours before the journey home. I will expect we will be pretty tired by this point. Nevertheless, we are going to want to see as much as we possibly can, same as we have on the rest of the trip. After all, I've never been to Barcelona. Who knows when we will get back there again!

Many people around the world are very proud of their hometown. People in Barcelona are no different. When I think of Spain, I think of vineyards and bullfighting, and flamenco dancers. Barcelona's different. They are very prideful that they are *not* part of Spain, but of Catalunya. Catalunya has its own flag, and a language that's only spoken in this area of the world. Although they all speak Spanish, and I'm hoping a few will speak English as well, Catalunya is the language children are taught in school. Interestingly, it's spoken with a deliberate lisp. They say Bar*THEL*ona, not Bar*SELL*onia, patterned after an early leader who had a genuine lisp, so as not to embarrass him. Odd things carry through generations. This is one of them.

I think of Spain in terms of Columbus, early colonization in America and elsewhere, the Spanish-American war. Their history is also quite modern. The Spanish Civil War was a biggie, fought between 1936 and 1939, which wasn't all that long ago. My *parents* were children during this period! Catalunya area was one of the last pockets of resistance against the fascist dictator Francisco Franco. There is a lot of national pride, national spirit, in Catalunya, and Barcelona is the capital of it all.

Many reviews I've read recommend the Hop On Hop Off bus. There are two bus companies that provide this service. We selected the Turistic Bus and bought discounted tickets from their website prior to our trip. There are three routes, all covered by one ticket. It will give us a good look at the city. Our plan is to take a Hop On Hop Off tour, and then walk down Los Ramblas, just for the experience. Los Ramblas is known for street theatre, street entertainers, and shopping.

Husband is a fairly brave soul, usually easy-going, willing to try new things. However, culinarily speaking, he's a coward. There, I said it. Someone had to! He clings to the familiar, and fears anything he hasn't already tasted a hundred times. In San Francisco, he actually ordered *chili* while I enjoyed sourdough bread and cioppino. In Chicago, Husband did order an Italian beef, but *plain* – no peppers. At Quincy Market in Boston, I had a lobster roll and clam chowder. Husband ordered tacos! They were so bad, he threw them away after one bite. Enchiladas in Maui suffered a similar fate, as they should have.

I think the worst example of this, though, was when we were in the International District in Seattle. In any other big city, that area would've been called Chinatown, but in the great Northwest, we are painfully politically correct. We were with my parents; in other words, time to make a good impression, but no. The restaurant we chose was Chinese, and I don't mean *kind of* Chinese. I mean, we were the only non-Asians in the place, we couldn't read the menu, we didn't understand what anyone was saying; that kind of Chinese. We managed to order by pointing and pantomime. It works in most places in the world.

My husband, however, said a shocking thing to our waiter. He said, and I quote, "do you have Veal Parmesan?" Worse than that, the waiter said "yes"! We were really scared because heaven knows what Veal Parmesan sounds like, translating it from your basic American tourist language into Chinese! Lo and behold, when our wonderful dishes of stir-fried glory came, a steaming plate of Veal Parmesan also was delivered to our table. Husband said it was some of the best he'd ever had. I still think they sent the busboy out the back door and across town to that Italian place. I just don't believe anyone who can cook Chinese food is good as my dinner was can make Veal Parmesan.

As we began planning this trip, Husband admitted that he's afraid of tapas. What?! Afraid of *tapas*? Why, that is as silly as being afraid of french fries or toast! Tapas just means "small plate," like an appetizer or an hor dourve, a little bit of exotic Catalonia or Spanish food on a little dish. How could that make a person uneasy? He's quite convinced he will starve in Barcelona. Unlikely—if nothing else, we'll still be full from all that cruise food! When Barcelonans go out to eat, they order tapas. They absorb the atmosphere and socialize and eat little tasty bites---and for one evening, I want to join them. Husband will survive. Actually, I think he will love it!

The planning for this Mediterranean cruise has taken months, longer than most trips by far. I hope it pays off!

PART TWO

The Planning is Over: The Trip Begins!

This part was written day by day, during the cruise. I took notes throughout the day, then gathered my thoughts back on the ship, and added more thoughts later on. First, a couple of things that stood out to me, across this odyssey: Water, and restrooms.

Water

We are Americans, and as such, are accustomed to simply drinking tap water at home and in public. We lucked out, having tasty drinking water in our area, unlike some places I could mention. Ever tried Florida's water? It either tastes like chlorine or slightly diluted swamp, and is best served well disguised. Water in Hawaii is vaguely salty, leaving me thirstier than before I drank it. Oklahoma water tastes oddly dusty, which is no mean feat, considering that dust, by definition, is dry, and water is ...not. Yes, water varies, but at home, as well as in local restaurants, tap water with ice is just fine.

We quickly learned that abroad, plain tap water for drinking water is not as ubiquitous as at home, and it comes with a lot more descriptors, too. We are not generally in favor of Profiling—we don't label folks as Potential Terrorist, or Stupid, or by perceived religion or political beliefs, at least not right out loud. In Europe, starting with the flight over, we quickly learned that profiling people by assumed water preference was common, and seemingly based on nationality.

Let's take temperature. One of our group is very fair, with very blonde hair. On the Iceland Air flight, the rest of us American-types were greeted in English, and given chilled water bottles upon boarding, and ice cubes in our cups of water, every time. Our blonde friend was greeted in Icelandic by the flight crew; I guess they identified her as "one of us." When she stared blankly at them, they quickly switched to English. When four of us requested water to drink, three of us were given iced water, while hers was room temperature. Three times!

Throughout the flight, all the flight attendants spoke fluent Icelandic and English. Every time they came by to offer drinks, they looked at us and asked "Can I get you something to drink?" Obviously assuming our blonde, slim friend was Icelandic, they'd say "hvað get ég fengið þig til að drekka ?" She'd venture, "umm...water?" hoping her answer was close to right for the question.

Our society frowns on "profiling" either by race, nationality, or gender, but we experienced it all over Europe in many forms; this was just the first.

We noticed that in Turkey and Greece as well. Buying bottled water was common, and a practice we quickly adopted. Newsstands and kiosks everywhere sold water, with prices ranging from half a euro to one-and-a-half. I quickly noticed that chilled water was given to us, but ambient temperature water was given to travelers who appeared to be locals. I guess The Cruise Addict looked especially American---twice, he was given half-frozen bottled water! We were still better off than Asian-looking tourists, whom I noticed were given cups of *hot* water. In 95+ degree weather, that did not seem refreshing to me.

It seemed funny that four people could approach a stand, ask for water, and be given four different types, with no discussion! Reminded me of my father, in that bakery in south Florida. He asked for "a loaf of that good Italian bread" and the clerk took a loaf from the bin and wrapped it for Dad. As he put away his change, another customer came in, and asked for "one of those Cuban loaves, please." The clerk gave him an identical loaf! As Dad gathered his bag, a third customer came in and ordered "a loaf of French bread." Without a word, the clerk reached in the same bin and pulled out a loaf of bread. Dad reported, "it was the exact same bread, every time!"

We learned new words for water, too. In restaurants at home, we are given a glass of ice water, or a pitcher, if The Cruise Addict, whom I swear can go through eight glasses during a meal, annoys the waiter, who'd like to keep the glasses full. When we asked for water with our meals on this trip, we were questioned. Would we prefer mineral, still, or sparkling water?

The first time, I ordered sparkling. I like sparkles---what fun, to have my glass of water sparkling during dinner! Alas, it not only did not have sparkles; it also tasted terrible, and was not at all refreshing. It tasted a lot like salty carbonated water, or like soda with no flavor syrup. Yuck. "Mineral water" sounds oddly nutritious, as if it ought to taste of iron or potassium or something. Turns out, it tastes like plain old water. "Still" water is poetic. Can't you just imagine peaceful calm waters, maybe with lovely blue-tinged scenery? Still waters...ahh. "Still water" seems to be the code word for plain-ordinary- bottled-water; not particularly poetic, but thirst quenching and reliable.

In restaurants, when we asked for water with a meal, we were given either 2 small bottles of water, one large bottle of water, or a jug of water, with a glass stopper. I don't know if the glass bottles were really bottled water, or just decanted out of the sink's faucet in the back room. In any case, they were always cold. We're Americans, after all.

Restrooms

Bathroom facilities were a concern to me. I had a few puzzling moments, but as it turned out, I only had a couple of uneasy experiences, including one hole in the floor, and a sign that still makes me shudder. It was at Topkapi Palace, in Istanbul. "Do not flush toilet paper. Place in bin, not toilet." Eeww...! The bin was an open basket, on the left-hand side of the toilet. It was a Muslim country, after all, and one would only use one's left hand for toilet procedures, reserving the right for other "clean" tasks such as eating. Seems to me, if you just pooped and wiped, and left your soiled paper for the next person to admire---and smell--- it really mattered very little which hand you used! All I could do in that case was what I needed to do, as fast as possible.

At the Mosque of Sultan Ahmet, alias the Blue Mosque, I encountered the one-and-only hole- in- the- floor situation. It had a concrete floor, with an open porcelain oval, level with the concrete surface, and two foot rests etched into the concrete . I did not look closely to investigate what lay below; it was a case of hurry up and get out! I'm still baffled by the porcelain, however. I have done enough pottery and ceramics to know that porcelain is a pain to work with. The wet clay texture ranges from mashed potatoes to heavy cream, and must be dried and then fired to harden. Firing a vase or plate in a kiln is no problem, but this was part of the cement floor, and you can't fire cement. It's a temperature issue; porcelain requires high temperatures, while cement would turn to dust if fired that hot. How was that "seat" manufactured?

I was concerned about locating toilet facilities on our journey. In America, at least in polite society, we have a wide range of words for that locale. Restroom, bathroom, potty, ladies', gent's, lavatory, loo, facilities, washroom, latrine, privy, john, powder room, men's room, little room, plus all sorts of euphemisms, including powdering one's nose and going to see a man about a horse. But in Europe, what are they called??

Turns out, they were easy to spot at a distance. I'm still baffled over the signs, though. In every country we visited, they were labeled "WC." WC stands for Water Closet, and is a distinctly British title. It also stands for Wesleyan Church, also very British, but let's not confuse the issue any more than needed, shall we? In Turkey, Greece, Italy, France, Spain, and Sweden, why would the British have such a hold on society as to impact this in the most personal of rooms? I know they were great colonizers in their day, but of all the odd influences to leave behind!

We are not accustomed to paying for the use of the WC, or whatever it's called. In North America, the little rooms are available in public places such as parks, schools, offices, stores, restaurants, museums, theatres, etc, and never for a fee. I think the only places we found restrooms on this trip that did *not* require a fee were in museums, hotels, and restaurants, and most were located so as to discourage non-customer's use. It became a policy to Just Try, like I told my kids when they were small. "You don't have to *go,* but you do have to *try*; who knows where we'll find another."

Some of the bathrooms were upstairs, around corners, tucked behind bars, etc. In a restaurant in Greece, the plainly labeled WC was blocked by a bar stool with a sign that read "ask." I did so, and was directed "upstairs, to the right." The steep curving stairs led up to a darkened second floor, filled with draped furniture, lit only by curtained windows. I had a genuine need, so I wandered around hopefully, banging my shins. At last, another customer bumbled her way up the stairs. I debated about jumping out to scare her, just because of the spooky surroundings...but I figured her screaming would cause one of us to wet one's pants, and I would just as soon it not be me. Besides, I was a guest in the country, albeit an increasingly uncomfortable one. She spoke no English; I spoke no Greek, neither of us could find a light switch or restroom. At last, we stumbled through a door marked Office, and there was a toilet! That's all there was; no office at all. It was not very clean; perhaps it had not been used in a long time.

Politely, she indicated I should go first. I did so, then stepped out to wash my hands. Uh, oh, a problem I had not foreseen. I had lathered my hands with the liquid soap on the wall dispenser, but could not turn on the water! The handles did not respond, and what was I going to do, coated in soap, and my lunch waiting below? Just then, the other woman stepped out, scolded me in what I assume was Greek---it sounded Greek to me--- and stomped on a small flat disk on the floor. Water half-heartedly dribbled from the faucet. It was grey, but it removed the nearly dried soap layer from my hands and I was grateful. She scolded some more, then put her arm around me and we made our way through the labyrinth of furniture and down the rickety staircase to the bustling restaurant below. Packing my little bottle of hand sanitizer seemed a like a very good idea at that point.

The more public (for a fee) restrooms were usually easier to spot. I suspect it was an economic issue; the WCs are money makers! Not a lot of money, granted. Most cost half a euro, correct change only. In a few places, there was a change-maker, who silently took larger coins or paper currency and slid change to the customer in line, making sure to subtract half a euro in the transaction. What a job!

Several had attendants, besides the money-takers; a sort of traffic cop. The ones I saw were uniformed women, who aggressively ordered men and women to step along sharply, not hesitating to push or pull one to the right spot in line. As usual, the men took less time using the facilities, so they were yanked out of the line and shoved in ahead of the women. Also, not a great choice of profession, in my opinion.

Even at a price, I found few clean-looking restrooms. I became adept at doing what needed doing, often while holding my breath, and getting out as fast as I could, while touching the least surfaces possible. I think the public one in Pompeii was probably quite clean. At least that is what the attendant told me. "Clean! is okay! Euro, please!" She had bustled out of a stall, waving a damp rag, with her hand outstretched. Not exactly extortion, but not the "free WC" advertised ten feet outside the door, either. I would have had to shove her out of the way to get by fee-free. As I stepped out, she hurried in, then emerged seconds later, telling the woman next in line, "Clean! is okay! Euro, please!" What a way to make a living.

On Our Way!

Our group of friends planned to make our own way to Venice, and meet up on the ship. The twelve of us booked various flights to Paris, Amsterdam, Rome, and Frankfort, on five different days, and every one of the flights had a layover in Iceland. I tend to be an optimistic soul. Really, I do. But the odds of all of us making our way that far, on that many routes, and ending up on the very same piece of floating real estate in Italy looked unlikely. Ah, well, the whole trip was to be a grand adventure. And at the very least, I knew I could keep tabs on The Cruise Addict and myself. The rest ...well, they were on their own.

Our first destination was Stockholm, which required a layover in Iceland. There is exactly one flight per day from Seattle to Reykjavik. This seems to be the main way to go anywhere in Europe. Look at an Iceland Air map; every flight from the USA to Europe swoops through their capitol city, making the map look like a busy bowtie. Reykjavik is the knot.

Checking in at the airport in Seattle was easy. The agent took our passports, and questioned where we were going, and how come we were only going one way. We explained that we were going on a cruise, and would be flying to Stockholm, but home from Barcelona, on a different airline; thus requiring one way tickets. She accepted that explanation, then said sternly, "I must weight your carry-on bags. Remember there are strict limits on weight and size."

I handed her my backpack, while The Cruise Addict reached for *his* backpack. She did a double take. "Wait, are you sure that's all you have for carryon? You *are* Americans, right?" That was the first indication that I had not over packed, one of many to come. Looking back, now that I am home, that was a smart decision. There were several times when I simply could not have managed more than my single suitcase and backpack! Not to get ahead of the story, however. Keep reading.

I dreaded the long flight from Seattle to Reykjavik. This flight was expected to be 8 hours 45 minutes. That's less than that awful flight from LA to Honolulu, when the just-under-six-hour flight took just-over-eleven hours. Something about a bent jet stream; I'm not real clear on the reason, but I know it felt never ending! And at least that time, I was geared up for not-quite-six hours. This one would be much longer. With chasing time zones, we wouldn't land until the following morning. The flight to Iceland was 5813 miles as the crow flies. Not sure if the theoretical crow flew over the North Pole, but that was our route.

It was the longest flight I had ever booked. I planned on being miserable.

When we traveled with our young children, I put them in charge of their own entertainment. "What do you need to make you behave on the flight/car/train/whatever?" I'd add something else, like a roll of foil for crafts, snacks, maybe a road map to forestall the never-ending "are we there yets?" but, basically, they were in charge of behaving nicely after about age 3, and responsible for bringing whatever that effort required.

I approached this trip the same way; what did I need to get through the flight? My tablet and e-reader with about a dozen new books, and a keyboard in case I felt like typing, earphones, my ever-present notebook and favorite pen, inflatable travel pillow, my journal, some snacks. It seemed insufficient! I also carried the entire trip's paperwork in my backpack; all the tours, hotel information, receipts and reservations and tickets. My backpack also had about two pounds of assorted electronics, chargers, camera gear, flash chargers, and all. My backpack was 8.6 lbs when I left my house; significantly heavier on the way home.

I'm sure planes are clean, but I don't believe that, so I had my trusty package of disinfectant wipes. Before I even buckle my seatbelt on any flight, I swab all hard surfaces within my reach; armrest, tray table, and seatbelt buckle. Overkill? Perhaps, but I rarely get sick from flying. And when I do, I can usually blame the guy next to me, the one coughing his head off the whole flight. As a tip, we also go over every cruise ship cabin and hotel room with the disinfectant wipes, first thing. You don't want to think about what was on the remote control. People fret about the recirculated air on a plane, but really, those filters are about as good as a hospital's. It's the hard surfaces that'll get you.

A Product Plug

Mom recommended I just take a heavy-duty sleeping pill at Final Boarding call. I decided to ignore that wisdom; in an emergency, I'd need my wits about me. In a serious emergency, the kind where death was a probability, I *really* wanted my wits about me. After living this long, I'd want to meet my Maker with my eyes open, not in a drugged stupor. Besides, the flight left at 3:45pm. I knew I'd already be scrambled with all the time zone chances; sleeping midafternoon couldn't help. Well, yes, the overnight flight was to land at 7am, but *still*. No sleeping pills for me. I did take a couple of low-dose aspirin to ward off deep vein thrombophlebitis, blood clots that can form from sitting too long, such as on the longest flight I've *ever* taken.

I read about a product that sounded too good to be true. Dreading the flight, I decided the worst that could happen with taking the product was... nothing much at all. In the best case scenario, I might feel better! It's Jet Zone, a homeopathic tablet that claims to prevent jet lag. On a trip this size, I really didn't want to be dragging. I didn't expect much benefit, to be honest, but maybe the psychological effect would make a slight difference. Yes, I believe in placebos! I dutifully ate the little tablets as directed, before and during the flight. They tasted like dust, only a tiny bit sweeter; really no problem to dissolve in my mouth.

Surprise---I think the Jet Zone made a big difference! I didn't sleep much at all on the flight, but still arrived with enough energy to tackle Stockholm, feeling a lot like I do when I wake up at home. I had planned to stick to the time zones in which I found myself; eating at the local meal times, not napping, going to bed at a reasonable local bedtime, etc. I had expected to be tired and foggy-headed for a few days. I was surprised to realize I actually felt great and adapted astonishingly well. I hardly ever recommend a product, but I certainly plan on taking Jet Zone on any long flight from now on. I used it on the way home, too, and again on a cross-country flight to a New England cruise ten days after this trip (who plans these things? I did tell you I'm married to a Cruise *Addict,* yes?). The stuff worked great!!

End of Product Plug. Back to the flight.

Long Flight, Made Longer

I noticed right off that the International wing of the airport had a different atmosphere. Safer, maybe, or a little more upscale. Far be it from me to critique people, but I did note that not a single person wore pajama bottoms or other sloppy loungewear, as I have seen on almost every other flight I've taken in the past decade. Every passenger dressed like a grown up in public! I'm all in favor of comfort, but really, most flights I have been on look like a slumber party gone bad. I'm not saying we need to revert back to the days of white gloves and May Janes, exactly, but there is a big spectrum between that and slovenliness. As an aside, did you know that studies have been done where gate agents are 85% more likely to offer a random upgrade to a well-dressed person over a scuzzy looking person?

Reminds me of the time my well-to-do brother went to buy a new BMW. He's well off, owns two successful companies, and could have *bought* the car dealer easily. He showed up wearing his standard outfit; shorts, tee shirt, and baseball cap. Do you know anyone else who has a wardrobe of baseball caps? He went to the BMW dealership, and looked around at some cars. He noticed that the four salespeople were not busy; in fact, they seemed to be talking and joking amongst themselves. My brother was ignored. After wandering for 15 minutes, he approached the nearest salesperson. Before my brother could speak, the guy abruptly said," I doubt we have anything *you* could afford here. Have you looked at the used car dealer down the block?" My brother left. He went home, put on a suit and tie, and bought a BMW from a competing dealer across the valley, where the salespeople treated him with great respect. What is the commission on a $77,000 car? Point of the story: if you want to be respected, dress like you deserve it.

Me? I wore black silk pants and a soft knit shirt that felt a lot like sleepwear, but looked put-together enough for a cocktail party, should one arise. You never know. I had a pareo in my backpack, which I could use to dress up my outfit if needed, or to ward off the chill of the airplane's air conditioning. It proved totally insufficient for the unplanned hurricane in Iceland, however. I can't plan for everything!

We found out the day before we left that Brett and Melissa would be on the same flight to Reykjavik. We'd part ways there, as they flew on to Amsterdam and we went on to Sweden. We met up at the gate.

We liked Iceland Air, and would definitely take that airline again. Seats were comfortable, attendants were personable and polite, and even the safety video held my attention. Iceland is promoting tourism in a major way! The video was the standard wording, (with English subtitles) but the pictures were eye-catching scenery of Iceland. For example, when it talked about the emergency slide, it showed a joyful girl sliding down a waterfall. The life vest part showed people buttoning parkas by a glacier. It was beautiful!

I smiled as the flight attendant concluded the safety video with, "Sit back and relax or lean forward and be tense. Either way, we are going to Reykjavík."

One thing we wished we had known ahead of time was that Iceland Air allows a layover in Iceland for free, up to seven days, on any through flight. Had we known, we would have planned a few days in Reykjavik, coming or going. We certainly will go back! I've been in all fifty US states, and Alaska is the one that cast a spell on me. I left a part of my heart there, which is why I'm always up for another Alaskan cruise; it's fun to go visit my body part. I felt the same effect in our too-brief Iceland part of the trip, something calling me. I want to go back! I wonder if sitting next to a chatty Icelandic tourism agent on the flight home had any effect on me? As I said, they heavily promote tourism!

I hoped to sleep on the flight to pass at least some of the time, but failed in that. I read, wrote, watched tv, and found myself entranced with the sunset. The flight chased the sunset as we flew further and further north, over the Pole, across time zones. It was a gorgeous sunset, and six hours long! The glorious colors hung there, glowing in the sky, like God's own watercolors. I felt sorry for the passengers who slept around me.

Unexpected Hurricane

The flight was not as bad as I feared; it passed pretty smoothly, until the last two hours. It became too turbulent to read, or watch tv; I don't get motion sick, ever, but why provoke a first time? I tried to sleep, but it was just too bouncy. I found myself checking my watch...would the jerking motion ever end? As the plane descended into dark grey clouds, heavy rain pelted the windows and the turbulence increased.

After a very bumpy landing, the plane taxied for quite a while, then stopped. I still saw no terminal out either side of the air craft, or even any lights. It was unnerving to sit in a darkened parked plane. I still felt serious turbulence as strong winds buffeted the aircraft, as if the plane wanted to be back in the sky. The wind made even standing up tricky. That plane really shook!

The seatbelt sign remained on for long minutes. At last it went off, and people began to stand and gather their belongings, as usual. The part where passengers begin to disembark any flight always seems too slow to me. *Move, people!* It's not a surprise; you land, you get off, like that. This time, people stood, gathered themselves, stretched and chatted, and waited in the aisles. *And waited.* After a very long time, at least five minutes, the Captain made an announcement in Icelandic.

I knew something was amiss when those who understood let out a loud groan and plopped back into their seats. What?! The next announcement was in English: Sixty knot winds, not safe to bring the steps to the plane, everyone sit back down and wait for the winds to subside. Sixty knots is darn close to hurricane force winds! How long would we wait until the winds died down? What if it took hours, or days? We only had a 50 minute layover! I had looked forward to a restroom, a snack, a chance to stretch my legs and check out the airport shops. Now the chances of us even making the connecting flight looked slim.

Surely this couldn't take too long. Well, it might; weather is not concerned with human schedules. My heart sank when the cheerful flight attendants passed out more water, and lower still when they came by with coffee twenty minutes later. They assured nervous passengers that this happens often, but never this time of year; only in winter. "Not to worry; the whole airport is closed, so any connecting flights will have to wait. You must hurry, however, because they will wish to take off as soon as we are cleared, before the next wind comes in." After an eight-and-a-half hour flight, I was very ready to get off that plane. It was every bit as bouncy on the ground as it had been in the air! It felt as though the plane was determined to take off on its own. Let's see, what do I know about the principles of flight? Something about lift versus wing surface…Was this even safe?

After eighty-eight minutes ---why, yes, I counted—a cheer went up. Someone had spotted stairs coming towards the plane, through the driving rain. Uh, oh. As the locals around me began pulling out warm coats and hats from their bags, I realized I had a problem. I had not planned on being <u>outdoors</u> in Iceland! I had assumed we would just walk through the airport to catch the next flight. My knit shirt seemed inadequate against hurricane force winds and sideways rain! I had a silk wrap in my backpack, but it would be slim protection against the weather. I thought longingly of my nice jacket carefully packed in the suitcase in the baggage hold below. So close and yet so far!

I fly a lot, and I've never seen a protocol such as we saw in Reykjavík, Iceland. Finally, the door opened with a whoosh of chilly air. Row by row, passengers made their way through the aisle, down the stairs, and outdoors into the 50 mile an hour winds and sideways rain. They had us go down the stairs one at a time with crew members at the top and bottom of the stairs. I wondered if that was to see if the first would blow away before the second one was allowed to step out. When it was my turn, I half ran, half blew, down the stairs, hanging onto the railing so as not to turn into a kite. I dimly saw a bus through the pelting rain. I ran another twenty feet across the tarmac into the waiting bus. I've not seen a bus like that before – it had no seats, only bars to hang onto. I was grateful to be out of the rain, even for just a moment. I was also glad to see Husband appear a minute later.

I guess we lucked out. The bus was only half-full when another announcement was made on the plane and no more people came down the stairs. Another delay! The bus slowly drove away. It drove very far – I bet it was a half mile or more through the inky darkness. At last I saw the airport's lights through the blinding rain. The bus pulled up to the terminal and we ran again through the rain and into the airport, thoroughly soaked by now.

There was chaos inside, but it was a calm and polite chaos. Once again, I realized the difference between Americans and other travelers. Americans would not have handled that sort of a delay gracefully. I could imagine fuming people screaming at gate agents. Not here. The place was very crowded, as people of all nationalities and languages lounged about on floors; every chair was full.

We found a sign that said our plane would board in twelve minutes. That was not enough time to get a snack, or explore the airport, but at least it was enough time to find a bathroom. Oh, yeah I forgot, I'm not in America, and what I needed was a *toilet*. The signs in the airport were all in both Icelandic and English. There was quite a line at the bathroom-- excuse me— *toilet,* and our flight number was being announced as I raced back to The Cruise Addict. The winds were still howling and the rain was still pounding, but our flight was ready to board. It was a reverse protocol; onto a SRO bus, to the plane, through the driving wind and rain to the top of the stairs, onto the plane. How do disabled people travel in Iceland? I can't picture passengers being able to manage the stairs in a wheelchair, or even with a cane, especially in 50 mile an hour winds!

I doubted that the plane would even take off, as badly buffeted it was by the winds. I guess the pilot was rather a daredevil because we were barely seated before the plane was up and going, making up time. On to Sweden!

Stockholm, Sweden

As a rule, I'm the planner. I keep track of things. The Cruise Addict had lived in Sweden for two years, a couple of decades ago, so he took the lead here. We landed in Stockholm with no problem at all. No one even checked our passports or raised an eyebrow at us as we walked through the airport and out onto the street, as if we belonged there. It's harder to get back into my home country, America, from Canada than it was to enter into Sweden! People were friendly, they greeted us, but it was just a welcome, no documents checked at all. I immediately noticed that every sign was in both Swedish and English. Oh, good! I suspected it would be the last country on this epic journey where I'd be able to communicate freely.

First Impressions

The airport in Stockholm is not anywhere near Stockholm; it's a good 45 minutes away. We decided to take a bus to the city, once that we determined that a cab would cost over a hundred dollars. The bus let us off at the main terminal in Stockholm, three miles from our hotel. We still needed to take a taxi. as we settled in the back seat, the cabbie scolded, "this is not America! In Europe, we use public transit, not taxis !" Besides being startled at being reprimanded at my ripe old age, it seemed odd to be told not to use the very business that employed him... had we avoided taxis, us and everyone else, he would not even have had a job. Once he got that out of his system, he kept up an easy chatter as he drove.

I was excited to be in Sweden! Stockholm is based on an archipelago of eight major islands, and the first impression was beautiful. We stayed at the Elite Marina Hotel, right on the water. The Baltic Sea! It was a five star hotel and I was quite impressed. The architecture, the furniture was all very Scandinavian, which I guess is to be expected... in Scandinavia. Our suite was larger than expected. After all, I've always heard that European hotels are much smaller than American ones. Nope, we save that for Venice.

The hotel was in an old lading building for the shipping industry in Stockholm that had been converted to a very modern, very elegant hotel. The best part of it was the bed. It had a deep featherbed on it, with two separate fluffy duvets folded, one on each side, meeting in the middle. The way this bed was made was brilliant. Each person got their own thick comforter and I got to sink down into a featherbed that would be mine, all mine, all night. I could tell that I was going to be delighted, but for right now we simply we didn't have time to admire the hotel. Off to explore ASAP!

Wherever we travel, I find that the locals who live there know way more than I do about the area, and so we immediately turned to the desk clerk for advice on how to get to the main part of the city. She recommended we take the little ferry which was about 50 feet from the front door of the hotel. Did I mention the hotel even had red carpet? I felt so welcome there, and could've happily lingered just in the lobby alone-- but Stockholm awaited!

The little ferry stops at nine different stops around Stockholm, hitting all the high points. It was quite inexpensive and a lot of fun to be right there on the black water of the Baltic Sea. I think we were the only tourists on the ferry at the time. There were mothers with large-wheeled strollers, businesspeople with briefcases, residents with shopping bags, and us. The ferry makes a circuit which we eventually ended up taking, but for now we wanted to go into the Old Town.

Gamla Stad is the old part of Stockholm and I do mean *old*. There are buildings there from the ninth century. America is such a baby country; we simply don't have anything that old here. I have been to the oldest buildings in America; Saint Augustine, Santa Fe, Roanoke, and the missions in California, but we simply don't have anything from the ninth century!

The square in Gamla Stad looks like Disney made it, as if Walt himself said, "Alright, make a really old square with very old buildings around it, and cobbled streets, and make it look believable and really authentic." My senses were simply overwhelmed at the idea of being able to touch buildings this old. My American soul was about to be overwhelmed over and over and *over* again.

As we made our way from the ferry uphill to the Gamla Stad area, we walked on worn cobblestones. We came to a giant rectangular building that The Cruise Addict informed me was the king's palace. I would not have guessed that-- it didn't seem very elegant to me; rather boxy, not palace-y, but then again what do I know? I've never seen a real palace.

I noticed a well-dressed guard or two at every corner and at every entrance. We definitely wanted to come back to the palace the next day, but for now we wanted to explore the area. This was a great beginning. Gamla Stad had a little courtyard in the middle of it, maybe thirty feet across, and fifty at most, with a sort of a fountain in the middle of it, complete with gargoyle faces. Quite scary faces, with rings coming out of their noses and mouths. It was pretty spooky, as Halloween decorations go. Only it wasn't Halloween. It was real! I found out later that this was where many people over the centuries had been killed.

Public capital punishments took place right here. Had I known that, I would not have enjoyed the atmosphere nearly as well.

The killings have stopped – Swedes are actually very calm, mellow, pacifistic type people – and now the square is surrounded by little tiny restaurants, each one more appealing than the other. We had been snacking across several continents, but I could not remember when we had last eaten a meal. I think it was in SeaTac, right after we dropped off our car.

Where's Dinner?

It was late afternoon by now and the sun was starting to go down, along with the temperature. Because it was still very warm ---relatively--and a beautiful day for being outside, people had gathered at the tables and chairs outside of every little restaurant. Each restaurant provided little fleece blankets to their customers. We saw groups of happy people eating, wrapped up in green fleece, while a few chairs over there, people wrapped up in red and orange. It just added to the atmosphere.

45° is really not picnic weather to me! We chose a wonderful little bakery. The kitchen area was smaller than my linen closet at home, but it displayed amazing, beautiful, enticing, fragrant, drool-worthy baked goods. We chose a thick slab of cream cheese torte to share and took it back outside to eat on a bench as an appetizer. About five inches tall, made of cream and cream cheese with cardamom and lemon. My taste buds were ecstatic.

However, even the best cream cheese torte in the world doesn't qualify as dinner. We wandered down a narrow side street... And I do mean narrow! Holding hands, as we often do, our shoulders nearly grazed the sides of the buildings as we walked. Husband insisted this was an actual street. I still felt like I had fallen into Disney's imagination of what an old, old street should look like.

We stepped into a beautiful little restaurant. *Very* little. There was outdoor seating, but I was chilled. It had probably four tables and a bar inside; most of their clientele were outdoors. I could see into the kitchen. Again, I've seen kitchens bigger in RVs at home. Clearly, my estimations of what size things 'ought to be' going to be challenged this whole trip. Another thing the challenged me was the prices on the menu, and everywhere else in Sweden. One krona equals fifteen cents in American money; all the prices on the menu were triple digits. Really, 689 in any currency seemed like a lot for dinner!

We ordered Swedish meatballs and Jansson's Temptation, to share. Jansson's Temptation is a recipe that Husband remembered from his days of living in Sweden. It's a rustic dish of thin sliced potatoes mixed with onions, anchovies or herring, and cream, layered like a gratin, with toasted bread crumbs on top. It's quite remarkable that something as simple can taste so heavenly.

The meatballs were amazing and made me think about my cookbooks. I collect cookbooks and I cook frequently. I have made several different versions of Swedish meatballs, but none of them were anywhere near as delicious as this plate. The steamy handmade meatballs were served with a warm, spicy gravy, little boiled potatoes, jewel-like lingonberries, and a plate of pickled gherkins. I'm pretty sure the pickles were homemade, too.

After this very satisfying dinner, we slowly made our way back to the hotel on the little ferry. It was dusk by now. The temperature was rather brisk, but the view from the harbor was delightful. This time we took the other route, going left, completing our tour of the harbor. I liked the whimsical sculpture of a graceful arch, like part of a rainbow, with a sprite of some sort on top, splashing water into the harbor as if out of a fire hose, with happy sculpted stars above him. Husband was puzzled by it; he's not much for modern art. He mused, "what's the point of pouring water from a hose into a harbor full of water?"

The sun was still setting, which I found rather odd. At home, near Seattle, the sun drops out of the sky into the night pretty rapidly. Plop. Sweden is farther north. Here, the sunset took *hours*. It kind of glided in on a low arching trajectory and it took a good three hours to finally set. Husband reminded me that during the summer the sun barely sets at all, and during the winter, it rises above the horizon just enough to set again.

A Palace

Our second day in Stockholm was spent exploring. We took the ferry over to the main center of town and wandered a little bit until we found a tiny café with a bunch of local workers. They look like construction workers to me, and of course, again seeking out local foods, this was the place for me. This is my first introduction to foods that I would've refrigerated, had I been home. There were trays of little sandwiches with meat and cheese in them, and hard-boiled eggs just laying out there, at room temperature.

We ended up with hot cocoa, tiny ham and brie sandwiches, and we split a huge pastry. Oh, that was the best part! It was intricate, like strands of ribbon heaped into a glossy haystack, and it was fabulous. I asked what the flavor was. Cardamom! I didn't know that I like cardamom. I want to find some recipes, when I get home, for foods that include cardamom. Not for the pastry ---there is no way I would have that much patience to make something that intricate, only to have it eaten.

After breakfast we made our way back to the Gamla Stad area, the old town. We walked off the ferry, up towards the palace. Just as we came to the first crosswalk, we heard music. Wait, was that a band? A parade? At 8:50 AM in the morning on an ordinary Tuesday, what could be going on? Just then an entire marching band in uniform, playing loudly and very well, came around the corner of the King's palace. We noticed a crowd gathering across the street and lining the cobblestone walkway up to the palace. As we went to join them, crossing behind the band, we heard people talking about the Changing of the Guard. What perfect timing!

We are Americans. We don't have a Changing of the Guard in America, unless you count the Tomb of the Unknown in Arlington. We quickly made our way up the sloping sidewalk, outpacing the band. Sure enough, when it came to the first entrance, there was a formality, a Changing of the Guard. The light blue soldiers replace the dark blue soldiers. The band continued on up the hill and around the corner, still playing. The band was not playing typical patriotic music, whatever that would sound like in Sweden. No, these were show tunes, and I recognized most of them! It just made it more fun. The marching band continued to the top of the hill and then around to the back of the palace, or maybe it was the front. I still have no sense of direction, and in my defense, the palace is square. The crowd was pretty extensive by now, several hundred people, and this level area had been blocked off to make the Changing of the Guard even more formal.

There was some shouting and some explanations, both in Swedish and English, and then the light blue uniformed guards were relieved by the dark blue uniformed guards with much formality. I enjoyed that. Then the music conductor announced in English and in Swedish that they were delighted to have the crowd gathering and they would favor us with a concert. They played their hearts out for a good twenty-five minutes, right there on the cobblestone courtyard, and I loved it. I'm a big fan of serendipity, of unplanned pleasures, and this certainly qualified.

It was a great start to the day. Being an American, I've never seen a real live palace and I was anxious for a tour. But first, a stop in the gift shop. I had to smile at a sign low to the floor. It read "be aware of pickpockets. They have been sighted in this area." Of course, in America we have pickpockets and crime too, but we don't announce it on formal gold-edged placards.

We went to the desk to pay for tickets to tour the palace, but the docent there talked us into buying a Stockholm Pass instead. I flinched at the price. The conversion from kroner to dollar was rather appalling. It would cost us close to 4000 kroner! He insisted we needed the Pass, so we bought it. Good advice-- we used it over and over the rest of the day. We ended up saving a lot of money on entrance fees and transportation. It even covered the cost of the little ferry which we needed to take everywhere else we went that day.

I've never seen a palace before. I was awestruck, over and over, by the art and the history and the opulence. It's a working palace, not just a museum. We went in the royal apartments. We walked through the King's Counsel and Audience rooms, and the room where he greets foreign ambassadors. We saw the long table where decisions of state are made. Heavy law books were arranged down the center, a clear reminder that the law must be followed. The king's chair at the very end was the fanciest we saw! There was a silver throne, and a gold one built in the 1600's.

I was stunned by the incredible artwork. One room had a ceiling that took my breath away. There were beautiful clouds, a painted heaven, interspersed with angels. Some of the angels were painted, others sculpted, three-dimensional, looking so life-like they could have swooped down to speak their piece at any moment. Just breathtaking. The huge wall tapestries were intricate with exquisite hues. Twice I mistook mosaics for paintings, because the shading was just that good. I am no artist, but I appreciate artwork. This was amazing and I loved it! My only complaint was because it is a designated Sensitive Military Site, photography was forbidden. My camera itched in my pocket. However, I wouldn't want people taking pictures in my home, either, and in the king and queen actually do live there. We bought a book at the Royal Gift shop, loaded with pictures. It was the best I could manage.

The palace is an uninteresting square outside, flat and fairly plain with a massive courtyard in the center. I guess I expected turrets and peaks and towers. This was basically just right angles. Ah-- I saw a model and it all made sense. The actual palace was constructed <u>inside</u> the courtyard originally and towered over the stone sides. It was destroyed by fire, centuries ago, then it was rebuilt using the castle *wall* itself. The current palace is actually inside the old walls. Clever!

In nearly every room there was a well-dressed and polite person just standing there, perhaps to answer questions or to enforce the no photography rule or perhaps to prevent theft. One approached me when I was looking into the courtyard through a large beveled window and explained that, while they no longer had moats, or fires burning to protect the king, security was still very high. This was not the first palace that I that I was to see in our travels, but certainly a very impressive one. I guess my impression of Swedes has always been that they are reasonable, friendly, optimistic, logical, no-nonsense, nonviolent type people. As I spent the day in Stockholm, it was simply reinforced.

One of the things I wanted to see was a real live Swedish Church. We were in luck; the national church was right nearby. It's where the royal family worships and where the entire lineage of Swedish kings are buried. Again my frugal soul flinched at the number of kroner required to go inside; a quick conversion came to almost $18 a person. I hesitated. Husband noticed a sign at the desk. Entry was included with a Stockholm Pass! Already I was happy with the purchase, and the guilt free entry.

We went through the big heavy doors, and I gasped. I've never seen such a place in my life~! Gold pillars, realistic statues, intricate mosaics, a stunning altar area, towering organ pipes draped with sculptured linen... opulence isn't a big enough word. The worn tombs of kings and the floors in the crypt of the site were interesting, dating back five centuries before my country was a country. I was enthralled with the soaring gold sculpture of Saint George slaying his dragon. This was a very worthwhile stop.

At home, we had booked a Hop On Hop Off tour in Stockholm, figuring it would be an efficient way to see the most places in our limited timeframe. In most places, a HOHO involves a bus. In Sweden, because the city is built on a series of islands, the HOHO is a boat. It was a good idea at home, at our computer in our living room, but if we came back to Stockholm, I wouldn't do that again. The little ferry cost much less and went more places, plus-- bonus -- ferry, subway, and buses are included in the Stockholm Pass. I flinched at the original outlay of cash for the Pass, but it became a great savings for us.

A Warship

Our day plan included the Wasa Museum. The *Wasa* was a 17th century warship that sank twenty minutes into its maiden voyage. Excellent workmanship; poor engineering. It lay in the harbor, untouched, for over 300 years! Due to the cold temperatures and the pollution in the Baltic Sea from the city's waste, the ship did not deteriorate much beyond the iron rusting away. The museum itself was beautifully done. The six-story building was completely filled with this giant warship in such good condition that it didn't even look real. Maybe I spent too much time at Disneyworld as a child...again, it looked like stepping onto a movie set! The *Wasa* was huge and so well restored it looked ready to sail. Well, except for the faulty engineering, the part that caused it to tip over right in the harbor.

I was pleased to see that every information plaque was in both Swedish and English. I think Stockholm would be the last place on this trip where I could count on being part of the conversation. The *Wasa* was astonishing with gorgeous workmanship, and much, much larger than I expected. The restoration was incredible. After it had been pulled off the bottom of the harbor in the 1960's, workers had injected the rotting wood with a sort of polymer. That preserved the form and shape of the wood, and gave it an oddly plastic texture.

We could plainly see which parts were the original; they were dark. Missing parts, such as the wooden disk where the bottom of the rigging was tied on was made out of plywood, so we could clearly see the difference. There was very little that was not original. It was a complete warship, rigged and ready to sail! Husband observed, "The *Wasa* is the only ship from that time. Had not sunk, it wouldn't be here for us to look at."

Even parts of the sails' fabric endured for centuries. We wound our way up on ramps and stairs to the top floor, admiring every level, to the crow's nest. The workmanship was breathtaking; remember, this was long before power tools were invented. Back on the bottom level, we explored the area that told about how the restoration actually took place. Multiple bodies had been found on the ship, preserved in in place in skeleton form. With the modern technology used by crime forensics, the faces of the people who were found on the ship were able to be restored, and displayed. They were so lifelike; had they spoken, I would not have been surprised.

And… The Wasa Museum entry fee was again covered by the Stockholm Pass. That was a really good purchase!

Next we went on to Skenson, also included in the Pass. It was a laid back place, described as "Historic Sweden in a nutshell." Old buildings from across Sweden had been brought to this island and restored to a living history site. I really enjoyed seeing the different homes, the overview. By this point, we were very tired from so much walking, so I also appreciated taking advantage of the benches with pleasant scenery overlooking the city. We had korv for lunch. Korv is a traditional street food that looks a lot like a long hot dog in a short bun. It was surprisingly tasty.

The ferry took us back to the downtown, the main modern area of Stockholm. We enjoyed an hour of walking, window-shopping, people watching, and resting in a sunny park. When I travel, I generally have a Quest, a local item that I would like to own. In Stockholm, I hoped to find a good solid cheese plane. This seems like a very ordinary thing to want, just a flat tool to slice cheese with at home, but they are remarkably hard to find in America, at least ones that will cut properly. We asked a few locals where to find one. They universally suggested IKEA! Too far without a car. Finally one recommended a local store, three blocks down.

Husband complained that, while he was still fluent in Swedish, every single person who greeted us spoke to us in English. Obviously, they marked us as Americans. Husband was hoping to practice his language skills. We found a beautiful cheese plane, and he went to pay for it while I wandered off to another area of the store. He returned, looking sheepish. Without his dark-haired companion, me, the clerk mistook him for a Swede. She greeted him in Swedish, at last! That would've been fine, but then the next question she asked Husband was out of his expertise in the language. She asked him what his "member association number" was. Sure he had misunderstood, he had to answer her in English. Rather disappointing, but at least we know that it was me, holding him back.

Our time in Sweden was almost over. I enjoyed Sweden much more than I expected. I would not hesitate to come back. I was impressed with the kind, polite people. Several times I was surprised to be walking down the street and have a random stranger come up, welcome us to his country and ask if he could help us find something, or recommend a good lunch place, or ask how did we like the city so far. We are too often in our own world at home—to be greeted warmly by strangers was charming. People did not seem to be in a rush, although is a very efficient, clean city.

I felt very much at ease, knowing I could ask anyone for help if needed and make myself understood. That likely will not happen anywhere else on this long journey. We head for Italy tomorrow. Italians, Greeks, Turks, French, and Spaniards don't automatically speak English. We are off to the more *foreign* foreign places next. We've a flight to London at 6am.

On Our Way To Venice

Allowing for the too-early trip to the airport, we had to take a taxi at 4:15am. My ears were still ringing from the scolding the taxi driver had given us about using public transportation when we arrived, but there are no buses at 4:15 AM. We grimaced at the $100 taxi fee; no way around that.

And we flew to London. We went to London city Airport, saving almost $200 per ticket per person over Heathrow. London is another place I'd like to visit someday. Not this trip; we have a cruise to catch. As we flew low over the city, I could recognize little tiny landmarks down there. Kensington Palace, the London Eye, even Big Ben and the Thames River. No time on this trip, but I'll be back to London.

The London City was arranged differently than any airport I've seen. There was only one central meeting area, not the individual gates we have found in all other airports. There was a giant electronic board that listed all of the impending departures, with gate numbers listed for only the top four. We kept a close eye on it. Gradually our flight number made it to the top four on the list. Instantly, the moment it was announced, it began to blink "warning! Final boarding call!" How could that be? We were late and had to run, seconds after it was announced! We grabbed our backpacks and took off sprinting through the airport, with a bunch of other running people. The gate agents boarded passengers, urging everyone to hurry. Apparently this is protocol! I'm learning a lot about airports on this trip.

Venice, Italy

My first glimpse of Italy was preceded by a sharp elbow to the ribs. Apparently I fell asleep on that flight from London, finally. Venice was a beautiful city, even from above, with buildings very densely packed in close together on the islands in the murky lagoon. Venice is described as a fish shape. You hardly ever see fish with steeples and old buildings on them. I didn't quite see the fish shape, but I could see Venice was beautiful, even as the plane landed. I couldn't wait to explore!

We had researched how to get from the San Marco airport to San Marco Square, close to our hotel. The airport is on the mainland and the Square is the center part of Venice itself. A private water taxi cost $400; that was out. The Vaporetto was a second choice. A Vaporetto is like a public bus, only it's a boat that holds maybe 50 people and has open windows on the sides. Making our way from the airport terminal to the Vaporetto stand was no problem at all, a walk of maybe 500 feet on level ground. Signs were clear. We took the Red Route, the one with fewer stops along the way. It cost 18 euros; not bad!

Tantalizing scenery passed at a very slow speed as we traversed the lagoon. The lagoon, until you get to the Grand Canal, is a 'no wake' zone, and I guess there must be pretty stiff penalty for making a wake because we were barely, barely moving. I'm pretty sure I could have rowed faster. I was getting anxious. I wanted to be there already!

We passed Murano, the famous glassblowing island. The workshops were open to the water, and at that speed, we had a pretty good view. Of course we admired their famous art everywhere all around, including in our hotel, later on. After what seemed a very long ride, we began to see canals and bridges – VENICE!

When you're coming into Venice a day early for a cruise, you have two choices. You can stay on the mainland, which makes it easier to get to the cruise ship, but inconvenient to explore Venice. The other option is to book lodging near Saint Marco, on the island itself. That makes it easier to see Venice, but more difficult to get to the cruise ship. We decided that it was more important that we enjoy Venice proper and worry about how to get to the cruise ship later on.

Our group of friends had made their own arrangements for lodging in Venice, independently. We laughed when we heard that all ten of them were staying at the Best Western in Venice! *Best Western* – we could stay at those anywhere. This was not the time for familiarity! Our hotel, after minor debate, was chosen for Old World Charm and it was all that. We chose the San Gallo Hotel, just off of San Marco Square; a good central location.

San Gallo hotel was rather a chore to reach, I admit, from the Vaporetto station, once we reached the terminal. I would have greatly appreciated a nicely tipped bellhop at that point. We pushed /pulled our suitcases over cobblestone, and up over an arching bridge along the waterfront and then diagonally across San Marco square, through a portal in San Marco Square, all the while dodging crowds of people and swarms of pigeons. It was a bustling place! I longed to stop and soak it in, but checking in at the hotel and jettisoning our bags was a priority.

The Cruise Addict had an etiquette issue as he walked across the giant cobblestone square. Etiquette says, when you see someone taking a photograph, you pause, so as not to get in the picture. Rarely is photo bombing welcome! After he stopped three or four times, he recognized that he was only going to be able to walk maybe two steps at a time before he was in another photograph. We were not going to make any progress at that speed. He ducked his head, apologized repeatedly as he walked, and we made our way across San Marco Square.

Our directions to the Hotel San Gallo told us to go to the second portal on the east side. That led to a small, narrow walkway, up over a canal, complete with bobbing gondolas and there we were in the courtyard that we'd seen on Google Maps at home. We stopped to rest a bit. I was winded by this time from dragging my wheeled suitcase over uneven cobblestones that far with my heavy backpack on. I was grateful that I decided to fit everything in one suitcase. It was not the first or last time I had that thought!

Cisterns

The tiny courtyard had one of Venice's very old cisterns in the middle; a good spot to rest. Venice has a very interesting and historic water filtration system. Considering the city was built in the middle of a salt lagoon, they found an ingenious way to get fresh water. They built barely sloping courtyards in the city. With each rain, the water drains into underground cisterns. Each courtyard space had a waist-high fountain or faucet that pumps water filtered through naturally occurring sand deposits. Voila! Fresh drinking water!

These public fountains are no longer relied on, but are still in place throughout Venice, and they still dispense perfectly safe water to drink---after hundreds of years! Generally, I'm very hesitant to drink water out of anything less than a sealed bottle when I travel outside of North America. I'm not over the episode in Mexico City. I was fanatically careful not to drink the water, and yet I still ended up getting deathly ill. There was about a day and a half where I was afraid I *wasn't* going to die. All I can think that I may have done wrong was brushing my teeth using the water from the hotel sink. Since then I've been very careful about drinking water or anything that doesn't come in a sealed bottle when I travel in unfamiliar places. From everything I've read, that won't be a problem in Venice. There's something kind of cool about drinking from a fountain that has stood for hundreds of years. Just imagine all the people that have stood by that very fountain, filling pitchers and talking!

San Gallo Hotel

We found a small oval Hotel San Gallo sign by the old wooden door. We pulled open the door and faced two very, very long flights of steep marble stairs. Thirty one worn steps, to be exact; we counted later. I was already so tired! How were we going to get those heavy suitcases way up there? It didn't look like a hotel at all. Just then two women, tourists, probably, walked down the stairs. As they passed us, we asked if it was indeed the Hotel San Gallo. They shook their heads. "No, Murano Glass display studio." Thoroughly confused, I sent Husband up the stairs to be sure we were in the right place. I was not interested in hauling my heavy suitcase up those daunting stairs more than once, if I could help it.

Oh, good! Husband returned promptly with two Italian men, Venetian men, who greeted me profusely in Italian. Mercifully, they did not kiss me, although it looked like a risk for moment there. I'm not big on kissing. They took our suitcases and bounded up the stairs, two at a time. Legs aching, I followed. At the top of the stairs, I could see the confusion with the tourists. On the left was an open Murano glass display studio, but if you turned to the right and went up three steps and through the other door behind the wall, then up four steps, there was a hotel lobby.

I loved it immediately. The hotel was charming! Old and well-kept, clean and shiny, and exactly what I expected for Venice, had Walt Disney designed Venice. As we checked in, the owner gave us three keys; one to open the door at the bottom of the steps after hours, one that opened the hotel just in case the owners were not there, and one that opened the door to our room. I have never had the key to a Venetian hotel before! I'm not sure I could diagram the hotel's layout; it was a warren. To get to our hotel room, we were led around the hotel desk, to the left, down a short hall, up three stairs, down a passage to the right, up eight stairs to the left, ducking under the stairwell, around two more corners, open the door and there we were. Piece of cake!

The Hotel San Gallo was a quaint, old, delightfully typical Venetian hotel. I was instantly comfortable. I'm sure it had nothing in common with the Best Western, where our friends were staying. On the other hand, *they* probably had room to move around their hotel room. We did not. The whole room was about fifteen inches larger than the bed, which was in the center, so tight we literally had nowhere to put our suitcases. We set them in the bathroom. When one of us wanted to walk around the bed, the other had to step into the hall.

The hotel owner escorted us to our room. Rather sheepishly, in good English, he explained that it was smaller than American hotels, but since we're going on a cruise, we should be grateful because, certainly, our cruise ship cabin would be much smaller.

Turns out he was wrong, by at least half. I probably would've been claustrophobic had I stayed at the hotel San Gallo for a couple of weeks, but for just a couple of nights, I really liked it!

The room had two windows, one in the hotel room and one in the bathroom, both made of leaded stained glass in a diamond pattern. I love stained glass! I leaned out the open window, and was met by the view of assorted rooftops, very close. The stained-glass window above the bathtub was propped open, letting in a delightful mixture of smells just begging to be identified.

I immediately recognized the light fixtures and sconces on the wall as being authentic Murano glass, which just added to the charm. The wallpaper, curtains, bedspread, and the cushion on the ridiculously tiny chair all were made of the same large silvery paisley print. It somehow reminded me of an Old West bordello theme; not that I've ever seen such a place, mind you. It was a little overwhelming, but authentic, and I liked it rather a lot. The point of travel is to see new things, isn't it?

Bring On Venice

We dumped our stuff and then headed out to explore Venice. We were to meet Clint and Mary at five o'clock, right in front of San Marco Basilica, which still sounded like a postcard location to me. They had flown in from Paris that morning. Still seemed strange to me to make an appointment to meet someone over 5000 miles from home for *dinner!*

I was determined to see San Marco in three different ways. I wanted to see it in the middle of the afternoon, which was now, after dark, and again first thing in the morning. I find when we travel, that's a good way to get an overview of the place. The atmosphere and pace of a place changes throughout a day; it's an easy way to get a feel for a new city.

We didn't have much time to explore on our own today, but we had enough time to be amazed. We headed back out into San Marco Square, unencumbered by luggage. It was *very* crowded. There were tourists, tour groups trailing guides like wayward ducks, people juggling suitcases as we had done, children, vendors, all in a colorful blur. We even spotted several pickpockets plying their trade. The restaurants were open and thriving, but the architecture is what impressed me the most.

The architecture of San Marco was *designed* to impress visitors to the Empire when it was the center of commerce in its heyday, to stun visitors into knowing they were not in a trifling place. The effect was successful! The statues and sculptures, right there on the square, were breathtaking, along with the many- pillared structure itself. Why, with our great technology and power tools and laser cutters and all this free time we have in our modern society, why do we build rectangles?

We were anxious to explore in more depth tomorrow. For now, we just walked around and admired the architecture of the buildings, got our bearings, and soaked in the feeling of the place. I admired the vendors, selling little gondolier outfits and hats. I bought a lacy scarf, the first of ...well, many. Scarves and wraps make me happy. They are light, pretty, versatile, they go with everything, they jazz up any outfit, they pack easily, and *I like them*. I ignored Husband's mutter about "Another?"

Eventually we made our way through the crowds to the Basilica entrance to find Clint and Mary. I had not met Clint or Mary. Husband works with Clint. The Cruise Addict is guilty of bragging, and it seems he mentioned, just in passing, he assured me, that we were going on this cruise. An hour later, Clint announced "we're coming with you." I was very pleased, once I met them, that I liked them immediately. We spent a lot of time together over the next fifteen days, and I really did enjoy traveling with them. Good thing!

I was also a little intimidated, truth be told. As we got acquainted, Mary mentioned they had just had their eighth great-grandchild, last week. Clint mentioned that in their lay-over in Paris, he and Mary had decided not to wait for the elevator, and instead climbed to the top of the Eiffel Tower! 1021 steps to the second level's platform ---who does that??

Gondolas

Husband had made arrangements with his co-worker and his wife to have dinner that evening and to share a gondola ride. Ah, gondolas – not my thing! Think about it; in every Venetian movie or documentary you've ever seen, dull faced people are plopped in gondolas. That's a typical tourist behavior and I don't enjoy doing typically touristy things when I'm traveling. My style is to avoid the predictable tourist traps that everyone else does. I like to step off the beaten path, and a gondola-riding sounded like falling right into it. I was not excited, but I was outnumbered. And polite, of course; unfailingly polite.

So we set off to find the typical touristy gondola ride, which I had no intention of enjoying. As we walked around the area, we noticed multiple gondola "stops." We discarded the idea of taking one out of the Grand Canal because of the crowds, which seemed to be increasing by the minute. I wanted somewhere a little more quiet, at least, if we could find one away from the masses. We found a likely looking gondolier by the Hard Rock Café ---what was *that* doing there? The mix of very old and modern jarred me; one of many times on this vacation! We settled in on the omni present velvet and tasseled seats, and the gondolier pushed off. I sat back, preparing to be bored. I wasn't going to enjoy it, regardless.

Oh, but I was wrong! I ended up loving it. The gondolier took us down sleepy canals, across the busy Grand Canal, under low bridges, against crumbling walls, places we couldn't have seen on foot. Some were so narrow; had we been walking, I would've called it an alley. It was like a peek behind the scenes, where the throngs of walking tourists could not see. The ride was about 40 minutes long. All the while, the gondolier ignored the four of us, and called out in Italian to the locals, and other gondoliers. I'm pretty sure he knew every local we passed personally, but did not seem to even see the tourists waving at him from byways and bridges. It was a surprisingly calm ride, and quiet, except for him shouting every so often. I enjoyed getting a feel for the city, crumbling walls and all. The parts of the city most visitors see are lovely and well kept, but it's a façade, of sorts.

Venice is sinking; that's part of the problem. Building on islands in a lagoon is really not a very stable place, even linked together by the little bridges. Hundreds of years ago, thousands of whole tree trunks were sunk as pilings in the lagoon, and the buildings were built on top of that. Well, it wasn't designed to last forever. We could see places, first floors, that have already submerged, with water gently lapping under the doors. From the gondola, crumbling steps and walls were clear to see. It is been said that 'Venice is in a state of elegant decay.' I agree, both about the elegance, and the decay. Some of the walls we saw looked *perfectly* decaying, almost fake. The gondola ride was actually a highlight!

Dinner

Although it was way early for dinner, comparatively-- Europeans don't start dinner until at least nine or ten o'clock-- we'd been traveling so much that we were not even sure what time zone our bodies were on, and we were hungry. Husband was heart set on spaghetti in Venice. As we were checking into the hotel, Husband asked the owner of the San Gallo to recommend a good place for dinner and he did so. He assured us it had the best squid ink pasta in Venice! *Squid ink?* I seek out local fare, but I draw the line at glossy black slimy stuff on my plate.

Husband asked the owner, "So, they have good Italian food?"

The man drew himself up proudly and said, " No, Sir! They have excellent *Venetian* food." Whoops-- another boundary to trip over.

We four were on our way to go to the restaurant that he had recommended, but as we wandered down little side streets, away from the crowds of tourists, over little bridges, over canals we realized that we were *surrounded* by small restaurants, and they all looked excellent. We chose one near a candy shop. Like all the other restaurants we had passed, it had menus posted in the window, with pictures. A waiter standing in the front doorway greeted us with a bright, "Bon giorno!" and a broad smile. This was as an authentic as we could get. This was going to be great!

The Cruise Addict was happy. His goal, stated at home, was to eat spaghetti in Venice, pizza in Naples, gelato in Florence, gyros in Greece, and something on a skewer in Turkey.

Of course, the menu was in Italian. I have only about twenty Italian words in my vocabulary, but I speak Food fluently. I recognized most of the main menu words and read avidly, trying not to drool at the descriptions. Mary and Clint were overwhelmed by the language barrier and quite concerned about finding something they would like to eat. They finally said, "We give up. All we want is American spaghetti. What's that called here?"

I happen to know that American-type spaghetti sauce doesn't even exist in Italy, but I would do the best I could to order something the culinary cowards would enjoy. I ordered some homemade linguine Bolognese for the three of them, figuring that was as close as we could get. They were surprisingly uncomfortable, but as they munched on their breadsticks, they relaxed. I ordered some handmade rolled pasta with clams for myself. I knew that I was going to be happy when the waiter brought me a little empty bowl to put clam shells in. My delicious pasta had about 45 whole littleneck clams in it. Guessing at some of the words, I was able to pick out a nice antipasti misto, made of wonderful local cured meats. The antipasti had Parma ham, salami, prosciutto, and a pale salty meat I did not recognize. It was delicious! I was terribly thirsty all that night and the next day from all the salted meat, but it was worth it.

Communication between the waiter, who spoke only Italian, and I, who spoke almost no Italian, was ...well, *I* thought we did rather well. He obviously was questioning himself and so he had the cook come out to verify our orders. Husband chuckled when he met the cook, who spoke passable English, and perfect Italian, as well as Japanese... because she was from *Japan*. So much for Grandma's authentic recipe there in Venice!

Venice at Night

We parted after dinner, planning to meet on the ship on the first sea day. Clint and Mary were staying back in the Best Western and wanted to get back there before it grew too dark. For us, there was plenty of time left to explore Venice, in a new light. Er, dark. Husband and I slowly headed back towards San Marco, leisurely exploring the side streets. Venice has no road signs, but on most corners, painted arrows indicated either "Per Rialto" or "Per San Marco," major landmarks. Also, every shop had business cards with a 'you are here' map on the back. Venice isn't big enough to get very lost, in any case.

Even after all these years, The Cruise Addict is still under the mistaken impression that I love to shop. He is wrong. I am very good at shopping, but I don't love it. I didn't shop much in Venice, but it's fun to window shop. Our first stop after dinner was the candy shop next to the restaurant. Italian candy reminds me of my childhood. My grandparents were from northern Italy, and always had a bowl of those little rice-paper-wrapped nougats on the table. We acquired a few treats to munch as we walk. Travelers need sustenance, after all!

Dusk had fallen, and the atmosphere was very different than it had been in the afternoon. Venice seemed more mellow, quieter. A lot of the tourists were gone, those with suitcases had apparently reached their hotels by now, even the kiosks had folded up for the night. In San Marco, the nightlife was in full swing. Outside almost every restaurant bands were playing on the square. Folding chairs and linened tables had popped up. People were meandering and eating and smiling, dancing to the music. We walked, hand in hand, absorbing the atmosphere. My soul was happy.

The plan for tomorrow: an early start! The hotel provided a full breakfast, on the rooftop terrace---in *Venice*! I usually disdain breakfast, but this sounded special. Besides, we had more exploring to do; I'd need fuel. Even before breakfast, I wanted to get out onto the streets of Venice, very early, before the crowds and tourist arrived. Real people live here, behind those narrow little balconies. I looked forward to sampling the city as it woke up.

Venice in the Morning

We woke to heavy rain pounding against the stained-glass window. The stained-glass window over the bathtub did not close all the way. As I had a shower, I had *two* showers, warm water, interspersed with gusts of cold rain water as the wind blew. I did not dawdle. We planned to enjoy the day, and a little ---okay, a lot of ---rain was not going to stop us. After all, we're from Seattle. Our philosophy has always been, if we wait until the rain stops, we're going to miss an awful lot of our lives.

Husband's favorite meal is breakfast, so we had a slight adjustment in the timing of our morning jaunt. I think we could have made an earlier start, but for the rain. We looked forward to breakfast on the rooftop terrace, but due to weather, it had been moved into the charming hotel lobby. The Cruise Addict was too tempted to just walk past the breakfast laid out on the sidebar. The food was interesting, not the greasy eggs-and-hash-browns of home. Room temperature juices, coffee, teas, hard-boiled eggs, cold cereals, but unfamiliar ones, muesli, jams, jellies, nice little pastries, whole oranges, yogurts, thick milk, and fresh bread. Even not being able to read labels, everything was recognizable. And tasty!

The toaster was interesting. I haven't seen a toaster like that. At home, I slide a slice of bread into the toaster slot, and when it pops up, it's done. This looked similar, except the bread goes in a little slot-sized wire basket with a handle, and the whole thing is lowered into the toaster. A timer clicked, but nothing popped up. To retrieve the toast, the diner took up the whole rack and slid the toast onto a plate. No burned fingers-- actually rather a good idea. The novelty made even toast fun.

There were maybe seven other hotel guests in the lobby, all very friendly. Everyone was talking and greeting each other. We met three other Spirit passengers who were from New Zealand. They said that they wanted to stay in a 'hotel with atmosphere.' We chuckled and agreed that that's what we had found.

And we met Debra! Debra was traveling by herself and we had actually made arrangements on line with her to share a tour in Naples, so we're very surprised to meet her in our little hotel at breakfast. What were the odds of meeting up there? She asked about our room experience, and we told her. Her story was different.

When she reached the San Gallo staircase, Debra hauled her two heavy suitcases up the steep 31 stairs by herself. After she wrangled the luggage that far, she sat in the lobby, panting and puffing. Debra is a very slim woman. She was told that her room was back on the ground floor, in the rear of the hotel, around the building. Without missing a beat, the hotel owner took her suitcases to the stained-glass window there in the lobby and swung it open. He tied a nearby rope to the handle of each of them, then lowered the bags out the window to the sidewalk three stories down! Pulling Debra's arm, he ran down the steps to ground level, retrieved the luggage, crammed the rope in a back pocket, then calmly escorted Debra to her hotel room. We laughed as she told the story—we are not in Kansas anymore! Was that standard operating procedure?

After our enjoyable breakfast, we headed off into Venice. I knew that Europeans tell time differently than Americans do. And I probably tell time differently than that. I'm an early morning person. Italy, Europe in general, doesn't get going till what I consider midmorning. At this time of day, the city was barely awake. Luckily, the rain had stopped. Bright sunshine sparkled on the puddles. Venice seemed a different place altogether! Gone were the crowds, the merchants; even the gondolas bobbed sleepily under their tarps and covers on the canals. I loved seeing Venice before the crowds arrived!

Early morning was the time to prepare for the day's commerce. We passed foodstuffs and linens being delivered to the hotels and restaurants. Delivery trucks, which looked a lot like big wooden wheelbarrows, rushed up and down the narrow streets, with cries of "mi scusi!" There are no delivery trucks or any motorized vehicles in Venice; it all comes by boat. No noisy taxis, no honking trucks. Everything was offloaded from boats, then run through the streets at high speed on little carts of one kind or another. Residents called to one another in Italian. Women hung laundry high above the street on clotheslines, adding to the postcard effect.

It must have been trash day. People lowered little trash bags out of their upstairs windows by rope. A man with a trash bin on wheels would come along, and untie it. A shouted greeting, a wave, and the rope was pulled back up, over and over. Later the bins were dumped into a trash scow in one of the larger canals.

It was a totally different atmosphere than last night. I soaked it up happily as the two of us wandered up the little narrow streets. It was not time for tourists to be out and about, and we were functionally ignored. I enjoyed the sneak peek into life in Venice, before the "show" begins.

San Marco

But now it was time to get into tourist mode. We went to Saint Mark's Basilica first. It had a long line, but once it opened ten minutes later, it moved very fast. The line forked once we reached the lobby area; upstairs to the right or through the Basilica itself straight ahead. The majority of people aimed for the Basilica's floor. I wanted to see the Square from a high vantage point, so I detoured to the sign that said Marciano Museo Terrace. We climbed a long flight of very steep marble stairs in a narrow curving stairwell, hardly wide enough for two people to pass. They were uneven heights, some knee-high, worn from centuries of monks and priests climbing them. Halfway, my legs were screaming.

Not at the bottom, mind you, but at the very top, was a sign that said "five euros." I was out of breath, so I just looked at Husband. I didn't climb that far for no reason! He knows that look, and silently reached in his pocket and paid the fee. Oh---it was worth every penny! It set my perspective for the rest of the trip, seeing the artwork up close.

We ventured out onto the terrace; more of an uneven rooftop, really; sloping, with marble rain gutters. To be able to see out on the balcony and over the Square, and eye level with the famous copper sculptures of the Horses of San Marco, was a view I will not forget. I also will not forget the flash of terror as my foot slipped on the slanted marble roof, before Husband grabbed my arm. Let's just say the structure would not have passed US building codes!

We lingered on the roof for a while, happily soaking in the view of ant-sized travelers below, then went inside to see the Museo section. It was awe-inspiring to see the intricate mosaics, mere inches away! The museum displayed ancient mosaics, very, very close, within a foot of my face. I could not touch them, but they were that close and changed my perspective on all the art that was to come. We saw so much mosaic art across Europe as we traveled on this trip; this was just the beginning. To be able to see the precise half-inch squares and how they were set made me look at the rest of the artwork we saw on this trip with a fresh eye. Some of the tiny tiles were covered in glittery gold leaf, and put together so delicately to make the shading look like paintings. We took many pictures, but they simply don't do it justice.

I was very grateful for that perspective. I was also puzzled; with all of our modern technology, free time, and smart modern brains, why don't modern people do fabulous art anymore? I guess we lack the patience or tenacity to stick with a project that delicate. It seems a loss.

We made our way back down the treacherous stairs, clinging to the walls. I'm telling you, the laws in the United States simply would not allow stairs like that. I rather liked it, even as I was very mindful of where I placed every footfall. How many thousands of feet had made that same climb over the centuries?

The Basilica itself was stunning. It is still a working church, centuries old. Imagine, worshipping in a place with art like that! Funerals, weddings, regular services; made our home church look pretty bland. I image children would not be bored. If they had trouble being attentive, they could make up stories about <u>this</u> statue going to visit <u>that</u> one, and so on. Photos were not allowed in the Basilica. I tried to absorb it as best I could, making memories as we wound our way through the church with a few thousand others. The route led us through the obligatory gift shop before spilling us back into the sunshine. I bought a slim book on San Marco square, with history and a lot of photographs.

Rialto Bridge

Husband and I walked to Rialto Bridge, crossing over many canals, over bridges. We passed two wedding parties--- what a great backdrop for wedding photos! I liked seeing the signs of prosperity, the embassies, the elegant architecture. It contrasted with the pitiful beggars once we neared the famous bridge. Rialto Bridge was mobbed, as we expected, a sea of humanity, moving up and down and through the shops, constantly posing and taking photos. We had seen it from below last night from the gondola, as we turned onto a smaller canal. To be on the bridge now gave us a dual perspective. There seemed to be more people on the bridge than spaces to put them!

The Rialto Bridge was a serious touristy spot, and sadly, the only one most visitors flock to, missing the side streets altogether. It is been said that 80% of tourists who go to San Marco never venture beyond the Rialto area. I was much happier seeking out the little narrow byways with quirky little shops. That's more my style.

Think how many movies you have seen this bridge in! To stand there was still worthwhile and awesome, looking out over the busy Grand Canal. The streets were wider around the Bridge, with upscale shops. I recognized the shops' brands as being very high end. The Rialto Bridge used to be lined with fish markets. There is still a fine market there. The small fish such as local sardines and octopus and squid come from the murky lagoon itself. The bigger fish come from farther, but either way, if you can't find fresh fish in Venice, you're doing something wrong.

On to the Museums!

Our Venice Pass covered entrance to six of them, and saved us time, too. We just breezed past the long lines of people buying entrance tickets. We bought our passes at the tiny visitor's center by the Alilaguna station, but our back up plan was the Correr Museum, since it typically has shorter lines. It cost €16, quite a bargain.

In America, museums' treasures are kept under glass or at a good safe distance from people. Not so here! To be able to be nose to nose with the sculptures was breathtaking to me. How did the artists, sculptors long ago, make ruffles, draped fabric, folds, tassels, even *curls* out of marble? I have worked quite a bit with clay and pottery, as well as textiles. I would have trouble making folds that flowing with soft clay! Marble is a lot less forgiving. The craftsmanship was stunning. Remember, too, they didn't have lasers or power tools back then. These lifelike sculptures were literally the sum of their life's work.

It seemed that the main architectural feature of Venice was stairs. It seemed everywhere we went that whole day was upstairs. Many stairs up up up, and then go around the corner and up more and more and more steps! This happened at the Doge's Palace, the Correr Museum, and again at the Basilica. Oddly, no matter how many steps we went up as we explored, we exited out on ground-level every time. I'm still little confused about this

.Doge's Palace is situated right on St. Mark's Square in Venice, an impressive first view for visitors coming by boat. They all did, in the days before the recent bridge construction over from the mainland. Its goal was to intimidate to visiting dignitaries, letting them know without a word that this was an important place. In Italian it's called Palazzo Ducale. It was the Doge's, or duke's, grand home, and it's still as if he walked away from it last week. The exterior architectural alone was astonishing. The interior includes a courtyard, grand halls, dramatic frescoed walls, gold-leafed ceilings, stunning murals, and intricate statues. It was opulent, huge, and quite impressive, but I found myself comparing it to the light, bright, brilliant colors of the only other palace I've ever seen, the one recently in Sweden. The ancient art was amazing, but I do like light and bright colors!

Casanova was held for many years in the Doge's Prison, accessed through the Bridge of Sighs. Legend says the doomed prisoners would peek out across the lovely city as they crossed the last bridge into the prison, and sigh mightily. The Italians are a romantic lot! The prisons were used until the 1950's, but had not changed much since they were built centuries ago.

The Correr Museum was our next stop, on another corner of San Marco Square. The Correr Museum was surprisingly uncrowded and gave us a good overview of Venetian art, along with a glimpse into what ancient Venetian life was like for politicians, aristocrats and other citizens. The Correr Museum is a must-see! It was fantastic to admire such artwork close up. I was surprised at how accessible the pieces were! Ancient works, right at nose level, not behind glass or protected by anything beyond respect. I suspect had I tucked one under my arm, it would have been a different story. It was delightful to be able to admire the paintings, sculpture and mosaics in their own places, not in a documentary or book.

Our next stop Academy Gallery, Venice's Museum of Art, is a monumental art gallery and contains the world's most complete 13th- to 18th-century art collections. Masterpieces by the Venetian greats who specialized in Byzantine and Gothic art of the Renaissance period such as Giovanni Bellini, Giorgione, Titian, Tintoretto, Veronese and more were on display. These masterful Venetian artists not only shaped the history of Venice art, but European art as a whole. Some of it was surprisingly familiar. Who said those college art history classes were not useful?

The Archaeological Museum was next, right nearby. I marveled at the coins from 2000 years ago, coins that were in circulation when Christ was alive. It displayed pottery and weapons and swords, early guns, maces, and an astonishing array of academia, manuscripts, and more art—gorgeous, every bit of it! I wish we had more time there. I could have happily spent an hour just on one or two sculptures. The Biblioteca section held texts from hundreds of years ago. I saw one from the 9th century! It had elegant, precise calligraphy with beautiful gold leaf artwork on the pages. It was a museum filled day.

Venice Midday

By late afternoon, our senses were overloaded and my back was in spasm from standing so long. Back outdoors, we noted that Venice has very few places to sit and rest, only a couple of benches. The steps on San Marco Square looked promising, but wandering uniformed people kept tourists on their feet. We were not ready for a restaurant. We took a break in a small nondescript church a couple of blocks off the square, just to be somewhere quiet where we could sit a little.

Once our eyes adjusted to the dim lighting, we were again shocked. The art! Mosaics! Soaring towers! Gold at every glance! Just think of all the people actually worshiping here, from the medieval ages, and today as well. The stories those ornate walls could tell if they would only speak to us-! This was far more meaningful than those upscale shops back by Rialto!

The church featured a sculpture that made me choke up. I was grateful for the dim light as I wiped away tears. A smiling young Virgin Mary held her pudgy little baby Jesus on her lap, gazing at her infant with love in her eyes. She seemed oblivious to the chubby cherubs ringing her feet, watchfully taking in the scene. I thought of our daughters, raising our precious grandchildren. Do unseen angels surround these young women as they love and raise their babies? Is Heaven's help just that close? Do we fail to notice, in the daily-ness of our lives?

We headed back to San Marco again. By this time, we were hot and tired and hungry. It must be time for gelato! Husband chose cherry. I had sweet cream, and both were wonderful. A short break, and we were off, exploring little byways and shops.

I very much enjoyed walking leisurely around Venice, to be able to absorb some of the history and notice the details in the narrow streets. I expect a lot of tourists don't even leave the main Rialto Bridge area. They really miss out. As we walked, often we would come over another little bridge onto another little island and find ourselves in another little courtyard with a square old blocky edifice in the middle of it. At first it looked like a good place to tie a horse, but of course there are no horses in Venice, either.

We had come upon some very early hydro engineering! Rather ingenious planning was required when the people of Venice first settled onto the lagoon. They realized, living on an island, that fresh water was going to be a problem. And so the early residents built cobblestoned or brickwork courtyards, with a slight incline down towards the middle. When the rains fell – and the rains do fall in Venice-- the rainwater would be channeled underground through sand to filter it. It could then be pumped out, using the pumps there in the middle of each courtyard. It was an ingenious cistern system that enabled people to live there for many years. Modern plumbing was added in about 1910, which really isn't all that long ago, when you think about it. The courtyard below our hotel boasted a cistern, as did almost every other wide spot we came upon in Venice.

We contacted our daughter at home, probably for the last time until midway through the cruise, barring crises. She said that her two-year-old son kept asking, "Where's Grandpa? Where's Grandma?" On the other side of the globe, of all places!

We were so tired! All those stairs. All these hours of walking. All those bridges. We enjoyed Venice so thoroughly that even I admitted we were done in. It was late afternoon and we had covered so much area, walking and exploring since breakfast. There is no question in my mind that we saw more of Venice than people who have been there a week. We didn't have to be on board the Spirit until 11 PM, but we were frankly worn out. We decided to go to the ship, earlier than planned.

To the Ship

We purchased Blue Route tickets on the Alilaguna water bus that would take us right to the cruise terminal. We hiked back to the hotel to retrieve our suitcases, which we had left at the desk. Oh, no, those thirty-one steep steps again! We gathered our two suitcases and our two heavy backpacks and made it down the stairs without falling. We retraced our route of the day before, through the courtyard, over the bridge, across the canal, up the stairs, back across San Marco Square, diagonally, while dodging the increased crowds, the tour groups and the pigeons, over the cobblestones, past the vendors and pickpockets, up over the bridge to the Alilaguna dock. Whew!

There was only one ship in port that day, the Norwegian Spirit---ours! The Blue Route on the Alilaguna bus was supposed to take us to the terminal, but since there was just the one ship, someone announced it would take us right to the ship, saving us a good long walk. As we waited at the Alilaguna dock, we ran into people on who will be on the cruise with us, including several that we met on the way from the airport the previous day. It was fun to talk with them again, and compare notes. We also saw Rick Steves over there, ready to board the Red Route. Of course I've seen all of his documentaries on PBS. He looks about ten years older than that, but he was recognizable, just the same.

The water bus came. We loaded up and off we went to the cruise terminal, taking many more photos as we went. The Grand Canal is just beautiful. I'm awed by the old buildings, the history, the big palaces, the merchants' houses, the obvious influence of the government and the Catholic Church, the charming atmosphere...I do love Venice.

As the water bus passed down the Grand Canal, we again glided past the Medici mansions. Generally, the Medici was a big family that was based in Venice. We were to run into their influence all over Europe on this trip. They were an all-powerful family, probably corrupt, but pervasive. As they set up all of their riches and all of their wealth and all of their trades and political tentacles, they forgot one important detail. An heir! You would think that passing along the family business would be critically important. And even if you couldn't have children, it would've made sense to adopt one, make somebody next in line. Instead, when the last Medici died off, all of that wealth reverted to the countries in which they were based. Prior planning!

We enjoyed talking to people and visiting with them on the Alilaguna on our way to the Spirit. A cheer went up from the passengers as soon as the cruise ship came into sight. It was fun to be with happy, excited people, all thrilled to be going on a twelve day Mediterranean cruise. We dropped our luggage off with a porter, and then we began the check in process.

Checking In—and a big surprise

Norwegian generally has a pretty smooth check-in process. They have different lines for passengers; for the loyalty levels, for the suites, for the elite, for everyone else, and we are very familiar with it. We've been on quite a few Norwegian ships before, after all. Did I mention Husband is called The Cruise Addict?

It all seemed very ordinary as we checked in, until it didn't seem ordinary at all. The agent took our photos, verified our credit cards, joked with us about our passports; all very normal until he reached to get our key cards at the end of the process.

A funny expression crossed the agent's face. He seemed suddenly... What was that? deferential? flustered? Hastily excusing himself, he almost bowed as he stepped away. What was going on? He quickly returned, apologizing for making us wait those fifteen seconds. He had our cards in an envelope; that hasn't happened before. Was there a problem?

He said, "Please, come with me. I will escort you to the VIP lounge where the concierge will assure your arrival at your cabin." VIP?! What was he talking about? We were not VIPs! We were just travelers, booked in a not-exclusive cabin. Had we been mistaken for someone else?

Acting as if this was normal – and I do mean *acting* – we followed along. The agent introduced us to the concierge who greeted us by name and turn to a uniformed man nearby. "This is Carlos, a butler. He will escort you to your cabin, and I will stop by shortly." Still acting, but stunned, we smiled as Carlos reached to take our backpacks. Mine was heavy, and I appreciated not having to carry it any more. I figured, we were good, until someone realized the mistake.

We followed Carlos and our backpacks over toward security. I glanced at my husband, who was about to speak, and simply said, "Don't." I could see that he wanted to pelt the man with questions; we have been very married a very long time. Husband closed his lips.

Carlos guided us through security. Husband set off the metal detector. This happens a lot. I think he might have metal supports in his shoes. Husband stepped back, took off his belt buckle, set the metal detector off again, and he stepped back again. The second time, Carlos said something quietly to the security guard. The guard's face changed. He stood up straighter and, "Oh, so sorry, Sir, I did not realize." The security guard waved Husband through and said, " Please, sir, excuse the inconvenience. Do not let this color your trip." <u>What</u> is going on here?!

Carlos, the butler, led us to an elevator, and to our cabin. Surely at this point, I figured, he would notice something amiss; this was not the penthouse, only a very big ocean view cabin. Carlos unlocked the door, set our backpacks down, and told us the concierge was on his way. The room steward immediately bustled in and welcomed us; the only thing that seemed normal at this point. Seconds later, the Concierge came to the door, and the steward fled.

He was very welcoming and he said, "Your VIP status entitles you to an elite breakfast and lunch at Cagney's." I know only suite passengers can go there. He further said that, of course, we were invited to cocktail parties with the Captain, and he gave us two invitations. He also gave us his card with his phone number on it. He encouraged us to call with "any little thing." He smiled, "I make things happen. Let me do my job, in any way you desire." Promising contact throughout the cruise, Ryan smiled and closed the door.

After he left, the room steward stepped back in. I asked her for some extra hangers when she had a moment ---I usually pack a few wire ones from home, but I was very weight conscious this trip. I expected her to bring them, but the next door knock, moments later, was the head of the hotel department herself with our suitcases! I've never seen luggage arrive at a cabin that fast, and certainly not delivered by an officer. She asked to be sure that we had everything. Both she and the steward seemed surprised that we only had one suitcase each. Well, it wasn't easy packing that light, but had I known about the Hotel Gallo's stairs, I would've brought even less. Extending her card, the hotel director left. The room steward followed, but returned seconds later, apologizing for failing to give us our Latitudes upgrade. She held a packet.

Latitudes is NCL's loyalty program. Our level entitled us to free laundry, discounts in various areas, two more cocktail parties, and four (two each) free dinners at the specialty restaurants, on top of the free dinner vouchers that the concierge, Ryan, had already given us. At this rate, we may never even see the dining room! Just as we shut the door, yet another knock came. We had a full on parade! This time it was canapés with a note, "compliments of Captain Lars Bengston, Master," addressed to us. Wow, just wow.

We were totally confused. As we sat there on the bed, happily munching the intricate little treats, we really could not figure this out. It's true we had a very nice cabin, the largest in its class by double, but it was only an oceanview, not a penthouse. Actually it was a *very* nice cabin, number 8500, one of only two that size on the ship. It was more than double the size of any balcony or suite cabin we've ever seen on any other ship, but it was still a lowly oceanview. We had booked it at a tremendous bargain price and we were not VIPs. What on earth is happening?

All I could think of was perhaps it had something to do with us hosting the Meet and Greet for the Cruise Critic group that would be the following day. The Cruise Addict was still anxious to ask questions about our sudden rise from frugal travelers to VIP status, but I am not one to look a perk in the mouth. If they're willing to indulge us, I'm willing to let them. Especially at breakfast; a lovely exclusive breakfast in a quiet steakhouse beats the cafeteria-like buffet all to heck. Fine. Pamper me. I can take it!

One of the first things we do on a trip is to go over every surface with disinfectant wipes. I'm sure the place is clean, but the risk of somebody forgetting to wipe a hard surface is not going to spoil my vacation. Unpacking took under ten minutes---we have it down to an art form. We were anxious to go see the ship!

First Impressions of the NCL Spirit

The Spirit was originally built for the Asian market, and I was quite concerned about it being small and cramped. Actually, we had more closet space than is normal on cruise ships, and plenty of room to spread out. There was about eight feet of empty floor space, which was handy for spreading out papers. Husband immediately took over the desk for his laptop and writing projects. As long as I could keep chocolate in the drawer, I can share. The cabin had a wide picture window over the bed, a chair, and coffee table, with another chair by the desk. I was happy to find a makeup mirror with good lighting. The closet was double wide with a new-looking safe, and robes that weighed about four pounds each, with slippers.

The bathroom was a good size, not huge, but bigger than some others and fine for our needs. I appreciated having a shower door. I like taking showers by myself, and to be grabbed in an intimate fashion by shower curtains doesn't make me happy. One of the perks was fancy upgraded Elemis bath products; good, that mystery soap in the wall dispensers is waxy. I always travel with the bar of my favorite soap, however, since that trip to the southern Caribbean. I had no soap, the waxy stuff in the dispensers was just awful, and the first three days of the cruise were sea days! It was a long wait until I could buy a bar of good soap. It's the little things that ease our way; I like nice soap.

We immediately noticed the ship had several things in its favor: smiling staff and crew, the ship looked very clean, and there was live music all over the place. This is going to be a wonderful cruise!

We did not plan to be on board in time for the life boat drill, but we were, so we went ahead and attended to get it out of the way. There was a makeup drill the following day. I heard that fully 75% of the passengers attended. However, we did not see them up wandering the streets of Venice at 6AM, as we were!

With an itinerary this port- intensive, we figured we'd be participating in a lot less ship board activities than usual. We found that in Hawaii, too---the ports were so close together, and we were so worn out by the time we oozed back to the ship, that pretty much all we did was eat, and take in a show before falling exhausted into bed. On this first day, we leisurely checked out the ship end to end and deck to deck, enjoyed the live music, then it was time for dinner. We opted for the Windows main dining room. Service was very good, and the food was just fine. I don't record much about food; it's so subjective.

Husband wanted to go to the show, Duo Dillon & Antonio. I was exhausted, and chose to go back to the cabin to read a while. I was happy to find a plate of elegant little chocolates on the bed, with a card that read 'Compliments of The Master of The Vessel.' Two were even remaining when Husband returned from the show. He reported later that the jugglers were pretty good, but how many jugglers does a person need to see in a lifetime?

NCL hosts a dance party pretty much every night. Tonight's was "Cruise Like A Norwegian" theme. I'm no dancer, and I was tired. We went to bed early, so as to be up in time for the sail away. Maybe it was a nap...75 minutes of sleep isn't really the same as going-to-bed.

The sail away at 1 AM was a stunning thing! I was glad we went up on deck for it. Even at that hour, I could still see people on the bridges in Venice. I was surprised to see a couple of hundred people lining the rails at that hour. The ship glided almost silently past Venice, down the Grand Canal, and out into open water. It felt like slipping into a dreamy postcard. The moon rising over Venice's lagoon left a wide streak of light on the water that made my soul happy. A moon rise over the Adriatic Sea—aahh! Goodbye, romantic Venice.

The Norwegian Spirit

I plan to tackle the rest of Part Two day by day, but now seems a good time to talk about the ship itself, The Norwegian Spirit.

It's not a new ship, built in 1999, with frequent upgrades and a dry dock since then. The Spirit lacks some of the bells-and whistles that I disdain anyway. Central Park atmosphere---isn't that why I vacation, to get *away* from that? If a ship's "Dazzle" factor is extremely important to you, the Spirit may not be the best choice. However, this cruise was selected based on the ports of call, and not the ship. With this great itinerary cruising the Mediterranean, we viewed the ship as simply a comfortable method of transportation, not the destination. We did enjoy this ship.

I will tell you that I think we pretty much explored every public room on the Spirit. And we found some places that quickly became favorites, as well as anti-favorites.

The Galaxy of the Stars quickly became one of our favorite places. This venue is used for things such as the past cruisers' loyalty program cocktail parties, and small evening shows. Some of the competitions and games are held there, along with dance classes. A Zumba class was held in there every day on this itinerary. The loud, raucous bingo games-- highly competitive ---were also held there in the afternoons. This lounge is in the very front of the ship, with floor-to-ceiling windows on three sides and plenty of comfortable furniture for lounging, good spots to relax and watch the sea go by. In the front, there are two punched out nooks with four chairs that extend past the sides of the ship. From that angle, one could see down the whole length of the ship. We found ourselves there on several lazy afternoons, just talking to our friends and meeting new people.

Being in the front of the ship, this lounge is right above the bridge. There is a little spiral staircase just to the left of the dance floor that leads down in the bridge viewing room. It's not really a secret; it's right there in the middle of the room, but we were surprised by how many people did not know that it was there. On Day Four, we ran into people who still had not found any way to observe the bridge, and wanted to!

At night, the Galaxy of the Stars becomes one of the main venues, with live music, and dancing. One party or another was held there every night.

We also enjoy having a Promenade deck that goes all the way around the ship. After all, the ocean is the point of cruising, right? It's nice to look over the side, but to be able to look over the whole scenery, 360°, while having a leisurely walk in the fresh air, is something truly special. Plus, I like teak and the promenade deck is made of teak with lounge chairs all around. Melissa says I do *not* like teak, it's a pain to maintain, but this is not mine. I'm not responsible and I do like it!

The Promenade deck has a shuffleboard court, built in; on other ships, it's made of a different material. The Cruise Addict I enjoy shuffleboard on cruises, although frankly we're not very good at it. However, I will have you know I took the all-NCL Pearl shuffleboard tournament on another cruise; I have the mug to prove it. Okay, only one eleven year old boy and I showed up, but take the glory as it befalls you. We found that the teak shuffleboard court was not a great idea. Pretty, but the shuffleboard biscuits simply did not slide, especially on nights when it was a little misty.

We tried a lot of the onboard restaurants, but for dinnertime dining, our favorite was the Windows restaurant. It's in the very back of the ship and has windows on three sides. I like windows. The Garden restaurant is on the same deck, more midships, with a quite similar menu. It has windows on two sides and a more intimate feel. The acoustics are not as good there. It seemed to echo, and voices were loud enough to be distracting. I preferred the more elegant Windows.

NCL Spirit had not yet had a retrofit when we were on it; a major one was scheduled for two months later. At the time we were onboard, it still had it had a Blue Lagoon on deck eight, just above the atrium, and it became an easy spot to grab a quick snack. It has since been replaced with O'Sheehans, with a similar menu. The Blue Lagoon served won ton soup and wings, fish and chips, burgers, that sort of thing. On other NCL ships, a hot breakfast was served in the Blue Lagoon, but this one had only a cooler with yogurt and milk, and some pastries.

A couple of places quickly became our least favorite places on board. The buffet, unfortunately, topped the list. The buffets on NCL ships tend to have a surprisingly good variety of food. They really make an effort to cater to the different nationalities as well, including grilled tomatoes and baked beans and fish soup for breakfast. I found the ambience sadly lacking. It was chaotic and loud, and it seemed to bring out the worst in people. People were shoving and pushing as if they feared there never be enough food for them. Some of these pitiful people must have been near starvation, after having not eaten for several hours!

There were simply not enough tables to accommodate all those who wish to sit and eat, although the Italian restaurant was available for overflow seating at lunch and breakfast. Also, the back deck was open. However, after you've taken your hot food and hiked that far, it's no longer warm. I'm really not a big fan of congealed eggs first thing in the morning. Especially at breakfast on port days, the buffet was crazy- busy as people rushed to grab sustenance against the day's activities.

The grill, just a few steps from the pool, was a good spot for grabbing a quick snack at lunch or midday. Burgers, grilled chicken, hotdogs, french fries, fruit, potato salad; easy, quick stuff to grab on the go. On port days, we found that we did not eat lunch on the ship at all. I'm a big fan of local food. I think it adds to the experience, eating what locals do and so we had lunch on the ship just a couple of times, on sea days.

In our exploration of the ship, we came upon the Maharini's Lounge & Nightclub, which is accessible only through the casino. It has an Indian influenced décor with velvet curtains and plush daybeds and a whole lot of red velvet. We heard it had a very happening atmosphere in the evenings and late at night, but it seemed like we always had somewhere else to be, and of course getting up so early, we really weren't in it for the nightlife. The only time I saw 1 AM on the whole cruise was at sail away out of Venice.

The Spirit was built for the Malaysia-based Star Cruises' SuperStar Leo line, which is sort of a shirttail relative of NCL. Transferred to NCL in 2004, Norwegian Spirit kept its Asia-inspired décor, with surprises around every corner. Artifacts on display – a full scale terra cotta warrior, random antique vases, a Samurai costume, all with little museum-like signs telling what's-what—made for an interesting atmosphere. The Spirit lacks the typical, sometimes gaudy décor that Norwegian is known for, with the exception of the hull---you can spot the NCL ships at a goodly distance by the brightly painted hulls!

The passenger dynamics on this cruise were different than others we've been on. Part of that was because it took place during the school year, and it was a 12 day cruise. It's tough for families to pull their kids out of school that long, so there were just a few children on board. We saw several toddlers, but only two school-age kids, siblings in a family from New Zealand. I'd say that, other than children, the demographics of this trip were fairly evenly spread out across ages. We met newlyweds, and older couples, and a lot in between. The oldest ones we met were the couple celebrating their 75th wedding anniversary. They were easy to spot, burning up the dance floor any time there was music playing!

There were 2206 souls on board, from ten nationalities, not including the crew. That surprised me; I would have expected more variety. The crew represented another sixty countries. We noticed that the activities on the ship were a lot scantier than on some other cruises, probably because of the very intense itinerary. Usually we get very involved in ship activities, games, classes, and such. On this trip, we were so tired from all the walking we did in every one of the ports that we really did very little at all, once we were back onboard, beyond dinner and the main show in the theatre every night.

We saw some signs of wear on the ship, but overall and generally we found that the Spirit was very well up kept. The staff and crew were cheerful and enthusiastic and wonderful, going out of the way to make things easier, greeting people, helping them whenever they could. It made a big difference!

A crew member told me a tip: any time you exit any elevator onboard the Spirit, you're facing aft. Neat, huh? For a person with no measurable sense of direction, this helped a lot!

Another tip: The terraced seating section with tables overlooking the kid's pool on the ship's aft end rarely had more than a couple of people there. The noise from the kids playing below did not carry up, nor did the noise from the chaotic buffet space a few steps above. It was a good spot to take a book, snack, or admire the scenery off the aft of the ship.

The Spirit has an air of elegance, somehow melded smoothly with comfort. The Atrium's mellow atmosphere includes glass elevators and waterfalls. Oddly, however, it lacks seating. On other ships, the Atrium becomes a gathering point, the heart of the ship, as well as being another venue for events. On the Spirit, the heart beats, but only as you walk through. The only seating nearby is at the coffee bar, or outside Henry's Pub, which we promptly claimed as our group's port day morning meeting spot.

The Stardust Theatre has comfortable red velvet seats, and NCL's trademark awesome-in-any-lighting stage curtain. The theatre tended to fill up fast for the evening shows. I blame/credit the quality of the shows for this: they were too good to miss, and word spread! How can one cruise ship garner that much talent? The Production Cast and show band were excellent. One thing I found very odd. The entrance was in the *front* of the theatre. So if someone needed to slip out early, they had to walk in front of the stage, or hike up to the second level exits.

The Spirit is an older ship, and I did notice a few minor problems. The toilets have a pretty significant delay. They don't always flush. If they do make up their mind to flush, it may take up to five minutes after the button's been pushed. In our family we have a rule --no pooping in the cabin bathroom, on any ship, at any time. This is what the public restrooms are for. The ventilation in the cabin leaves something to be desired. You're better off just going on down the hall and not inflicting yourself on your cabin mates. With the delay in flushing, this rule was especially valuable!

We never did figure out how to do the wake up calls. Every evening, we ended up calling Guest Services to set a wake-up call for the following morning and every time we were told "oh, no problem, it is a very complicated system." No, I don't think it should be that complicated. On every other ship and in just about every hotel I've ever been in, the process is very easy. You pick up the headset on the phone; you push the button that says wake-up call. Follow the prompts, and there you are. Not that difficult! On this ship, I would pick it up, push the indicated button, and nothing would happen... day after day after day. It was not a big deal, just a minor annoyance.

Behind the Scenes Ship Tour

Provisions

On one of the days-at-sea, Husband and I enjoyed an exclusive behind the scenes ship tour. Fascinating! I like food, and I'm pretty knowledgeable about it. Not as good as my son, who can write a recipe for a dish after tasting it once, but I do like the stuff. I found the provisions, kitchens, and food preparation areas most interesting, although we covered a lot of area in the tour. The Spirit has eleven restaurants, plus eight bars and lounges, all serviced by the same storage and prep areas. Several have their own kitchens for last –minute food preparation, but the preliminary prep all takes place in the bowels of the ship.

The food storage takes place on different decks, depending on whether or not the food is considered to be clean or dirty. "Clean" food is packaged and dry goods, raw meats and seafood, and also prepared foods such as peeled onions and chopped carrots. "Dirty" is any food requiring further prep before cooking, like baking potatoes still in the box that need scrubbing, carrots that need to be peeled, onions waiting to be peeled and chopped, and meats or fish that have not yet been butchered into serving portions. Peelings and dirt and leaves and trimmings never make it to the main galley; only ready-to-cook foods are delivered to the chefs and cook staff, by people pushing carts at breakneck speed, using the designated elevators. Separate "Clean" and "Dirty" *elevators*---wow!

Including crew, staff, and the passengers, an average of 10,000 meals per day are served on the Spirit. And you complain about making dinner couple nights a week!

I was impressed with how close to the mark the ordering of provisions manages to be. There is very little waste---how do they possibly predict that? I don't do that well in my grocery shopping at home, and there are a whole lot less people at my dinner table!

The Provisions Officer explained to us that the order he makes ahead of time varies, considerably, by the passengers. It's made one month in advance. The Captain is provided with a passenger list with ages, nationalities, and, of course, the number of passengers on board; a full cruise ship obviously requires many more provisions than a less-full sailing. The Captain gives the list to the Provisions Officer, the Provisions Officer consults with the Executive Chef, then makes an order, okayed last minute by the Captain. The Master of the vessel is responsible for overseeing everything, even details like how many eggs are ordered.

The provisions order is influenced by many criteria, including the time of year, age of passengers, their nationalities, and even the expected weather on the cruise itinerary. Orders for the buffet and the grills on board vary much more the main dining rooms or specialty restaurants, which are fairly steady. If there are a lot of kids on the cruise, say, during summer and holiday vacations, they lay in more french fries, pizza, chicken tenders, and a whole lot more ice cream. If there's an older clientele, such as on a longer itinerary, they order in more fruit and sweets, especially prunes and dessert ingredients. For some reason, older people crave sweets. And prunes; don't think about it.

If the population has a large European contingent, the cruise line orders more wine, chocolate desserts, and extra red meats, such as lamb and duck. On more casual itineraries, such as in the Caribbean, or when there are a lot of American passengers on board, they make sure to have extra burgers, hotdogs, a whole lot of coffee, craft beers, extra beef, chicken, and less of upscale things such as caviar and escargot. When a lot of Germans are on board, extra pork and bacon are ordered; not so when Israelis make up a significant part of the passenger list. This isn't exactly racial profiling; certainly, categorizing by age and nationality, though! It'd be easier to argue, if they weren't so amazingly accurate.

Holidays and time of year also affect the provisions required onboard. More cookies in December, more prepackaged kosher meals over Jewish holy days, more fresh fruit during summer months. When you think about it, it's probably the same thought process you use to make up your own grocery list---only on a much larger scale!

If the ship is going somewhere colder, such as Scandinavia, or perhaps Alaska, they lay in extra coffee, more hot cocoa mixes, and they plan on going through a lot of soup. If the passenger list includes a lot of Asian nationals, plan on extra rice noodles and fish, plus extra rice ---although the crew alone goes through 400 lbs of rice per week!

On cruises with a lot of high- priced suites booked, and elite cruisers, VIPs, or upper-level loyalty members, the Provisions Officer plans on additional large strawberries for those daily big juicy chocolate covered strawberries in the cabins, along with extra fancy items such as prosciutto, cheeses, caviar, champagne, large shrimp, extra lobster, more chocolates, and high-end meats.

Think about cheese. Plain old American cheese is the best for melting on a burger, but not suitable for a fancy cheese tray at an Owner's Suite party. Someone had to plan that, and that is just one item!

Besides nationality and climate, the cruise line also factors in quality. When we were on the Spirit, I personally noticed at least four sizes of shrimp. There was salad size in the buffet salads, and medium-size shrimp appeared on the surf and turf in the main dining room. In the specialty restaurants, the shrimp cocktail had a larger size. The biggest ones I saw were offered as hors d'oeuvres at the Captain's VIP cocktail party. That's a lot of variety, and it's only *shrimp!* Meats, such as steak, also come in varying quality and size, and must be ordered according. For example, in the main dining rooms a plain strip steak is on the menu. In the steakhouse on the Spirit, a 16 ounce rib eye was on the menu. Depending on the demographics of the ship that particular cruise, they may anticipate a run on the steak house, or the buffet may be more popular. All of this changes the provisions order.

I wanted to know where the ship's provisions came from on this particular itinerary. We noticed that, for example, that the milk and other dairy products were different than in any other cruise ship we had been on before, although we still saw very familiar items as well. I was told that they provision in Venice and again in Citivecchia, which is Rome's port. Ten containers come from the USA, sealed shipping containers, the size that goes on the back of a semi-truck. TEN of them---for only one cruise! Those are referred to a 'heavy store' and it includes dry provisions and canned items. All the frozen meat and fish also come from North America; from Miami, in this case. That vision you have of the chef plying a fishing pole over the aft deck catching your dinner isn't based on reality...but it does sound fun!

On this cruise, the ship takes on fresh foods, including fruits and vegetables, non-frozen meats, and all dairy, in Venice and again in Citivecchia (Rome's port). That's why, for breakfast, we could find Kellogg's Frosted Flakes, but the milk was a little different than we were used to... kind of thick, kind of almost – yogurt flavor and texture. We didn't like the milk. Personal preference!

Ten minutes after the ship makes port on Embarkation Day, the ship's Provisions Officer and his staff are already busy with their clipboards, checking every pallet and crate of food as it is delivered to the ship. Besides keeping a fanatically accurate count, they check for any spoiled fruit and vegetables. Each pallet is then directed to the proper area, to be stored at a specific temperature. Red wine goes into a warmer room than white wine, beer, and champagne, for example. Blueberries never share space with flour. All food categories are stored separately; the fish never meets the flour, the fruit never shares a room with the chicken. Every bin, bowl, cart, or bag is carefully covered with clear plastic wrap to protect it. There are different lockers for different meats; red meat, poultry and fish all have their own refrigerators for thawing and freezers for storing. The degree of organization was mind boggling!

The Cruise Addict and I were able to wander through the provisions rooms on the behind the scenes tour, including the dry storage, freezers, refrigerators, proofing rooms, thawing chambers; pretty much all over. I recognized many of the brands and was impressed with the quality of the NCL purchases. The provisions are stored floor-to-ceiling in the beginning of the cruise. Towards the end of every cruise, it gets down to nothing much at all; just a day or two of foodstuffs remain. The ship always has extra ice cream and meats onboard; being frozen, those items have a much longer shelf life than, say, fresh berries. This ship had enough ice cream alone to fuel a couple of elementary schools!

The Provisions officer explained that they plan for the length of the cruise, plus two days, to account for delays, such as port problems or weather issues. If the ship is unable to make the disembarkation port for any reason, throwing together another meal or two is taken in stride. Good planning—if they were to run out of food, there could be a mutiny onboard! We've heard horror stories about the Carnival ship that had engine trouble and was not able to return to port, about how people survived on crackers and Spam and mayonnaise sandwiches. That kind of story is bad PR, among other things.

A Shopping List

The Provisions Officer gave us this list of stores onboard for a typical seven day cruise. Remember ours was a 12 day cruise, so the numbers are even bigger!:

24,236 pounds of beef

5,040 pounds of lamb

7,216 pounds of pork

4,600 pounds of veal

1,680 pounds of breakfast sausage

10,211 pounds of chicken

3,156 pounds of turkey

13,851 pounds of fish

350 pounds of shelled crab

2,100 pounds of lobster

25,736 pounds of fresh vegetables

15,150 pounds of potatoes

1800 pounds of butter

20,003 pounds of fresh fruit, including 680 flats of strawberries

3,260 US gallons of milk (from Italy; different taste than American)

1,976 US quarts of heavy cream

600 US gallons of ice cream

9,235 dozen eggs

5,750 pounds of sugar

2,500 lbs butter

2,600 lbs cheeses

2,000 lbs sugar

3,800 pounds of rice

1,750 pounds of cereal

450 pounds of jelly and jam

2,458 pounds of coffee

2,450 tea bags

120 pounds of herbs and spices, both dry and fresh

3,100 dozen eggs, plus liquid whole eggs for baking, and white for meringues

3,400 bottles of assorted wines

2000 bottles of champagne

2000 bottles of gin

290 bottles of vodka

350 bottles of whiskey

150 bottles of rum

45 bottles of sherry

600 bottles of assorted liqueurs

10,100 bottles/cans of beer

...and the list goes on!

All told, about 750 pallets of food, fresh flowers, beverages, and other supplies are loaded on the ship on Embarkation Day, along with passengers' luggage, at the same time the trash from the previous cruise is off loaded. Your suitcase not in your cabin as fast as you're like? Cut them some slack!

Food Prep

There are five butchers on board the Spirit. Just five! They break down the larger meats into serving portions. At the time we were there, one butcher was frenching a mountain of lamb chops for the dining room menu the following night. I thought five butchers was an awfully small number for the whole ship, until I saw this guy's speed! His knife moved so fast it was blurry. It looked extremely sharp and I was pleased to see that he had a metal chain mail glove on his other hand.

We learned that there are three sub-cooks in charge of produce preparation. Chefs and cooks do not prepare their ingredients

The chefs must order what they need for the following day; say, ten pounds of diced onions. Down in the bowels of the ship, one of the produce workers will peel and chop a sufficient amount of onions-- only ten pounds was a lot less than the real number! By the time the chef reaches for them, those onions have been cleaned, peeled, chopped, weighed, and wrapped in plastic. While we were there, we talked to one of the crew, who was peeling carrots. He said that that he would peel and dice 200 pounds before the day was over. Carrot soup on the menu? The kitchen crew works twelve hours a day, yet still had warm smiles for us interlopers. Imagine spending a twelve hour shift peeling onions and putting carrots through the dicer, knowing the sacks of cabbage have your name on them next?

Norwegian Cruise Line has the best bread on the open sea, in my opinion. I especially enjoy NCL's croissants and pretzel rolls. All bread, including rolls, specialty breads, croissants, hot dog buns, sandwich bread, those yummy pretzel rolls, and all desserts are all made on board from scratch. This saves space in storage. Of course the bread products are fresher and they tend to be tastier than packaged items. On a personal level, it's kind of a nice thought to think of people making bread in the middle of the night so that I can have fresh challah for my French toast for breakfast. I hope they take a nap later on.

Norwegian makes beautiful desserts; elegant, fancy, nicely plated desserts that I find frankly... tasteless. Even in the specialty restaurants, desserts were disappointing. For some unknown reason, I find a lot of Norwegian Cruise Lines' desserts are gummy, as if they've too much gelatin or thickener in them. This is true of the fruit pies, cheesecakes, puddings, and the unnamed but pretty square desserts with fancy chocolate toiles on top. Maybe it has to do with stability or transportation from the lower galleys. I'm not sure. I guess I give them points for consistency –and I guess I appreciate them sparing me those extra calories... although I make them up with the delicious breads and croissants!

In the bakery, I admired the state-of-the-art equipment; sheet rollers, dough rounders, proofing racks, glass fronted ovens leaking enticing aromas. Two crew members were very busy making the multigrain rolls for dinner that night, weighing out individual portions on a scale. I'm not sure the weight of all that dough, but I know I could not have contained it on my kitchen table. It may not have fit in my grandchild's wading pool, either. And that was only one product.

The quantities were overwhelming! We saw trays and trays of cookies, cakes, and beautiful desserts, all lined up, ready and waiting for the night's dinner service. Whole turkeys were roasting in the ovens, pans of braising lamb shank, along with vats of soup and heaps of fresh vegetables waiting their turns. Baked pastries and breads cooled on tall racks, while unbaked items slowly rotated in the proofing area. The Cruise Addict made a new friend—not sure how, but Husband ended up with a warm cookie!

Cleanliness is taken very seriously by Norwegian Cruise Line. Cruise ships are very sensitive to illness outbreaks in any form, and they go to pretty extreme lengths to avoid the food-borne variety. Sanitation is about as good as your local clinic. There are two elevators for dish transportation; dirty dishes have their own elevator, while clean items never cross their paths. We noticed that the clean utensils all had plastic wrap on them, from hotel pans down to the smallest whisks and ladles. No one has to ask, "Hey, is this clean or dirty?" like we do at home. It's a good idea, but not one I'm likely to adopt.

The preparation areas in the galley looked immaculate to me, but being nosy, I took time to step aside and peek into a floor drain. I figured if there's any gunk or dirt, that's where it's going to be.

I happily report that the tile floor drain was pristine and white, as clean as a countertop. Not clean enough to eat off of; it was still a floor drain, after all, but you get the idea.

Water

One of the questions many first-time cruisers ask is "where does the ship get fresh water?" (That question is followed up by "Is the water in the toilets safe to drink?" That's just weird! Do people drink out of toilets at home, or only when they travel?) The answer: they make most of it, on board. In some ports, the massive storage tanks are refilled, but for the most part, fresh water is part of the ship's process.

Think about it---all those passengers and crew, cooking, drinking, swimming, showering, flushing, washing dishes, mopping a deck...that requires a LOT of water! Some of today's biggest cruise ships can use more than 260,000 gallons of fresh water every day. The Norwegian Spirit is smaller; still, a substantial amount is required. It would be nearly impossible for a ship to carry all this water from the embarkation port, or rely on local ports of call for refills. Instead, ships transform salty sea water into fresh drinking water by a process known as desalination.

The desalination process on a cruise ship uses either flash evaporators or osmosis. Flash evaporators boil sea water and re-condense the steam vapor, producing fresh drinking water. This method is similar to the natural water cycle, where sea water is heated by the sun, rises as steam to form clouds, and then falls back to earth as rain, only a whole lot faster. The second method, osmosis, filters sea water through a series of fine membranes to separate pure water from salt and other minerals. Cruise ships do not desalinate water near ports or close to land, because coastal waters are the most contaminated.

Either way, the water is then tested for impurities, sanitized, and the pH is corrected before it's pumped into big storage tanks on board the cruise ship.

We learned on the tour that the trash and waste is very seriously controlled by international law. Food waste is separated from other items, and is ground to pulp, a sort of fine slurry, and then discharged into the sea in specified areas. This reminded me of the time when I was on a Royal Caribbean ship, and I noticed that there were dolphins out, bouncing along the waves, just a couple, and then there were dozens, and then there were hundreds. As I admired them over the railing, a crew member walked by and commented "see, we're discharging the food waste." The sea life in this area had actually been trained to recognize the sound of that particular ship's engines and they came for the feeding frenzy! I suppose it's the same for the Spirit as well. The slurry is discharged at least 12 miles from any shoreline.

Crew Only Areas and Theatre

The tour also included the off-limits crew living areas. I was surprised at how small the crew bar was. There were several game tables, a bar, a few places to sit. Our guide told us ruefully, "after working twelve hours, and smiling at passengers all day, most just don't feel like a wild time socializing. They may grab a beer and be on their way, except for nights when there are planned parties. Then, you can bet they whoop it up." I found it interesting that when there is a crew party, there are *two*, 12 hours apart, so all can participate, regardless of their work schedule!

The crew on the Spirit is mostly Indonesian, but represents more countries combined than the United Nations (gets along better, too, from all indications). A commonly asked question is "does the crew eat the passengers' leftover food?" Besides being demeaning ---these are hardworking humans, not farm animals--- the very idea of leftovers would probably cause an uproar. No, the crew has its own galley and dining room. The chefs try to prepare food the crew will enjoy, including familiar flavors from home, as much as possible. The crew on the Spirit alone goes through 400 pounds of rice per week!

The theatre's backstage, storage, and performers' areas were tiny, and jam packed. Even for skinny performers, I should think being hit by a random elbow would be a risk. The costume manager told us she spends six days a week, nine hours a day, just making sure the performers have what they need to be onstage. Washer, dryer, a commercial sewing machine, all very organized in a tight space. The dressing areas looked so small; how ever do they manage those quick costume changes? The manager told us the quickest costume change they have is seven seconds. Whoa! The longest is eight minutes, "but that still may not be long enough, if a zipper breaks!"

Laundry

The ship's enormous laundry facility was overwhelming to me, especially when I learned how very few crew members work there! For one thing, the idea of being stuck in a laundry, without windows or fresh air, dealing with untold heaps of dirty laundry twelve hours a day seven days a week for a whole 9-12 month long contract sounds awful, and I know these crew members are some of the lowest paid. The ship produces a mountain of bedding, plus tablecloths, thousands of linen napkins, and towels. Our guide smiled, "This is an easy itinerary for towels; not like the Caribbean, where the striped pool towels are never ending!" Along with the bare-bones laundry needs of the ship, the facility also cleans and presses all staff and crew uniforms, and passenger clothing that's sent for cleaning.

I have never sent clothing to be cleaned a on a ship, fearing it would not end well, although free laundry service is part of the loyalty level for us. Oh, also the VIP status, come to think of it, on this ship. I *like* my clothes, and wondered if they would shrink from the commercial dryer's high heat. After seeing the care taken on this tour, I bravely filled the laundry bag in our cabin .... with The Cruise Addict's shirts and pants and socks. The next day, the clothing reappeared, neatly washed and folded, layered with tissue paper in a pretty basket. I admit, they don't look that good at home. Next time, I'll be more confident in sending my own stuff off to be laundered. Perhaps.

Day One: On Board

The itinerary for NCL's Grand Mediterranean cruise is a little confusing; deceptive, even. It says that Day One is Venice. But sail away was at 1 AM, passengers had to be on by 11 o'clock last night, and the Spirit sailed all night, all day, and into the night again. By all rights, this is not a day in Venice. It is a day at sea, and those with plans to tour Venice today were out of luck. I wish Norwegian Cruise Line had made this more clear. We were able to be where we needed to be, but there were people who were complaining all over the ship.

We had a VIP breakfast at Cagney's, feeling like imposters. We were pleased to be greeted by name. Again, Ryan, the concierge, came to us and asked what he could do for us this day. Reservations for the spa, dinner reservations, perhaps an in-room movie? Anything we wished, he said, we had only to ask. Actually we were doing quite well and we are pretty self-contained travelers, but I did appreciate being asked. With a smile, Ryan reminded us, "I make things happen." I had Crab Cake Benedict for breakfast with a bowl of berries and cream. I debated about the Lobster Brioche. Perhaps tomorrow.

Meet and Greet

The Cruise Critic Meet and Greet was at 10 o'clock in the morning on this, our first sea day. Husband, alias The Cruise Addict, had set it up and kept the people on the online roll call informed. I thought it was successful, although most people arrived after the senior staff had come and introduced themselves, and left. About 35 people attended and I think maybe ten of them were there on time. Quite a few were disappointed that they missed the staff, who had come and gone by the time they moseyed in.

We met Gio, the Cruise Director, and liked him right away. He became a good resource all cruise. He and the First Officer greeted me and The Cruise Addict *by name* as they entered, which I found rather disorienting. Had they checked our security photos or what? Well, I guess so; I expect to do them to do their job, after all. The head of each department was there as well, and greeted us nicely, then introduced themselves. They handed out cards to everyone with direct contact information, and urged everyone to let them know of any issues. NCL is careful not to let passengers write negative reviews and they do everything they can to make things right on board.

We had not seen most of our friends since home, and this was our chance to meet up. Oh, good-- they all made it from points unknown! After the officers left, we lingered, meeting and greeting, putting names to faces.

Today was a leisurely, lazy day at sea. We played a trivia game first thing in the morning and again before dinner, and won both. Some of our friends were very happy to participate in the Zumba classes. We also played in the shuffleboard tournament. Oddly, we were the only ones who knew how to play and so ended up teaching the four other passengers who showed up. They beat us. Seems we are better teachers than players.

At lunchtime, there was a German Bavarian buffet on the deck. Wonder why? We were nowhere near Germany! The weather was so beautiful that we decided to skip our regular lunch and just have a sausage and some German potato salad out there in the sunshine. It was beautiful, watching the water go by. A cruise is for relaxing!

Lucky Friends

The casino was already open and it was a very, very popular place. We ran into Clint and Mary our way through the casino. Clint said he was just getting his feet wet. Did he mean it! Later on that night, The Cruise Addict, who has insomnia, happened to be wandering past the casino when he heard a sharp cry go up; a shout, followed by cheering. He stepped in to see what happened. There in the middle of a congratulating circle was Clint and Mary. They looked stunned. Clint told Husband that he had just won $2800 from that slot machine right there. As Husband congratulated him, Clint squeaked out that he had won $2200 right before that! We notice that particular machine was shut down the rest of the cruise, with an "out of order" sign on it. $5000 on the first night! We have some lucky friends.

The rest of the first day was leisurely. Gio, the cruise director, sought the two of us out on deck, and we got to know him pretty well. Gio was very good at answering questions. He seemed to be just everywhere, the whole cruise. There's a guy who's in the right profession. He obviously loves his job. The whole ship seemed to be in party mode today. Everywhere we went, there were people eating, dancing, partying, drinking, laughing, lounging about in the warm sun. Everyone just seemed really happy to be on the ship. We are off to a great start!

I was surprised at how calm the waters have been today. We've only seen a few islands all day. It's very wide, this part of the sea, and this stretch is known for rough water. Not today; it has been as calm as a pond! I've seen puddles with more turbulence than the Adriatic Sea had. Could we be this lucky the rest of the cruise?

We met up with our friends throughout the day. I'm still pretty amazed that that many people made it that far, all on the same little piece of geography, over 6000 miles from home. Everyone seems happy to be to be on this adventure, after so many months of anticipation. I think the group is going to be fun; so far, everyone is getting along great.

Dinner For Twelve

Someone suggested all of us to get together for dinner. The question was, could we get reservations for all twelve of us, with just a couple of hours' notice? Husband stepped aside, silently, and pulled a card from his pocket. A quick phone call to Ryan, the concierge, netted us a near instant reservation, right at the time we wanted. Yes, I could get used to this VIP stuff! We're not going to tell our friends that we have VIP status. Boasting is not becoming and I simply wouldn't do that. However, if it allows us to make dinner reservations easier, that's all to the good. We may avail ourselves later of Ryan's help for the tender days, also; I hear the wait can be painful. We don't wish to hold our VIP status over our friends. I hope they didn't notice that we were greeted by name, all evening; at the dining room desk, the waiters, even as we all made our way into the variety show later on.

Dinner was fun, with all of us talking and laughing, and impeccable service. Tomorrow will be another sea day, and it's important to me that the group all gets along well because we are going to spending a lot of time together over the next week and a half. I'm pleased to see that our friends immediately liked Clint and Mary, whom they had not met before, absorbing them into the circle as if they had always known them.

The show tonight was really good! It was a variety show, an introduction to the other shows later in the cruise. There was a dynamic Bee Gees legacy trio who were quite talented. They got the audience up and dancing. As one who avoids heels, I gotta say they did really well on those platform shoes, too! I usually yawn at magicians, but Sander and Allison were amazing. I've seen production cast in Las Vegas that were not any better than this one. And of course the spectacular Spirit Production Cast was great. NCL's definitely improved their shows, we think, in the last few years, now that the Jean Ann Ryan Company has been replaced. I'm pretty sure we will be at every other show. After all, we paid for them!

Back in the cabin after the show we found another treat, along with the Freestyle Daily with the next day's offerings; our "mail." The treat was four perfect little handmade chocolates, all different, with a note that read, 'compliments of the hotel director' with her signature. Oh Yum! Our 'mail' included three more invitations to different cocktail parties, one for past cruisers, one for Latitudes loyalty program, one for the VIPs with the Captain, and another one for high-level past cruisers with the Captain again. Really, I must find a way to take this relaxed feeling home with me. It feels healthy to me.

Day Two: Sea Day

This is our first official sea day, although we were at sea yesterday as well. I rather wish that the sea days could have been spread out. After this, we will have ten straight days of ports back to back to back, with only one more sea day tucked in there. I planned on today being a lazy day, but it turned out to be quite busy with activities, games, and impromptu gatherings with our friends all day long. I love the brilliant sunshine; felt so good to feel its warmth. Does the sun really shine brighter at sea?

One of the things we enjoyed most on this ship was its lighthearted attitude and the prevailing, yet tasteful, sense of humor, along with the good-sport outlook of the captain. For instance, one of our invitations read "free drinks on the Captain (we mean, with the Captain)". Not sure other Masters would go for that!

The past-cruisers-loyalty party was midafternoon, for all Latitudes members (which is anyone who's ever set foot on any Norwegian ship). It was crowded, but the staff did a great job of serving free drinks and assorted hors d'oeuvre to everyone. I was concerned about the guy in front of us. He announced "free drinks! That's why I'M here!" as he sat down, and promptly downed six glasses of white wine. I saw the bar server say something to the man, quietly. The guy waited until the server was gone, and called another over. The new server gave him four more glasses of wine, then it looked to me that he was deliberately not coming towards our area again. Maybe word had spread.

We were told at check in that all non-European Union passengers must relinquish their passports in Greece and

Turkey. We knew about this ahead of time, but never did hear the reason. Uneasy about this...seems Turkey would be the one place I'd *want* my documents! We had a letter as we checked in advising us to turn them in at the theatre today, promising that they would be available on Day 10 after Kusadasi. Not to be. At breakfast today, the concierge, informed us that he would personally see to them so as to avoid us dealing with crowds. Oh, all right; I'm okay with skipping a line, any time, any place. We gave our passports to Ryan at breakfast, and he gave us a receipt. Too easy! Later that afternoon, our friends said that it took them two and a half hours in line to turn in passports and get the receipt, although NCL had assigned times to turn them in by deck number. It should been faster than that!

The VIP status is almost funny. And it's only early in the cruise! Lunch was lovely, calm, elegant, and beautifully prepared in Cagney's. We skipped dessert, knowing the menu would be the same all cruise, and we went to the buffet to peruse the desserts. Instantly, I felt my bread blood pressure rising, that knotting feeling in the back of my neck. What chaos! Noise, crowds, constant motion, people elbowing each other to get food as if there never going to be any more, not enough tables, raised voices....I'm afraid it didn't take me long at all to feel spoiled with the VIP status.

However, on a couple of evenings, later on, we did return to the buffet after dinner for dessert. The desserts in the main dining room and the specialty restaurants, for that matter, were nothing to write home about. In the buffet every night, there was a warm cobbler of some sort, which Husband loves best of all. Better than that, there was a crêpe station, made-to-order crêpes with three or four different kinds of fillings and fruits and cream made right there in front of me---my kind of dessert!

The show on Day Two was a Production Cast performance of "Soul Rockin' Nights." High energy performances of Motown, soul, and rock n' roll. The audience sang along, which made it even more fun. Our group seems to have taken over row 2, center.

It's also NCL's Night Out, the rough equivalent of a formal night, for anyone who cares. The main dining menu was more upscale, photos taken in the atrium with the Captain, that sort of thing. We saw quite a few glittery dresses on the ship, but it seemed many passengers had opted for dressy/casual attire, not black tie by any means.

Today's highlight was cocktails at 7 PM with the Captain in the art gallery, a VIP gathering of less than twenty guests, plus senior officers. We recognized a few from the Meet and Greet. Husband and the Captain immediately hit it off. He is from Sweden and my Husband lived in Sweden for a couple of years. The Captain seems really approachable on the ship. On some other cruises, we barely knew who the Captain was; this one seems to be out and about and everywhere. I even ran into him today, jogging on the promenade deck in shorts and tee shirt. Can't hide that flowing mustache.

Day Three: Athens, Greece

Athens, Greece! A hundred times today, I told myself 'I cannot believe that I'm really standing here!' Athens is *old,* older than antiques, older than any place I've ever seen in our own country. I loved the experience of being able to experience the culture from close to three and four centuries ago, like stepping into history. The port of Piraeus itself is kind of rundown, industrial-feeling, but it was truly awesome to be able to go to Athens itself.

Would the months and stress of planning the private tours pay off? We had arranged a private tour around Athens through PK tours, online, sight unseen, and our group would be all together. That means, either we have a fabulous day, or the day is ruined for a dozen travelers. Butterflies in my stomach? No, this felt more like frogs.

The Tour Begins

Demetrius-- yes, that was really his name-- met us at 7:30 AM, immediately after the ship docked, fifteen feet from the gangway, holding a sign with our name on it. The first thing I noticed about him was his elegant handmade Italian shoes. We settled comfortably into the twelve passenger van. Demetrius handed out cold water bottles, with an invitation to get more from the cooler any time. Nice touch!

I liked Demetrius right away, and more so once he began describing what he had planned for our day. He listed amazing places, and concluded with, 'but of course we can skip or add anything else you have in mind. You must feel free to talk to me." We didn't feel hurried, but I'm surprised at how much we saw in just the few hours we had together! Demetrius kept up a running commentary as he navigated scary narrow streets, about the city, its history, government, people, as well as fielding the questions we asked. He was very informative, and funny too.

Our group ranged in age by fifty years or more, with varying degrees of education and background. Demetrius effortlessly kept us all very interested and engaged the whole time. His English was quite good, with a rolling Greek accent. He seemed laid-back and relaxed, yet efficient at the same time. Throughout the day, once he noticed we were interested in more than the typical tourist talk, Demetrius talked about the Greek economy, the oppressively high taxes, the corrupt government; a theme we were to hear later on throughout our cruise in other places as well. As we drove, we passed shady part of the city, with much graffiti on the walls, similar to what we see at home. Our guide firmly corrected us: graffiti is *art*. What we saw on the side of the buildings was "tagging by youth who care not at all." Well, yes, that's what it is.

Acropolis

Demetrius said that he usually started the tour at the Acropolis Museum, but today, because of the dynamics of our particular group, he decided to start at the Acropolis itself. The *Acropolis!* We would get an early start to the Acropolis complex before the buses and crowds arrived, "and I am sure you will appreciate it much more." He was not kidding. Oh, my goodness. Not to say Demetrius was a wild driver or anything, but we made such good time, it was scary.

We arrived so early that a contingent of armed Greek soldiers was just coming down. They raise the flag over the Acropolis every morning. I'm not sure why that task required 15 armed-to-the-teeth uniformed military men, but we hastily stepped aside as they ran in formation to their Humvees. The door slammed and they were gone, that fast.

Feet. Oddly, on this whole entire trip, I found myself thinking about the feet of all of those who had walked those very same paths before me; those who had walked on the cobblestones of Saint Mark's, and climbed to the top of the Basilica up those worn marble steps, and now, the feet of those who climbed up these very same steps to the Acropolis over hundreds and hundreds of years, eying the changing landscape far below. To wear down *marble* is a pretty impressive thing!

We were so early; there were probably two dozen people on the entire site. It was an imposing structure, and to see it still standing there after so many centuries was overwhelming. In America, it seems like any building over twenty or thirty years old is threatened to be torn down. Why, yes, I guess I am still bitter over Seattle's Kingdome, which was torn down 21 years before it was even paid for!

The Acropolis is being restored. Part of the Parthenon on top was hugged by scaffolding. There were no workers on the building, though, on this bright morning. Demetrius explained later that they have two seasons, in an effort to increase tourism and cut down on visitors' complaints. There is "tourist" season and "get work done" season. As we drove throughout the day, we saw many construction sites with partly built buildings, but no workers on site. Demetrius explained that is to avoid disturbing the tourists with loud construction noises. There is no building allowed, for three months out of every year. This didn't make a lot of sense to me. Wouldn't you want to build when the weather is the best? On the other hand, we once stayed in a hotel that had an air compressor running out in the street and I can't say I enjoyed that. I appreciated the consideration, I guess!

The Parthenon is one giant and elaborate optical illusion. Besides the age and sheer size, I was very impressed with the workmanship, especially the pillars. For instance, the giant columns that hold it up are not straight, although they appear so. They narrow at the top and they bend ever so slightly; if they were to continue on up another few hundred feet, they would actually cross. This gives the illusion of strength and solidity. If they were perfectly parallel, they would actually look weaker.

The floor of the Parthenon isn't flat. It's seven inches higher in the middle; another optical illusion, and a really clever one. Had it been a straight, level floor, when looked at head-on, it would've looked to be sagging in the middle. With it being raised in the center, it gives the appearance of being perfectly level. That degree of engineering skill is pretty remarkable, even for now, and remember, it was built close to 3000 years ago, by people who did not own a laser sight. How did they manage that precision?

Each of those massive columns took *20 to 24 years* to build, measured in man hours. Demetrius explained that three generations worked on some of those individual pillars. Fathers, sons, grandfathers; just imagine the stories that were passed down as those three men worked together! I'm a big believer in the power of story, and oral history. The columns were fitted together without mortar. Greece has frequent earthquakes, including the 5.0 one last week. How did the ancient builders know that stacking column sections would endure better than gluing or mortaring or cutting one solid piece?

I was surprised to be able to see incredible art and structures that I've only seen on documentaries right out there in the elements! The statuary, the buildings themselves, was just incredible to me. The Parthenon was largely intact until there was a war in which it was damaged by cannon fire. Then an Englishman named Lord Elgin raided it and hauled away a lot of the sculptures, which Greece is still trying to get back. The parts that were left were just breathtaking to me.

The word 'Acropolis' means 'edge of the city.' There are Acropolis in many other cities across Greece, and cross the Mediterranean. They are all built on the very highest point of the city area, the edge, but not this one. In Athens, it's built on the prettier site with the more commanding view. Actually the highest point in Athens is Mars Hill, which we visited later.

The view from the Acropolis was 360° of solidly packed city down below. Even from that dizzying height, we could see ancient ruins in among the modern buildings far below. We could even see our cruise ship way off in the distance in the glittering water; from that height, it looked about three inches long. Demetrius told us that there is a law that no building can be built taller than the Acropolis in all of Athens. The exception to this is seven buildings that were built during a coup and never torn down.

We explored, we admired, we lingered, we imagined, we took many photos, and we pretty much had the place to ourselves. I loved having time and space to leisurely dream, to think about the history, to feel the spirit of the place.

Demetrius told us that we would arrive before the crowds, and he meant it. There are several ways up to the top. We walked up the main wide walkway and we took the narrower walkway off to the side as we made our way back down to the van. I was horrified to see hordes of people arriving as we were leaving! There were dozens of vans and buses, disgorging hundreds and hundreds of people all at once. So many people flowing up the main path that we could no longer see the steps or the marble walkways at all, just a solid wave of people, probably fifteen abreast and moving fast, oozing up the steps and the walkways where we just been. I don't think those people were able to think about feet, other than protecting their own from being stepped on. They were probably jostled and buffeted by the crowds around them. I was really grateful to have been there early. Demetrius, our guide, earned his tip right then and there, and the day had just begun!

Temple of Zeus and Mars Hill

The Temple of Zeus was our next stop. Demetrius drove with a running commentary on the way. I was surprised as we drove, and throughout the rest of the day, to see ruins of ancient statues and art, just right there, touchable, exposed to the elements, accessible. Modern museums' displays are often under glass. Love it! It seemed as I laid my hand gently on the marble scriptures, pillars or stone, that I could sense the people who made them. Like today, they raised families, sought recreation, worked, enjoyed life, had dreams of their own

On this cruise, we are not in any one place long enough to see it all. We can't really spend hours admiring the fingernails on one statue, although I could have done so, happily! The goal is to get a good taste of a place, to decide later if we would ever like to come back and spend perhaps a week in Athens alone. We told Demetrius we wanted an overview, to see as much as we could in the short time we had. In this, Dimitris was an excellent guide; I doubt anyone else could have done better! I highly recommend PK Travel.

He drove next to the highest point in Athens, with the city spread out below, even higher than the Acropolis. Gorgeous, to see Athens sprawled out below! We rested on Mars Hill, where the apostle Paul preached, then left, finding the Athenians disinterested. You will note there is no epistle to the Athenians in the New Testament. We wound our way down to Odonis' temple – these people love their ancient gods, and temples were everywhere! – The ancient Gate of Zeus was still standing, and looked very much like my high school history book's photo. The chariot track was still visible, being crossed now by a slow-motion tortoise. It was midmorning by now, and really hot. I was very happy to have the ice cold water that Demetrius kept giving us in little bottles from his cooler, and grateful for my floppy hat. So much for looking classy in pictures! Not passing out from the heat was a better goal, I thought.

Changing of the Guard

Demetrius narrated as he drove and kept each of us engaged with his knowledge and humor. He asked "is anyone interested in the Changing of the Guard at the presidential palace?" Oh, *yes!* Remember, we're Americans. We don't do that, except for the Tomb of the Unknown at Arlington Cemetery. To have the opportunity to see another Changing of the Guard after seeing the one in Sweden did not go up for a vote in the van. I wanted to see it, and was certain the others would be as delighted.

One of the advantages to being in a small group as opposed to one of the crowded buses is that the van could go places the big buses were not allowed. Demetrius mused, "I could take you to where the buses all go, but let's go around the side instead. It is the same ceremony, same Changing of the Guard, but there will be no crowds. You will be able to get very close, and see much better." Man after my own heart. He took us to the presidential residence, the side entrance. As he drove, we passed a mob the size of a rally; who could see through all those bodies? Our place had about twenty people gathered to watch, including our twelve.

Demetrius had us stand just across the street, probably fifteen feet from the guard, where we could get a good view, but not be in the way of the guards who would come down the street. He said, " I want you to stand where you can see the details closely, but not to be trampled by the guards." With a grin, he said, " I've seen it happen. They do not stop, even for tourists from Iowa with fancy cameras." We obeyed.

The Changing of the Guard was precise, with careful pageantry, as the new contingent moved down the block and replaced the standing one. The Changing of the Guard was silent, except for a few shouted commands, and the clanking of the heavy shoes. Demetrius quietly told us it takes place hourly, and that each guard stands for four hours, twice out of every twenty-four hours.

The uniforms are interesting to me. They represented Greek blood, tears, and 400 years of slavery. The uniforms are wool, long-sleeved, and on that hot day, the poor guard had obviously sweat clear through. The kilt-like skirts have 400 pleats, representing 400 years of Ottoman oppression, made of *38 yards!* of wool. A long red tassel representing Greek tears fell from the fez. Their shoes weighed seven pounds (3.8 kilos) *each*, made of wood and red leather, with 60 nails in each sole. The handmade shoes turn up into a point, covered with a black pompom.

The Guard would halt, frozen as still as any stone statue, with his foot raised for two full minutes , then he took a few more precise steps, over and over. It ached to watch! The nails of the shoes striking the brick strip in the sidewalk were loud. In a muted voice, Demetrius pointed out where the brick work on the sidewalk was worn down from the shoes of the guards clanking their feet during the ceremony, hourly for years. He shrugged, "It needs to be replaced, but there is not time for new cement to set."

The guards were so precise! Demetrius said that they could only blink, not move any other body part, until they are relieved. If they have an emergency, such as bathroom need or a desire to faint from the heat, they may blink, twice. A separate guard and two police officers guard the guard, against harassment. Demetrius kept up a muted commentary, telling us what we were seeing, and we appreciated that.

He told us that the guards took their assignments *very* seriously. During a demonstration in front of the Parliament in 2001, he said, a Molotov cocktail was thrown at one of the wooden guardhouses, which promptly was engulfed in flames. The guard standing right next to it did not even blink his eyes, let alone move! Quickly, the guard of the guard ran to him and ordered him to step lively. With a scorched and smoking uniform on one side, the guard was relieved.

Awesome experience!

Authentic Greek Food

By this point, we were hungry. We told Demetrius that we wanted authentic Greek food for lunch, preferably gyro. I was surprised that several of our group had never head of this fabulous meal! They were game to try new things, however. Demetrius assured us he knew just the place, as he took us to the Market Square. He instructed us to enjoy lunch at any of the places nearby ("but this is my favorite"), then walk fifty feet down the path to the left, and turn right at the gate to enter the ancient Agora. That was puzzling ---we appeared to be in a busy modern marketplace, not near anything ancient! Demetrius had not steered us wrong yet.

I really like Greek food, and I seek it out whenever we find a Greek community in the States. I like gyros, especially. It's pronounced yee-row, everywhere except in the Northeast, where they say jiy-roh. They drop their R's, too; can't be helped. A gyro is seasoned ground meat, usually lamb or beef, cooked on a rotating spit, then sliced very thin, piled on soft pita, and topped with lettuce, tomato, onion, and a garlicky yogurt/cucumber/mint tzatziki sauce. It's a messy, four-napkin sandwich of deliciousness. My taste-buds were dancing long before we reached Greece!

Well, it turns out, much to my dismay, that I like *Greek-American* gyro, not the authentic variety. I guess it's like the Cruise Addict, who loves Tex-Mex more than Mexican foods. These gyros were very different than the any I have had in many Greek restaurants in America. They had *french fries* in them! and the tzatziki sauce was mild, like plain yogurt, with no garlic at all. The Greek salad, however, was gorgeous. Very ripe tomatoes, cucumber, thin sliced red onions, peppers, greasy wrinkled olives and about a five ounce slab of salty feta, drizzled with herbs and olive oil. It was delicious! We ate outdoors at a corner restaurant, and our friends were delighted with lunch, having nothing to compare it against. I will try more gyro when we get to Mykonos, just to see if they are any different.

Nearby, street vendors sold pastries, 12 inch diameter crispy rings coated in sesame seed, and giant donuts, about as big as a Frisbee. Authentic? Oh, yeah!

We were already in the habit of paying €.5 for any restroom. Our rule quickly became, do as your mama said: just *try*. When we came upon a free one, such as at a museum, or a restaurant, try anyway. In this case, the restroom was truly scary. It had no seat. It was very stained; the floor, the walls, the toilet itself. Shudder. There was no paper, but as they say, when you gotta go, you better go. Once again I was prepared with my little drawstring bag of paper and wipes.

As I passed through the restaurant, I saw the gyro meat cooking on a rotating vertical spit. This is common in Greek restaurants at home, too, but this packed meat had to be at least 125 pounds! I don't know how they lifted it! Another thing I found odd was that there is no lamb served at restaurants in Greece. I can't imagine why this is. Demetrius warned us ahead of time, and said we should order chicken or beef. He shrugged, "It is the way things are. We are in Greece." Well, I can't argue with that.

After we ate our satisfying meal and guzzled another bottle of water – drinking a lot of water today – we made our way up the dusty path that Demetrius had indicated. This area was lined with little shops and little cafés and street musicians and pop up vendors with card tables, selling ancient coins. I wasn't sure about the legality of even owning such an antiquity, or the authenticity , so I did not purchase any, but I certainly admired them as we went by.

What is it about dogs and Athens? We saw dozens and dozens of dogs, just lying on the dusty streets or on marble steps. They don't appear to have owners. They don't appear to have food or water. They don't appear to have any motivation to move, either, like regular dogs; they just lay there like heaps of overheated fur, ignored by people. And cats! We saw a lot of cats all over Greece, but at least they were in motion for the most part, behaving like familiar cats. Cade began taking pictures of cats on this trip. I think he ended up with a couple of hundred photos of cats by the end of our trip. No one knows why.

Agora

By now we knew that Agora means 'central place', like a plaza or town square. The Agora was the center of political and public life in Athens, back in the day. It was a large open area surrounded by buildings, including shops and stores, political offices, religious venues, and even military activities such as drills, took place there. The legislature was nearby, along with the courts of law and the local government offices. It was the heart of the city, much as a downtown functions in our modern American cities. But where was this one? Demetrius said it just "just down that way," but we saw only modern things, until we were right upon it, just a couple of hundred feet from the hustle and bustle of the modern city.

We were once again catapulted back into history! Relicts of ancient temples, pillars, fountains, and sculptures, all exposed to the elements, all totally accessible. Once again I was awed by the history and the spirits of the ordinary people who dwelt here

2000 or 3000 years ago. Of course, people lived on the American continent that long ago, as well as here, but we just don't have the visible remnants of the cultures that are available here in Greece.

After an hour or so of happy exploring, our group met back up with Demetrius. I was grateful to get back into his air-conditioned van and take another bottle of ice cold water out of the cooler. I'm enjoying the tour very much today, but I admit I'm also half cooked in this heat.

Marathon and Stadium

Demetrius then drove us to the stadium where the first modern Olympics were held. Melissa is a runner and she was extra impressed, even wishing she had time for a run. It did not affect the rest of us that way. Demetrius told us a story of the marathon. I've always wondered why it's an odd distance, 26 miles and 385 yards. It's because of the legend of Pheidippides, a Greek messenger. Demetrius told us that he was sent from the battlefield of Marathon to Athens to announce that the Persians had been defeated in the Battle of Marathon in 490 BC. Abandoning his exhausted horse halfway, he ran the rest of the distance in his full battle regalia. Pheidippides burst into the full stadium and shouted "Nike!" – *Victory* – and then collapsed and died right there. Ever since then, the distance of a marathon is 26 miles, plus the distance Pheidippides ran into the stadium.

Another thing I found odd was the restroom situation. Because we hadn't had a stop in a while, we decided to avail ourselves. This one had a table with a man making change for the line of tourists. There was also a sort of a traffic cop pulling people out of line, an authoritative-type woman; men to the left, women to the right. It made me think about career choices.

Can you imagine going home to Mother one day and saying, "Ma, I decided what I'm going to do with my life. I'm going to sit at a table in a smelly restroom all day long and make change for tourists. They will give me money. I will give them change. We will never make eye contact and there will be no interaction whatsoever," or perhaps "Mother, when I grow up, I'm going to stay all day in a windowless, airless bathroom. I'm going to pull people who need to use a toilet out of line. I will tell them when they can go and when they must wait and I will have no mercy upon their desperate faces." I was again grateful for the opportunities in America.

Past old churches, and statues, and the oldest library we drove, slowing down for photos, with Demetrius narrating along the way. He described the ancient universities, upon which our own education system is based. In one library, there is a volume from 1900 BC-- can you imagine?! At one intersection, he stopped to show us a sculpture, Marathon Man, made of sheets of green glass, running. It was a massive modern art, with the illusion of motion, and I was quite impressed. All day I was swept away, awestruck, by the old and the new muddled together.

Acropolis Museum

Demetrius had earlier explained, "We usually come to the Acropolis Museum first to give an overview, so you know what you're looking at, once you get to the Acropolis. But I thought your group would appreciate missing the crowds, and so I reversed the order." It's impolite to hug a tour guide you just met, but I felt like it. So on to the Acropolis Museum!

The building is three stories. The whole wall facing the Acropolis was made of glass. In fact, the whole building was tilted; laid nice and straight on the grid on its foundations, to fit the site. But the top story was canted, angled to face the Acropolis. It was truly breathtaking to be able to envision how it looked when it was fresh and new. To see the ruins all these centuries later, still standing, took my breath away.

The museum itself is built on ruins, on top of an ancient site-- it literally stands on archaeological dig! Some of the floors were glass, so we could see the excavations down below, including on the exterior entrance. I think I saw plumbing. I definitely saw a fountain. Again, it was tourist season, so no work was going on.

The Museum is amazing, bigger than expected, and quality. To be able to see actual pieces of sculpture and restored casts from the Pantheon at eye level was wonderful. We spent over an hour seeing the artwork close up, imagining what the Acropolis complex looked like in its glory. I wished we'd had more time just to linger. I could've spent the whole afternoon just admiring the curls on that one statue!

Much of the original artwork was stolen by Lord Elgin in the late 1600's, and still not returned. We learned that the British kept it, insisting the Greeks had no proper way to store or display the art. This was pretty shallow, considering how many ancient works we had seen already! Once the Acropolis Museum was constructed, the Greek government asked for their stuff back, but Britain again declined, saying :"we've had it so long, our people would miss it. " The fight goes on in international courts. I think the problem could be quickly solved by what I taught my young kids, long ago: If it's not yours, don't touch it. The artwork clearly belongs to Athens---give it back!

Successful Tour

It was almost time to head back to the ship. On the way Demetrius asked, "What else can I tell you? What else can I show you?" Melissa is slim, but she has a sweet tooth bigger than her head. She piped up, "you know what would make the day perfect? A sweet! Where can we get something sweet?"

Demetrius laughed, "My mother's house. She bakes the best treats, but you would miss the ship. How about some baklava?" Of course! He took us to a baklava bakery started in 1920 by some Jewish refugees. They displayed more kinds of baklava than I knew existed, coconut, pistachio pineapple, berry, pomegranate, lemon, chocolate, many more, all drizzled in gooey honey, plied high, and coming out of the oven right there. Oh, yum! Husband and I chose little ones, about an inch long and finger diameter. That way we could sample more flavors. It was a perfect end to a really successful tour!

Back at the pier, Demetrius shook our hands, and invited us to his father's house in December in northern Greece, when his extended family gathers to harvest and press the olives. It's unlikely that we'll ever see Demetrius again, but it's also unlikely that I will ever have an invitation like that again in my life. I was really very pleased with the PK tour experience, to have had that personalized tour, sight unseen, for such a good price. Oh, PK tours was great! I'd highly recommend them---we had an awesome day, and I'm quite sure we saw more than anyone else on the ship. My kind of traveling! Organizing this tour made for the best possible day.

Wrap Up The Day

Back on the Spirit, we were greeted personally, by name, by several of the senior staff as we walked to our cabin. It's becoming rather humorous to be known as VIPs, when we are really just plain old ordinary travelers, and frugal ones at that. We found another treat in our cabin; one every day so far! This was a cheese platter with brie, camembert, Swiss and a very nice sharp cheddar. We also had an invitation to dine with the hotel director on the following evening. This VIP stuff is over the top. I could adapt, mind you.

The shows are surprisingly good quality here in the Spirit, the show tonight was aerialists, Marta and Thomas. Very talented!

Tomorrow we will leave Europe for a little while as we enter Kusadasi. Turkey is the only continent in the world that straddles two continents, Asia and Europe. I admit I am slightly uneasy about going to Turkey. We have friends who've been on a similar cruise a year ago on their way to the Holy Land, and they said that Kusadasi was easily their favorite port on their entire cruise. I'm thinking their standards are pretty low. I'm also a little uncomfortable because we don't have our passports. It didn't seem to matter so much today in Greece. I felt safe. Turkey is the most *foreign* foreign place I've ever been to. Of all times to be without my passport!

Again, all twelve of us will be together on a tour tomorrow, and the next day as well. The further south we've gone, the warmer it has become. This afternoon was very hot. The forecast is for the upper 90's tomorrow. I'm grateful for my big floppy hat. I may look ridiculous, but if it saves my face from sunburn, it's worth it. Besides, it might make a good landmark. I *really* don't want to get lost in Turkey. It's rather a short day; we arrive at 7

AM and have to be back on board at 1:30 PM. Good thing we have a tour; with limited time, it's the most efficient way to see a place.

Day Four: Kusadasi, Turkey

Asia! Turkey! And I lived to tell! Today was really hot. I felt half melted as we toured Ephesus today. Temperatures were about 95° today, and very dry. People told us repeatedly , "oh, you are here at a good time! Just a month ago, temperatures were over 110°." Whew!

Our private tour was with Eklo Tours, and the same company tomorrow. The laws are different in Turkey, so this tour had a driver, who was functionally invisible, and a guide who walked right with us, all day. Hadi narrated nonstop, both on the van and as we walked---good thing he was interesting! All twelve of us planned to be on this tour. But Julie had had knee surgery recently and she decided she wasn't up to clambering the ruins of Ephesus, so she stayed on the ship at the last minute.

The port of Kusadasi is rather pretty, as initial impressions go, with ancient castle- type buildings next to neon signs, and the vivid red Turkish flag flying all around. I was relieved to learn from our guide that English is mandatory in schools. Every person has at least a basic ability in English, which is better than Americans do with foreign languages.

Ephesus and the Terrace Houses

We drove straight to Ephesus, past orange and fig groves. It's quite green here, and pretty in a stark sort of way. As we drove, every so often, we'd spot more ancient ruins; perhaps a wall in a field, or crumbled stairs near a well. What else is buried under the earth here??

Ephesus was once the capital of Asia Minor, a very busy seaport in its day. The apostle Paul's family was tentmakers and lived in the city, and he spent two years teaching Christianity here, right in the Roman theatre. We were anxious to walk the streets of this ancient city! Like the ghost towns in America, only completely different.

The driver obviously had a death wish. He drove so wildly, our friends had to hang on a few times! Hadi was unmoved; he stood in the van like he was on a sidewalk, telling us what we would be seeing throughout the day. We arrived at the entrance to Ephesus ten minutes before the huge outdoor museum even opened. That gave us time to visit the WC, buy chilled water bottles, and be barraged by multiple aggressive souvenir sellers. I felt oddly safer once we were inside the old city!

I was again surprised to be in an ancient city, an ongoing archaeological excavation site, to be to walk on, climb over, touch it, admire it, close up and hands on. I kept thinking about the residents of this busy city 2300 years ago. They walked these streets, rested under those arches. They parked their chariots, laid mosaic tiles, painted those frescoes. Real people shared bread, and shopped in the stores, ate in restaurants, and talked about their days, just as we do. They chased their children and fed their families. They worked and lived and watch the sun rise and set. They played games and told stories. They lived there, and 2300 years later, there *I* stood. I felt like part of a larger circle as I touched the walls, saw chariot tracks worn into the stones, peeked in the public ovens. Travel is good.

The excavated part of Ephesus is only 15% of the total city's area, as we suspected, driving to the site. The sculptures, inscriptions, and stonework through the city were simply breathtaking to me. Such fine workmanship. We don't do that well now! And the decorations-! These people lived long before electricity, lasers, power tools, and yet the paintings on the walls and the intricate mosaics on the floor were still clear today. Astonishing!

Hadi, our guide wanted to take us to the House of Mary, as described in the tour. I reminded him we had changed that by email at home, to the Terrace Houses instead. Mary may or may not have lived at the little house at one time. From what we understand, tourists file into the house and out the other side. Tour books call it 'nondescript'. We traveled too far for 'nondescript." We are not Catholic and so a religious pilgrimage to the area meant nothing to us. Skip it!

The Terraced Houses are part of Ephesus, the upper class area. They housed only five families. It seemed very large to me; elegant three story homes. They had thick walls, too, against the climate, against the hot sun beating down, and the cool of the winters, such as they are. The terraced houses are part of the larger Ephesus site, and the current archaeological focus as well.

Again, since we were there during tourist season, there was no active archaeological digging, but the archaeologists obviously left their mark, as if they had merely stepped away from their work. The whole Terrace Houses area is under a membrane, like a soft roof, open on the sides, specially designed for this site, to maintain the exact temperature and humidity level appropriate for archaeological digs

The 'puzzle room' was daunting to me; but I admit I don't even have the patience to complete a 1000 piece jigsaw puzzle. I didn't get that gene, but I did get a double dose of curiosity, and this place was fascinating!! It was right as we entered, there on the ground floor. Ephesus and the Terrace Houses walls had been covered in marble, over the brick work. Over the centuries, the mortar had let loose. Maybe age, maybe earthquakes; for whatever reason, it fell off, and it lay at the base of the walls.

There are heaps of marble, some crumb-sized, others slabs, just laying where it fell.

The puzzle room had giant tables where the archaeologists would literally piece the marble back together in massive jigsaw puzzles, turning the bits to make them fit. When a wall panel was completed, or when the pieces were used up, they would mortar and glue them together. They were hanging on the wall, so we could see the completed ones. Hadi explained that they used to do it all by hand. For a season, they decided to photograph every particle, from slab to speck of marble, and have computers work on the giant puzzle. Of course, the way the marble broke and landed, they couldn't tell what side was front, and so each piece had to be photographed from top and bottom, on all sides. They found that the photography was a great waste of time, and didn't match pieces any faster than humans, plus it was a major expense. Back to very, very patient people piecing it together using human eyes. It looked incredibly tedious to me.

The Terrace Houses' design was fascinating. The rooms were surprisingly small, with thick walls, staggered down the side of a hill, in terraces. Thus, the name. Stacked on top of one another, the homes were offset. The roof of the bottom house became the porch's floor of the next one, up and over. To have intricate mosaic on your roof-- how beautiful! The ancient steps to the side of the Terrace Houses where residents would've walked home are as old as the rest of the city, but much less worn than the main streets of Ephesus. I guess the only people who walked there, were actually going there, not across town. It's much like our neighborhood at home; it isn't on the way to anything, plus the roads are arranged like cooked spaghetti. The only people who drive here are going...here.

We walked through the open part of Ephesus first, detoured through the Terrace Houses area, and then finishing walking the rest of Ephesus. It was excavated from under eight to ten feet of hill side; just centuries of Nature reclaiming her city. The streets were made of rough hewn marble slabs, worn down by feet, and the elements over the centuries. Julie was right; she could not have managed such uneven walkways with as many stairs as we covered. I felt like I was on forbidden turf in this outdoor museum– I can actually <u>touch</u> that! Some parts were familiar, as if I fallen into a poster, having seen them in books and documentaries at home. The Nike carving, the Celsus library, the bakery, the chariot ruts in the roads. It was interesting to get a glimpse into people's lives from so long ago!

We sat in the amphitheatre in Ephesus. It was the site of dramas, music and orators in its day. The wealthy merchants at the time decided that they would prefer to live in a civilized society, and so they would arrange for speakers and performers to come in and perform for the populace, at no cost. Hadi pointed out that it was a good place to see and be seen as well. It was a bustling city of trade and commerce, so I would imagine there was an awful lot of variety in dress and status. Imagine attending a performance there?

This very amphitheatre is where the apostle Paul preached to 25,000 Ephesians, his hometown people. I could envision the audience in their finery , attentive enough to worry the merchants of the city. Ephesus worshipped Diana, and a good source of income for some merchants and metallurgists of the time was making and selling statues of the goddess of Ephesus. If people converted to Christianity, they would stop honoring the gods. The new religious movement became an economic threat. Turning to God is a good thing, but not everyone agreed when their livelihood was threatened. The apostle Paul spoke several times there. The last time caused a near riot right there, right in that theatre, right where I stood. Paul was imprisoned up on that tall hill, just outside the city. His prison was placed so he could look down into the stadium where he had caused such an uproar, and think about his actions. Standing there, I thought I felt Paul, smiling, suspecting that some who listened to him would act.

The baths were public, and in a particular order: a swift wash up, into cold water and then warm, hot, cold, warm and cold, preceded by a half-hour massage by slaves. Hadi said the lengthy process could be a deterrent to using the baths. He related, "people occasionally died of heart attacks in the bath from the shock of the temperature." Well, I can see why residents bathed infrequently !

We saw a flat marble stone with small circles engraved into it in the center of the agora, the main square. Hadi explained that it was a form of backgammon . He smiled as he translated the engraving for us, " have enjoyment while losing your coins gambling." 2800 years ago, real live people gambled in that square, never suspecting the game would endure far longer than they, or that we, centuries later, would see it!

We also found the brothel district in Ephesus, which I guess is not out of place in a port town with sailors coming and going. This part was made of very small rooms with erotica still visible on the walls and male fertility statues inside. I would think male fertility would be the last thing prostitutes would want! Hadi pointed out a sign carved into the street for out-of-town sailors to follow to it; symbols, in case a lusty sailor did not read the language. Hadi translated , "beautiful women will give you her heart for a coin." Societies don't change much.

I felt a spirit about Ephesus, an energy, that goes on even until this day. Ephesus quietly died out as a town. Later we were to see Herculaneum and Pompeii, which were suddenly destroyed, but Ephesus just kind of faded off into history.

Turkish Rugs

I know that most tours, either through the cruise line or private ones, go to a place that sells Turkish rugs. I very much hoped to avoid it. Several tour books I have read described exactly the procedure. The tour guide takes you to a rug factory where the group is introduced to the most important man, an honored man, who will do the demonstration. The group is taken into a very air-conditioned room and offered refreshment; alcohol, tea, or bottled water. The most important man, an honored salesperson, does a demonstration, laying out many many rugs, describing how they are each made.

A different salesman then comes in and begins to talk up the customers, trying to find a connection. Oh, you live in Seattle. I have a nephew's neighbor whose brother's girlfriend's sister visited there only 15 years ago; why it's like we're friends and neighbors, have you seen this particularly lovely rug? I've heard that it's time-consuming and considered most impolite to leave before the demonstration is complete. With our time being limited, this is not how I wish to spend it.

Brian and Pat, friends at home, have been to Istanbul and Kusadasi several times. They told us that it is one of their favorite places in Europe and the Mediterranean. I trust their judgement, to an extent. They lost it, when they visited the rug sellers. Brian and Pat were both completely awestruck at the process. Some rugs, the larger ones, can take many months to complete. They decided they must have one. The vendor who sold it to them, such an important man, offered them tea and told him his life story.

The seller said that during the busy tourist season, when they were there, he sold rugs. During the off-season, he had the pre-purchased Turkish rugs shipped to his sister, who lives in Salt Lake City. He would then fly over from Istanbul to Utah, rent a van or a truck, as his need dictated, and drive all around the United States. Taking a month, he would personally deliver the rugs to his customers! What kind of a markup was he making, to be able to buy the rug from the maker, sell the rug, ship it to the states, fly to the states himself, rent a truck, and personally hand-deliver every rug to every customer?! Apparently, he made quite an impression, because Pat and Brian's modern house now displays *six* large Turkish rugs, bought from the same enterprising merchant in Turkey! The Cruise Addict accuses me of being a world-class shopper. In actuality, Husband has no clue how frugal, efficient, or wise I actually am as a consumer. I do not waste time. I know that I did not want a Turkish rug in my house, and so what was the point of shopping? I very much hoped to avoid going to the Turkish rug demonstration. I talked to Melissa and Mary ahead of time, and they agreed that we simply were not going to stop there; we are strong women, after all, with a united front. A private tour means that we can decide where to go or not, right?

The plan was a good one, until Hadi suggested a rug factory be our next stop as we drove from Ephesus. Clint and Todd excitedly gasped in unison, "Oh, that's just what I want to do!" We women exchanged exasperated glances across the van. Sigh...it's their vacation, too. My heart sunk as we parked at a complex of rooms, a showroom, I guessed, with a handful of women outside working on rugs.

Their looms were protected from the searing sun under canopies. Their rug patterns, hand drawn with colored pencil on graph paper, were tucked between the warp and the woof of the loom. Brightly colored yarns hung from above, threaded into the pattern as they worked. Their fingers were blurry fast! Each woman made a yarn knot and cut it with a single movement, so fast I could not follow the motion. The well-dressed man who had met us at the van explained the process as the women worked in front of us.

He explained that the women were students from rural areas, taking a course at this school/factory, keeping the tradition alive. The fee-free session lasted several weeks, while they live on-site. They practice by making a rug. At the end of the course, each woman is given a loom to take home. She could tie rugs in between her work at home, in between taking care of the children and running her household. Thus, he explained, she could "earn money by emancipation," teach her daughters, and preserve the ancient craft. As their skill improved, the women would design their own rugs, increasingly more intricate and thus worth more money. The system works, as long as she agrees to sell her work to that studio, at least for a brief time.

It seemed a good deal to me; it increases the family income, yet it doesn't take the women away from the children or the home, while giving the wife and mother her own money and sense of independence. It increases social interaction, and allows rural families to stay in healthier areas to live. Plus, it preserves an art form that has gone on for hundreds and hundreds of years, and I'm all in favor of folk art.

As if the greeter had read the same tour books I had, he led us into a big room, a show room lined with padded benches, just like in the books, with a wide open floor. It was wonderfully air-conditioned; actually after the 95° outside, the temperature was almost too cold. Refreshments were offered, right on cue. The proprietor then politely inquired, "may I introduce you to you the most important man on the premises?" as if he had read his script.

The Most Important Man shook hands with us all, bowed, and said, "may I begin to demonstrate?" My heart sunk. Feeling trapped, I settled back onto the bench. He began to direct three men who magically appeared from between the rolled rugs lining the walls. They unrolled rugs of all sizes and colors across the wooden floor as he described each. The colors. The design. The artist. The time in the making. The finest materials. He said that each rug could be recognized by the artwork; the artist literally became familiar, much like we would recognize a painting.

The rugs flew faster and faster, arranged by material, by collection, by the artist, by color, deeper and deeper across the hardwood floor, six or eight rugs deep, before the Most Important Man finally paused. He said that we must get up, take off our shoes and walk on the rugs so we could appreciate their quality. I had to suppress a giggle. That, too, was in every tour book I had read at home; that customers would be invited to take off their shoes and walk with their bare feet. Several of us did. In the end, and there was indeed an end, although it took a lot longer than I thought it should have, Todd and Clint both bought a rug, small ones, only a few hundred dollars each.

I kept having flashbacks to my Syrian grandparents' house. I know they had many of these rugs, very similar ones. Where are they now? I still don't want one, even though the salespeople assured me that their value increases with age. At one point, after the Most Important Man was done, the salesmen schmoozed and one told me a story. There was an eight by eleven foot rug, ninety years old, that had been offered for sale there last year. The owner refused to sell it for the 180,000 euros the customer offered. While I honor the craftsmanship in these rugs, I still don't want to own one.

Back on the road, back to the port of Kusadasi. We went to a little market across the street from the ship. I wanted to look for a wrap or a scarf, and one for my daughters. I found silk ones priced at €15. They were beautiful, but more like a gemstone, when what I really wanted this time was the costume jewelry of Turkish scarves. By the time I had extricated myself from the very aggressive shopkeeper, I owned four silk scarves for total of €25. What a crazy stressful way to shop!

Melissa bought three 4-gram bags of saffron for six euros. It's Turkish saffron, which is actually a strong form of safflower, not as expensive or strong is the authentic saffron, but every bit as tasty, so long as you use a little bit more in your recipe. Since I know that, it'll work just fine. When I heard that Melissa had some saffron, I had her show me where she bought it. I also bought three 4-gram bags for six euros. The seller gave me a beautiful woven silk bookmark in the shape of a Turkish rug as a gift. He gave Melissa another bag of saffron, likely for bringing the business.

Husband went into a watch shop. I could tell that this was probably not going to be a good idea. He emerged a few moments later, chuckling as he showed me the package containing an Authentic Fake Watch. We know that it is; it said so right on the package!

Wrap Up The Day

NCL stages a welcome back party atmosphere at every port on this cruise. Today's included dancing, chilled washcloths, frozen fruit on skewers, and live music on the pier. A small thing, perhaps, but it made us feel valued. Back on the ship, we kicked off our shoes in our beautiful cabin, ate the chocolate covered strawberries that waited, compliments of the concierge, and reviewed the day.

Husband and I agreed that we had enjoyed the day more than either of us expected. The tour was successful, we learned a lot, and enjoyed being with just our friends and Hadi. We agreed we were wise to avoid being part of the bedraggled groups of tired passengers we saw pouring off the buses at the end of the day! I'm grateful that we booked our tours ahead of time--- it cut down on stress dramatically.

Ephesus was dripping in history and I was grateful to be part of it! Tomorrow we will be in Istanbul, a more bustling modern metropolis. Our tour is with the same company, going to both ancient and modern sites. I'm looking forward to seeing other places in this very old country. I'm also grateful to have a tour guide who guaranteed speaks English. It makes me feel a bit safer.

Our friends enjoyed the tour as much as we did. All that research at home paid off! While resting on some steps in Ephesus, Clint told Husband that he and Mary are happy about seeing much more than on any previous cruise, so appreciative, and they decided they intend to go with us to the Panama Canal next year. Wait-! I didn't know we were doing a Panama cruise next year. Guess The Cruise Addict has been talking again...

We ran into Todd later in the Blue Lagoon, munching nachos. He verified tomorrow's meeting point and time. As we parted, he said, "I just want you to know that Julie and I are having a fabulous time. You're fun and you're both great cruise tour directors. We want to go on more cruises with you in the future. Let us know time and place." It's nice to be appreciated, after all the stress of figuring out all the tours at home!

I keep marveling at Ephesus; I expect the memories of today will stay with me a long time. I was actually standing in *Ephesus!* The wooden roofs are long gone, but the pillars that supported them are in place, making it possible to imagine how it looked when the city was alive. The houses each had a courtyard and gardens; very different than American layouts. This is again why it's important to travel; trying to imagine how these people lived stretched my imagination.

Ephesus touched me. I'm going to remember being here for a very long time. Remembering should be easy. The cruise is only a third over and already the two of us have taken close to eight hundred photographs!

Part of the reason we wanted to have private tours was to be able to get to know a resident of the ports we visited, at least superficially. Our group made a concerted effort to talk to the guides in each port, asking questions, genuinely interested. Hadi, when pressed, admitted that the rising Islamic State is hurting his country. Refugees have fled into Turkey from Syria, far more than the refugee camps can sustain. They spread out into the countryside, camping in parks, etc. Hadi said, "Of course they must survive, but it is a hardship. It causes many problems for the residents."

Hadi continued, saying that even the Gypsies, or the Travelers, are afraid to wander anymore. They're making permanent camps, out of fear. How bad is a situation when even the Travelers will not travel? Hadi said that 1000 Syrian refugees were fleeing to Turkey every day and it was creating a serious hardship. "I do not see a good end," he sighed.

A thousand a day...yet two days after our return from this cruise, CNN reported that *160,000* refugees had crossed the borders in only a four-day span. There are no Western reporters in Syria – the last ones who were there were relieved of their heads – so the real story doesn't make it out, but how bad does it have to be for 160,000 people to flee for their life over one weekend? We are very far from home, very happy to be here, yet I wonder if this trip would even be possible a few years from now. Kusadasi and Ephesus will be in my mind for a long time. I'm grateful to be here!

Last night's dinner didn't go well. We were seated with another couple in Windows, the main dining room. That was fine; we like new people, but the whole wait staff was a little off. They brought Husband's and the couple's appetizers, but not mine. Thirty seconds later, the waiter served my entrée, while they were still having their appetizers! Plus, my entrée was stone cold. I didn't eat much. We left before dessert because service was slow, incredibly slow, and we wanted to see the aerialists in the theatre. Tonight, we have been invited to dine with the Hotel Director. I would expect service will be much better this evening.

later on. Oh, yes, dinner was fabulous. We had dinner with the Hotel Director and two other couples. The couple next to me were very interesting, from England, and I enjoyed visiting with them. A brash New York/Italian woman joined us. She barely stopped talking long enough to draw breath. Her husband contributed one sentence the whole evening. Yes, I counted. Dinner service was impeccable. I noticed we had the best table. Moreover, I noticed that there was sort of a buffer zone around us, with every adjacent table empty, although there was a line to get into the dining room. VIP ism, again. The Hotel Director was a truly charming host, making for a very enjoyable evening . We finished dinner in time to go to the second show. It was Bee Gees Magic Review, the legacy group. They had the audience up and cheering and dancing and laughing, like being at a concert. It was great fun!

Istanbul, tomorrow's port, is about 99% Muslim. I've never been a Muslim country before. I am uneasy. With the tumultuous history, and of course hearing about the radical elements on the nightly news at home, I'm being remarkably brave. Oh, well, so much of life is about acting. I can act brave. Probably. I'm good with trusting Eklo tours again, but I will quietly make it known that I am serious about refusing to go into the Blue Mosque. I'm on vacation; there is no benefit to being that stressed or uncomfortable! I'll meet the group outside.

Our tour in Istanbul tomorrow is scheduled to begin at 8:30 AM, but the Captain just announced that we will dock at 9 AM. I'm exhausted. I'm not going to worry about it. What I really need to do is go to sleep, but my mind is just racing. Main goal for tomorrow: Don't do anything that will land us on the evening news.

Day Five: Istanbul, Turkey

I survived Turkey! I enjoyed much of the day today, much more than I expected to. Istanbul is a very foreign place for this American woman. The busy city moves at a scary pace. I think I would've felt panic, had we been there alone, especially for such a short time, but we stayed with our guide and all was well. Most of it, anyway. It was not a relaxing day, but very interesting, and probably even important. It was certainly once-in-a-lifetime! Many people count Istanbul as their all-time favorite city. I am not sure I agree. I felt slightly off balance all day.

Meeting the Tour

We made port later than expected. We were supposed to arrive at 8 AM and our tour was at 8:30 AM. The ship did not get cleared to go ashore until after 9 AM. Our tour guide waited, as I knew he would. This is his livelihood, and private tour guides always check the ship's arrival, adjusting times as needed.

Our group has been really good about meeting on time at Henry's Pub, ready to go. Good—I hate mothering people! Today, we pulled out a deck of cards, and chatted with Gio (cruise director) until the announcement came. Actually, he got word of the clearance before it was announced, and suggested our group slip out, ready to go ashore as soon as possible, before the rest of the ship was notified. Small thing, but it saved us a few minutes.

It was a long walk from the ship to the terminal itself. Julie and Clint found a shuttle to take them out of the loading area; the rest of us hoofed it. Once we arrived at the terminal, Yazin was there to meet us, waving a sign with our name on it.

We had the same tour company as yesterday; with a different, but equally invisible driver, and a different guide. We were together, all twelve of us. I'm pleased at how well everyone is getting along! Again the driving was scary. We were in a large van going down narrow streets with two way traffic and tight parking on both sides. Why don't the vehicles show more damage? How can people drive here and not be in constant fender-benders?

Our guide was Yazin, who grew up in Istanbul. He was crisp and efficient and maybe a little overwhelmed by our talkative group, but he loosened up as the day went on. Our friends are really easy to deal with.

Ancient Hippodrome

Yazin, explained everything to us as we drove. We started in the Hippodrome. It was the site of the ancient chariot races in Roman times. *Chariot* races! There was a strange sensation of catapulting back through time, standing there in view of the old Blue Mosque and Turkish baths, with modern traffic whizzing past! When we stepped out of the van, we were immediately surrounded by ad hoc street merchants trying to sell us tour books, hats, trinkets. Suddenly they all scattered. A police officer in a three wheeled scooter was chasing them. Yazin shrugged, "they don't pay taxes."

All around us were ancient structures, mixed with modern shops. Sellers displayed their wares on little carts or maybe draped over their arms. Fourteen to twenty million people live in

Istanbul, depending on who counts, and it seemed that almost every one of them wanted to sell us some trinket!

All that remains now of the Hippodrome complex are the oval track, 2800 years old, and the obelisks. At one end stands the ancient walled Egyptian Obelisk, named after Constantine, who ordered its repair in the tenth century. He didn't put it there, though. At the other side, the Obelisk of Theodosius rises, where it has stood since at least the 4th century BC. Both were brought from Egypt, in one piece, so long ago, their exact dates are uncertain.

The Romans of the city had stolen the obelisk and transported it to Constantinople as a memento of their great victory. Later the Crusaders came. They ransacked the city and destroyed almost everything. We had seen this in Athens, too, where the invading armies destroyed a lot of the temples and shrines. War is like that – the warriors always destroy a place, and often the way of life that goes with it, as if to say 'we are here now, the old ways no longer exist, and you who have always lived here are subdued, right down to your gods, your shrines, and your buildings." That goes on today, as well. I was sad to feel that here, centuries after the fact.

Istanbul is officially 99% Muslim. Yazin admitted that about 60% are *practicing* Muslims. Turkey is a democracy, not ruled by religion, certainly not by the sharia law that some Muslim countries espouse. He assured us that he is personally very much against these strict laws that oppress women, and in many ways catapult society back into the Middle Ages.

We asked about education. Yazin said that education is very important, that there are 45 universities in Istanbul alone. He said that women are encouraged to work, travel, become educated and devout, same as the men, " for they rule the next generation." This is very much in line with my beliefs.

However, we still saw many women throughout the day, wearing burqa and hajib. Yazin shrugged, "what can be done?"

It rained early on in the day, and then again later on, for five minutes each time, an absolute downpour. The rest of the day was over 95° and sauna-humid. I was very uncomfortable in my light skirt and flowy blouse. My heart hurt for those women, my sisters, with no hope of even a breeze on their neck. I found myself irritated at their men wearing T-shirts and even shorts in the hot sun. I'm not a fan of double standards.

Today is Monday and Hagai Sophia is closed. We knew this ahead of time, and arranged to visit the underground Basilica Cistern instead. The day's plan also includes the Sultan Ahmet Mosque, (the dreaded Blue Mosque), Topkapi Palace, and the Grand Bazaar. Much of the tour would be walking because the places were quite close to one another. Traffic was so haphazard and fast-paced, I admit I felt safer walking than driving, even in a sturdy van!

I had hoped, at home, to have time for a boat tour of the Bosporus Strait to the bridge linking Europe and Asia, after the day's tour. Our guide explained, "You could do that, but you will miss the ship." The Spirit ended up berthed quite close to the bridge. I saw enough of both sides and I was content. Getting stranded in Istanbul was not on my life's goal list, at all.

Three per cent of Turkey is in Europe and 97% is on the Asian continent. There was so much history all around! The Bosporus Strait is the main channel up and into the Black Sea. The old city wall is still visible here, interrupted by elegant tombs of assorted rulers. Istanbul was the final stop on the Orient Express! The buildings go back many centuries. It was really too much ancient history to take in, but I did love trying. Well, I loved most of the ancient history, at least.

The Blue Mosque

I absolutely hated, *hated* being at the Blue Mosque, the Sultan Ahmed Mosque. I hated all of it. Yes, it was beautiful, with intricate mosaics and interesting architecture, with one large dome being supported by four smaller domes, but I was miserable. Islam's treatment of women, and the ghastly violence committed against innocents, makes me sick. Literally, physically sick to my stomach. Of course there are good, mild adherents, but the underlying tenets rattle me.

I had planned to wait outside while our friends visited the mosque. It wasn't fair for me to inflict my views on the group, any more than it was for the mosque to inflict its views on me. There was a long line, with one entrance and one exit; nowhere to wait outside safely. When I realized staying outside and meeting the group later would be impossible, I hoped the mosque would be closed. It closes five times a day for prayer, during which times tourists were not permitted inside. Five times---maybe we'd luck out and miss the tour. No such luck; our tour guide had factored that in, and we had plenty of time. Of all the days to be efficient...I was trapped.

Signs everywhere decreed the dress code. Men were required to wear clothing to cover the shoulders and knees. Women were required to cover arms, legs, ankles, necks, hair, all but faces and hands, officially, along with an outfit worn loose enough to disguise the female shape. It was not enforced beyond the headscarf and arms and legs being covered. They handed out lengths of fabric at the entrance, dark blue for covering shorts or legs and light blue for heads. Both women and men were required to remove shoes and were handed clear plastic bags to put them in.

At home, I frequently wear scarves and wraps and shawls. I'm fine with that. I *like* scarves and wraps, but this one made me feel queasy and claustrophobic. I had limited peripheral vision. I couldn't get enough air. No one else seemed to be suffocating; just me. I fought tears of panic and I could not adjust the head scarf thing to make myself feel better. I saw the others in our group did not feel the same. They even posed for photographs inside the mosque in their headscarves, while I was fighting waves of nausea.

Finally my concerned Husband helped, by twisting the length of blue fabric up off my neck so I felt less smothered. It was basically the same way I wear a towel on my head after I wash my hair. It was a little bit better, but I still didn't feel like I could get enough air. I hated the second citizen level in the mosque, with a high wall for separating women. The feeling of heart-pounding anxiety didn't dissipate until we were back outside.

Technically, Turkey is not a conservative Muslim country. Not like others that enforce the sharia law, but the mosque was bad enough and I was miserable. On the good side, yes, the mosaics were awesome. The carpet was beautiful. The dome was impressive; one major dome being held up by four smaller domes is beautiful architecture. I recognize the Blue Mosque is a very famous tourist place, and I'm quite sure that many other people go there and just love it. I still had one main goal, *get me out of there!!*

Basilica Cistern

The Basilica Cistern was nearby, and our next stop. Melissa chuckled, " How often do we get to walk in the city's underground plumbing system, and pay to do it?" Actually tickets were included in the Eklo tours price; another selling point as we debated which company to hire. As we made our way down the steep, wet marble stairs with no railing, my American mind thought "this is a lawsuit waiting to happen." No one slipped.

It was surprisingly cool in the cisterns, a definite plus on a day when the temperatures were so high. Colored lights at the base of the ancient columns sparkled in the water with an eerie ambience, spotlighting the bottom of each pillar. The shimmering lights danced as we walked around. It was both entrancing and a bit spooky, not like any place I'd ever seen before. The workmanship in the stones and pillars amazed me. I hope those photographs turn out!

The cistern was built in 565 AD by Emperor Justinian. There are 336 pillars, of different styles. Instead of carving all of the pillars as needed, the builders simply took some from captured lands. When in use, the stored water would have been up to the roof of the structure, but there was only a foot or so of water beneath the walkway now, with fish swimming, just for decoration.

I made my way down the slippery walkway to see the ancient Medusa heads. They were stone carvings, recycled rocks, Volkswagen sized, that once belonged to a former god's temple. Once she was dethroned as a god, the Medusa was plucked up, and chucked upside down in the underground plumbing, supposedly never to see the light of day again. This is a pretty serious way to disrespect the conquered ones' gods! The ancients could not have suspected their plumbing system would one day be a tourist destination.

Topkapi Palace

Topkapi Palace was huge, encrusted with jewels and intricate gold work all around. The last Sultan's immediate family (of four hundred) moved to a better place, but what on earth could be better than that? The grounds were so crowded. And yet Yazmin remarked us how lucky we were to come in on a slow day –! How could it get worse than this? Every room we moved around had long, snaking lines, and we ended up skipping the jewel room altogether. The grounds were full of tourists, along with obviously local Muslim families, people we recognized from the ship, so many people and swirling languages! I was glad much of it was outdoors, where we could enjoy the breezes as we walked from building to building on the Topkapi Palace grounds.

Back on the streets, we stopped to buy more bottled water. I realized that there's going to be a temperature issue again. I noticed that room temperature bottles were given to locals, right out of the case. North Americans were given chilled bottles. Husband was given semi frozen bottles, over and over. I'm not real sure what that indicated, but I'm sure it meant something.

I wanted to buy a few postcards outside of the Palace. I carefully mentally calculated the cost; Turkish lira into euros....got it. I must've added wrong. I handed six postcards and two euro coins to the kiosk owner. He violently shook his head, grabbed my arm, and hauled me to the other side of the kiosk. On top of the six I had chosen, he pressed two 20-postcard books, plus one of Hagai Sophia, as an apparent afterthought into my hand, along with a half euro coin. So much for my math skills!

Driving through Istanbul gave us a perspective I did not expect. The port area was surprisingly ugly and rundown, industrial. The Ottoman and the Byzantine influences linger, mixed with neon and modern shops in every block. As we drove, we passed many eateries, bakeries, and even a McDonald's, complete with motorcycles for delivery, and people – SO many people! Crazy drivers – if there are driving rules in Istanbul, they seem to be optional. People darted in and out of the front of cars, crossing the streets without a glance. Drivers did not hesitate to drive up onto the sidewalks and motorcycles buzzed in and out. It was a colorful place!

We wanted traditional Turkish food for lunch, but we didn't want to spend a lot of time eating it. At our request, Yazin took us to a fast food place of sorts, two-story, with a very steep semi spiral staircase.

Mercifully, the menu had pictures. It was delicious! We ended up with pita and meat rolls, and a very thin pizza- like food shaped like a flat canoe, served on a wooden plank. Husband asked "what kind of meat is it?" and the waiter calmly replied, "*Meat* meat." Oh. It was cheap, too. Both of our lunches cost only a hundred lira total; with three lira to a dollar, it wasn't much. Todd insisted on paying for our lunch. He keeps praising our skill in finding such good tours. He and Julie have traveled a lot, but they usually take ship tours. I doubt they'll do that ever again.

The Grand Bazaar

The last stop of the day was the Grand Bazaar, which is an ancient marketplace made of brightly displayed, neatly contained, utter chaos. It was begun in 400 BC, and added onto over the centuries. Finally, the city decreed 'it's done,' but the lack of available real estate did not stop merchants on foot from selling outside the main gates. It's arranged a lot like a shipwreck. The shops were tiny! Husband complained, " I don't *fit!*" when I wanted to show him something...I and one other customer were the only ones in the shop.

The array of items was dizzying; lamps, rugs, candy, leather, clothes, textiles, magnets, plates, pottery, jewelry, spices, teas, an endless display brightly arranged and tended to by personable, but aggressive, shopkeepers. Yazin had explained that the shopkeepers can speak 10 to 15 languages each, to be able to interact with their international customers. Maybe not 10 to 15 *fluent* languages, but certainly enough to discuss their own wares and to entice customers into their shops, regardless of the nationality. The four or five Turkish words I had memorized seemed pitiful.

We walked into a spice/candy store. The clerk in there was talking to the other clerk in Turkish. When we entered, he offered Husband a sugared date and told him, in English, how good it was. When another couple came in, he switched to Spanish. When they didn't understand him, he asked them, in English, where they were from, and when they said Germany, the clerk effortlessly switched to pitch to them in German-- rather impressive!

We did not venture far off the main section. Husband is a big guy, but not real courageous, and he was afraid that we would be lost forever among the 4000 shops. I did not think it would be an issue. I figured we could always back track, or ask anyone where is Gate One, where Yazmin had told us to meet. In between bursts of mosque anxiety, I guess I'm braver, although significantly smaller than The Cruise Addict. At any rate, we stayed not far off the main 'road' in the Bazaar.

We happened to be in the Grand Bazaar at teatime! I was delighted to be able to step back and watch the afternoon tea service being delivered to the little shops. A young boy, perhaps ten or twelve years old, carried a little metal tray hanging by three chains linked on a loop at the top. Several little cups made of glass, and a teapot, very tall and slim, maybe silver, rested in the middle of the tray. A small glass bowl of little balls of sugar perched on the tray, next to the cups. The boy would dart into a store, and silently approach the shopkeeper. The merchant would give him a coin and he would quickly pour the strong Turkish tea into a glass cup, drop in one or two sugar cubes, and scurry away at high speed to the next shop. It was like watching a hummingbird. Obviously, the boy was paid by speed, and he was very efficient. The shopkeepers sipped their afternoon snack, a tradition going back many centuries. I like seeing culture in action!

I bought some spices, some candy, the longed-for Turkish Delight in fabulous flowery flavors, and an embroidered scarf at the Grand Bazaar. I didn't bother haggling over the candy or spices---I'm not sure where my talents lie, but clearly it's not there. I did, however, hesitate over the scarf. Nothing had a price tag, and our guide said everything was negotiable, before he let us loose in the Bazaar. €35 seemed fair for the quality of the gorgeous hand- embroidered scarf, but it was still more than I felt good about spending on a silk scarf. As I moved away, the seller followed me, and the price dropped. I hesitated again, and now the price went down to €25. I bought it when he reached €20, without me saying a word. That kind of haggling, I can do!

Merchants were in-your-face aggressive. One followed Husband for *three blocks,* not accepting his emphatic "no." They politely tried to engage a conversation; *where are you from? oh, my nephew visited there! Come this way to see my beautiful rings, much finer than the other seller's, such a good price I will make for you...*

Outside the Bazaar was just as crazy, only the sellers displayed their wares on their arms, or in shopping bags. Unencumbered by geographic stores, they were free to follow potential shoppers. Toys, tops, puppets, pottery, pewter, pashmina, perfume, flowers, hair decorations, dolls, and of course headscarves and wraps. Some were very willing to make a great deal for all they had. Why on earth would I, or anyone, need 47 matching plastic toy tops?

Todd is a mild, laid-back, quiet man. I watched as he was offered knockoff perfume out of a shopping bag on a vendor's arm. One bottle for €10. Todd declined. "No. My wife doesn't like perfume." The vendor persisted, "for your girlfriend, perhaps. I make a good deal for you." As I watched, the price went to three bottles for €20, and then *five* bottles for €20. Todd kept declining, walking away, and the seller was right at his elbow. I got distracted by someone trying to sell me woven dried flowers for my hair.

When the group met back at the van a little while later, Todd sheepishly displayed a heaping shopping bag full of boxes of perfume! Bought all 38 bottles for €20. We had a good laugh. My own bargain-hunting was less impressive. A man displayed beautiful filmy pashminas on his arm, a weakness of mine, for €30 each. They were very pretty, like nothing I'd ever seen before, but I walked away. He followed. I declined. He offered two for the price of one. I shook my head. He took my arm. I hesitated – – and by the time I broke free, I had purchased three of the beautiful pashmina's for €13 total. It's really an insane system. Guess it works for them, though; they have been in using it for centuries!

Today has been exhausting. Istanbul is very interesting, very vibrant city. I'm glad I could visit, but I have no desire to return. As I sat on a bench, people watching and waiting for the group to gather, I leaned back to get one more picture of an ornate tomb of a Sultan. A light flashed on my camera. A message on the screen said Battery Exhausted. Yes, so are we all! Good thing we had two cameras with us.

Wrap Up The Day

The ship's main show tonight was the magicians again. They are fabulous, well worth seeing. Plus, it felt very good to sit, after so much walking today! The ship felt like a haven, a safe place to relax and let my guard down. I hadn't realized I was holding myself tightly, until I relaxed on the gangway.

Tomorrow is Mykonos, Greece. I liked Athens. I felt safe there. I'm happy to be going back to Greece! We don't arrive until 1 PM, so we can have a lazy morning. Our group has no tours booked; we plan to all be on our own in this port, with no plans to meet up at all. Our room steward had put VIP priority tender tickets on our bed, along with a plate of hand-dipped chocolates, which did not last long. We also had a note from the hotel director thanking us for an enjoyable evening last night. Next to the tickets was a note from Ryan, the concierge, advising us to disregard the VIP tender tickets. We were to simply meet him at the Cagney steakhouse whenever we wish to disembark, once the ship had been cleared. Oh, another VIP perk!

Husband and I would like to sleep in tomorrow, rest up, have a nice breakfast and lunch in the peaceful VIP venue, then go ashore and wander the town. I'm looking forward to it—a Greek isle! I also would like to find Wi-Fi or an Internet café to email our kids. Being out of touch is unnerving, and this is the halfway point in the cruise. We've been away from home a long time already. With only one sea day on this 12 day itinerary, I'm grateful for a quieter day ahead!

Day Six: Mykonos, Greece

Late start to the day; we arrived Mykonos at 1pm. It was rather nice to have a leisurely morning, starting with an elegant breakfast, including prosciutto, croissants, cream cheese roses, heaps of berries, all in the quiet elegance of the steakhouse. Yes, I could get used to this!

We ran into our friends a few times. Four of us played shuffleboard in the sunshine, and took in a Trivia game. We attended a cake decorating competition in the Galaxy of the Stars at 10:30 this morning. My ribs hurt from laughing! The Captain, the hotel director, the head pastry chef, and the cruise director competed for the title of Top Cake Maker. They assembled Black Forest cakes on the dance floor. By the end of it, the hotel director, Armando, had added so much alcohol to his that it was *leaking!* Cakes are not supposed to leak. Gio, the cruise director, and the pastry chef made beautiful cakes, worthy of display in any bakery. The other two... not so much. It was hilarious and a fun way to spend an hour. I enjoyed the Captain taking part; nothing stuffy or formal about this Master, although he obviously runs the ship with authority. He was approachable the whole cruise.

There was a Greek barbecue on the pool deck with live music. The food was not terribly authentic, or very good, for that matter, but it was fun to sit out on the sunshine on deck. I'm enjoying all the live music around the ship. It really has added to the fun of it!

I'm happy to be here today! There's plenty of time to relax. I even slept in past 6am; first time all week! Mykonos is known for beauty. I'm delighted with how wonderful this cruise is been so far. America such a young country and we just don't have any place really old. This awe-inspiring global perspective has been startling a few times, but I like it. I can feel my mind expanding. That is always healthy!

For example, I've always been taught, all through school, that the Crusaders were Good Guys who spread Christianity across Europe and Asia. Yazin, our Turkish guide yesterday, called the Crusaders "marauding conquerors, invaders who destroyed the culture and the religion, wrecking ancient art and precious idols as they invaded city after city, killing generations as they went." Definitely Bad Guys! When I get home I'll have to do some more reading on history, because the tour guides told us way more than I could absorb. It's a fascinating part of the world!

We will arrive in Mykonos in three hours. Mykonos is the name of the island; the town we are going to is called Chora, which means "village," roughly. I'm really looking forward to this port. We will be there from 1 o'clock until 9 PM. Plenty of time to explore a very small town and to leisurely soak up the vibe of a Greek island. Passengers will have to tender to the shore, in small boats today.

Tender Tickets

I am currently sitting in a small alcove on deck eight, midships, obviously writing. There are only four chairs here, tucked back in by the floor-to-ceiling glass windows overlooking the Mediterranean Sea. The sunlight is glittering on the ocean, which is about as smooth as any puddle I have ever seen, with no ships or land in sight. It's gorgeous! It should be very relaxing, but actually, I'm expecting bloodshed and mutiny at any minute.

Across the deck I see a very long line ---I cannot see the end of it-- of passengers waiting to get tender tickets. It was announced that people needed to be here at 10 o'clock to pick up tickets for their group and then they would be called, by number, and allowed to go on shore by tender. At the first announcement, at 8am, Clint called our cabin, offering to pick up tender tickets for us as well, as long as he was going to be standing in line.

It was awfully nice of him, but instead my Husband mumbled something vague and promised to call him right back. He promptly called the concierge. We didn't want to burden Ryan with our large group, or take advantage of our VIP status, but would two more make a difference? Ryan readily agreed to extend VIP tender privileges to Clint and Mary too. We are trying not to take advantage of Ryan's ability to pull strings, and certainly not bragging about our still-surprising VIP status, but I gotta admit, VIP-ism does come in handy!

The passengers waiting in line over there are getting louder, as the line is growing longer and more heated. I see four very harried crew members trying to maintain order. Now others are shouting because they ignored the repeated announcements and did not know they needed to get tender tickets. Handing them out doesn't even begin for another seven minutes. I hope they don't come to blows. My, this warm sunshine feels good on my shoulders.

Tendering

As arranged, Clint and Mary met us, and we went to meet Ryan, our concierge, at the steakhouse. We had not told them what we were doing; just 'don't get tender tickets, and meet us to get off the ship at 12:45 PM.' Ryan was waiting for us. Clint and Mary were clearly surprised to be meeting the concierge, but they greeted him politely. The four of us followed Ryan down the stairwell to deck four, past hundreds of angry passengers waiting in the tender line.

I felt kind of guilty hurrying past them all. Passengers were shouting, crew members were trying to organize the line of passengers into some sort of order, and several times crewmembers tried to push us back into line. Clint quickly learned the code phrase. He shouted at every crew member we passed, "we are with Ryan!" and they quickly cleared the way for us. At one point the hotel director barked, "Ryan! Get your people off the ship *now!* They must not be exposed to this crowd!" Who did they think we were? I tell you, I could get spoiled.

We settled into the very first tender. I think it was a local fishing boat; that's what it smelled like, anyway. As the boat pulled away from the ship, Clint eyed Husband suspiciously. "Ahem. Anything you want to tell me? What that was all about?" The Cruise Addict mumbled something about VIP status and Clint nodded wisely. "Oh, yeah, right, you just wait until the guys at work here about this." Husband sighed heavily, knowing he was in for some serious ribbing at work. Once we reached the shore, Clint and Mary took off on their own.

I love Mykonos! It's a dry island, very brown, with amazingly blue water and white stucco homes with blue or red trim, as if they were part of a postcard. All the buildings looked very straight to me, with no gables or sloping roofs, just various sizes of bright white boxes. All of the steppingstones on the walkways have wide white bands painted over the borders. The effect is just beautiful!

Husband and I decided to hike up to the old windmills, grist mills that have been in constant use for over 400 years. Partway up, we decided it was too far, too hot, too steep, and any way we are on vacation, so why should we strain ourselves? We started to head back, towards the town. I sighed. The part where the tender had docked was very touristy and I hoped to avoid that whole atmosphere.

A Greek Philosopher

As we made our way down the hill, I was glad to find an old man with a sort of a French-made tuk-tuk, like a miniature pickup truck, who offered to give us a ride. It had a rough plank laid behind the driver to sit on across the open truck bed. In American society, we are ruled by safely, with endless laws and rules protecting us, often from ourselves. We've noticed the difference since we left home – few hand rails, endless stairs, restrooms up or down stairs, apparently optional traffic laws, meats and cooked eggs and cheese displayed in restaurants in the heat of the day, unrefrigerated, on and on.

This vehicle would in no way pass US safety laws! Where were the seatbelts, not to mention, seats? It was tiny! The very idea of sitting on a loose board in an open vehicle was not safe at all! We hired him on the spot. "Show us your island, please, and then take us to a nice beach."

The driver had us sit in a way that would balance the little vehicle; he muttered something about tipping over on corners. The Cruise Addict sat opposite the driver, and I sat behind him. The man drove like a roller coaster over dusty narrow roads with blind corners, up and up. The hairpin turns were so severe that several employed mirrors! Husband and I braced ourselves. We finally stopped at a pretty overlook. The driver motioned us to come sit beside him on a wall overlooking the harbor. The bright blue water and the white buildings below were just beautiful.

Our driver turned into a real-life Greek philosopher for fully ten minutes, there in the sunshine! He talked about Greece's corrupt government, the graft. He said that when the stock market was devalued, he "lost over €300,000 overnight. No one cares." The country's infrastructure was collapsing. There is no medical care; even the unemployed must play stiff taxes. We had heard a similar story in Athens. He said three elderly people commit suicide a day in this lovely town all due to the corrupt government. "They get a diagnosis and there is no medical care, and so rather than slowly dying, they opt to die quickly. " and again, the resigned shoulder shrug: "What else can they do?"

The man asked if we had noticed how dry the island is. He said the ground was cursed; the rain didn't fall anymore, because of the unethical government leaders. The cisterns are dry and the celebrities and politicians bought up land that was owned for generations by the same families. He told stories of good, ordinary people who live there, who were suffering.

He said, "There will be a judgment. When you do good, good things happen. When you live an evil life and think of no one but yourselves, that will get you. *God* will get you, in due time." It was sad, but very interesting to hear from a local perspective. The man pointed out a knee-high rock wall built by 'a guy with too much money.' It was built in the Roman style, to mimic the old walls, and it wound all over upper Mykonos. What must that have cost? The old man told us that there were 6100 legal residents on Mykonos, "not including those with the funny papers they bought," and 600 churches. We flew past several little neighborhood ones on the wild ride uphill. He said sorrowfully, "Greece is very religious, but very corrupt."

He said in his younger days, he was a physical trainer and had always dreamed of going to America, "to seek the fortune that I know waits for me." Now he was too old; we could hear the longing in his voice. He said everyone on Mykonos had a relative who had emigrated, either to America or to Great Britain, to escape the corruption.

Then he asked us our opinion of President Obama, and do we think that Hillary Clinton will run for president, and what was up with JLo anyway? Did we think the stock market could hold its recent gains? Would the immigration bill before Congress pass? Was it possible for Tom Cruise to make a comeback movie? So far from America, it was startling to meet someone so informed about *our* country! It was a very interesting break, sitting on an ancient-looking stone wall, built only four years ago, conversing with a Greek philosopher, overlooking the beautiful harbor.

Back onto the truck, the man drove us to one of the ancient windmills we had sought earlier. The view from there was beautiful! Our driver suggested Saint Stefano beach, "where guests never go, yet it is within sight of your ship. It is the best on the island." Oh, yes! We waded in the warm Mediterranean, too lazy to even change into swimwear. This island lacks any sense of urgency, and it didn't take long for us to catch the laid-back spirit!

Still thinking about our young adult kids, we sipped milkshakes at a restaurant open to the beach, and connected to their Wi-Fi. We checked our email. All's well; the new grandbaby was getting fatter, the granddaughter took another award at school, the new was job going well, all were healthy. We tried emailing back, but the auto correct on my tablet fought back. Reading back over my email, I read "We are in Ammonia, Greece! We ate gyroscopes for lunch, and the Greek porpoises are very friendly. Several railings helped us find the orange velour giraffe feet that that I wanted. I am awestruck by all the ancient marble sandwiches, clothesline in the elements for centuries. We are having a great troop!" They may need to use a magic decoder ring to read it, but at least they get the general idea that we are alive. Goal met!

The same driver returned when we asked him to, and drove us down back in the town center, saving us a long, hot walk. We paid him, thanked him, shook hands, and wished him well. Time to resume wandering! But first, a snack. Husband was happy to find a bakery right there. He ate some flaky cherry pastry that he liked so well, he insisted we go back later to get another piece of it before returning to the ship.

Where Pirates Walked

Thus fortified, we walked around the town, past the crowds of sightseers, past the vehicle zones, up into the area called Little Venice, the residences, away from the tourist areas. I got some great photographs! The streets were purposely laid out in a confusing manner to discourage long ago pirates from going into the city, then escaping freely. At least, slow them down on their way out of town. The streets are narrow and twisty, all with those beautiful white-outlined stepping stones. I think, from above, the streets of Mykonos might look like a tangle. They felt pretty tangled at ground level, for sure! I don't have a sense of direction to speak of, but I knew that the breeze always blows out to sea here. I also knew that the ship was in the water, which was, by definition, at *sea* level, thus, downhill. So long as we headed more or less downhill, with the warm breeze at our backs, we'd get back. I loved it!

Husband, however, grew slightly anxious. The Cruise Addict thrives on order. He likes his routes to be nice and straight and predictable, preferably laid out in a grid. This apparent chaos, with its curving and twisting pathways, even when it was surrounded by beautiful shops and happy people, was making him decidedly edgy. The people were friendly and mild, and it wasn't big enough to get permanently lost. It was a charming place… He didn't think so. Perhaps a Quest would distract him.

The milkshakes we had earlier came with a little piece of candy. It was wonderful! It was a jelly, very flavorful and sweet, and I wanted more. I asked three different shop people about the candy. At last one of them said knowingly," oh, you want Moose Ticka! Turn right and then take two lefts." Husband was in no mood for a Quest, moose or not. Oh, lighten up, already; we are on vacation.

He grumbled when we came to the same tiny bank the fourth time. The first time was good; we used the ATM to restock our cash, but he saw no reason to repeat that task. We were not really *lost,* just a little disoriented. Well, I did have to ask two more shopkeepers after we got… not exactly lost, just a little temporarily misplaced… but we eventually found a delightful little candy shop, complete with Moose Ticka. At least, that's what it sounded like. I bought some of the wonderful candies and some olive oil soap. The soap came with glass anti-evil eyes. You never know when you might need one of those, after all. Oh, and as we walked, a couple more lovely scarves befell me as well. Did I mention I like scarves? I was really happy wandering in Mykonos.

But Husband was decidedly uneasy. I thought perhaps if we found some dinner, he might feel better. As we reached the busier part of town, where the walkways were wider, we passed a lot of expensive, very busy restaurants right on the shore. Figuring those were there for people who don't explore very much, we made our way to a little hole in the wall place back on the narrower streets, away from the crowds. It had outdoor seating, spicy gyro meat rotating in the window, and a waiter who was incredibly friendly, language barrier and all. I think that was the best food I've had so far on this trip! I had dolmas, grape leaves stuffed with lemony rice, and a pork skewer dripping with a tangy herb marinade. Husband had another gyro and decided that, indeed, we prefer the Americanized ones, without french fries inside. At least his mood brightened.

Wrap Up the Day

I loved Mykonos. It might be my favorite port so far. It was quite an experience getting there. The tender line I wrote about earlier literally did come to blows. Security had to be called to calm the passengers, yelling and shouting. It was pretty bad! People had already begun lining up for the tenders, too, long before the ship even arrived at Hora Harbor. Our friends later reported that the first passengers got off at 1:30pm; some were unable to get off until 3:15! Surely there must be a more efficient way. Once again I'm grateful for our VIP status. I know we will likely never see it again on other cruises, but I'm soaking it up now!

We finally took a tender back to the ship, and ran into four of our group on the boat ride. They said that they'd spend *over two and half hours* in the tender line with a lot of angry people on the ship! We were grateful to have avoided them! Making our way back to our cabin, we kicked off our sandy shoes and enjoyed the waiting hors d'oeuvres; big juicy shrimp and salmon pate on little toast squares. Nice, to have a little bit of edible artwork! There was also a bottle of Chilean wine and another invitation to go to any specialty restaurant, for free. Daily unexpected treats are fun!

The driver of our tuk-tuk earlier had explained to us that, yes, there was a lot of money here, but local people who had lived there for generations were suffering. He said that those people out there on the yachts, "The Wealthy Poor Ones," he called them, were hostages, prisoners of their own making. "They come all this way to be in the beautiful Greek Isles, but then they cannot get off their fancy yachts because of the paparazzi. They come up out of the woodwork and chase them with the cameras. To avoid that, they spend their vacations out there in the water in the harbor and never touch the Greek Isles at all."

The rising moon this evening over Mykonos was beautiful, enormous, showing details and texture, reflecting on the glassy sea... all in all, gorgeous. A big yacht in the harbor turned on underwater running lights as dusk fell. The glittery lights seemed to chase round and round the ship. Mykonos seems like a movie set. I thought of the poor pitiful celebrities, stranded out there in the harbor, missing the wonderful town itself. I am grateful for the freedom I have in anonymity!

Day Seven: Sea Day

I'm ready for a lazy day. We have seen nothing today but open ocean, calm as a pond. We did see one ship and a tiny sailboat, but no land. I'm surprised that there's no visible wildlife here in the Mediterranean, not even a bird. On other cruises, I've always seen something; leaping salmon, flying fish, whales, porpoises on cruises. This water here seems oddly empty.

The most ambitious things I did today was a behind-the-scenes tour, which I detailed earlier, and a Q&A with the senior staff in the Galaxy lounge. The captain told interesting stories! He was *four* years old when his father gave him his first boat; they were a sea-going family. The deal was, he could not even touch the shiny little sailboat until he could swim to his parents' satisfaction. The captain smiled, "never was a child again so motivated." The childhood imprinting worked; he was at sea full time at age 15, and worked his way up to Master of the vessel. Apparently there had been some sort of dust-up on the ship; he was called back halfway through his 90 day vacation to take the helm of this ship just before this cruise began.

We have lounged about the ship, enjoyed conversation and laughter on deck with our friends, played shuffleboard, cards, and ping pong, and we won another game of Trivia. Checking the big wall map by Guest Services, we estimated the ship would pass through the Straits of Messina around dinner time.

Cade reported that Todd was a little better today; we didn't see him until late afternoon. Todd received word late last night that his dearest friend of almost forty-five years had died. We all knew Ron, but not as well as Tom. The funeral will likely be over before we reach home again. Even mailing a card won't help; Todd himself will be home before it arrives. Email seems inadequate. Last night, Todd was so sad he barely spoke, but today he laughed a little as he told stories of the adventures he and his buddy had had over the years. He's obviously begun healing and I'm grateful to see it.

Today we found chocolate covered strawberries from the hotel director, plus a plate of intricate little pastries in our cabin from the events coordinator. Is all this just because Husband organized the Meet and Greet? Has someone found out that I'm writing this book? I do spread out on the wide open cabin floor when I write, but I am good about picking up all the loose papers when I leave the cabin.

NCL is going above and beyond to give us a positive experience! Several times a day, we run into senior staff members, who invariably stop to greet us by name and a chat a little. If we needed to complain, we certainly have had the opportunity to do so. But really, this cruise has been rather superior. Except for the stampede-a-comin' atmosphere of the buffet, one bumpy dinner, and the chaos of tendering at Mykonos – which we avoided – it's really been very positive.

All twelve of us had dinner together again in the Windows dining room. Suddenly, as we ate our appetizers in the main dining room, we saw a helicopter! It was startling, after not seeing any signs of life off the ship all day. The helicopters had search lights shooting down, low, right outside the back windows. The main dining room on the Spirit is in the very aft of the ship. We continued eating, figuring someone was in charge and it wasn't us. We noticed all the wait staff was making their way to the window to see what was happening; clearly, this was not a typical occurrence!

The Captain announced that it had come to medically evacuate a passenger who had appendicitis and "there would be a delay in transfer, so please enjoy your meal, and ignore the helicopter."

It was hard to eat with the bleating of the rotors so loud and close. It hovered a good forty minutes, just hanging there. Abruptly, out of the darkness, a small ship with red flashing lights approached the Spirit, out of nowhere.

The Captain updated us: the planned transfer to the helicopter could not be made, after numerous attempts, and the patient's condition had deteriorated. He suggested passengers pray, which I found startling, but always a good idea! After the helicopter had flown all the way from Rome, at great expense, to rescue the passenger, they had to abort the attempt. The passenger would be transferred to the boat that had come from Messina, and to the helicopter once they reached land. I guess transferring on land to the helicopter would have been safer than jostling a sick patient in a rescue basket, but neither option sounded good! I felt sorry for the poor passenger. To lose an appendix far from home in a foreign country is bad enough. Being that much pain and unable to be even be evacuated; to transfer to a boat, then a helicopter, while dealing with appendicitis, is just a terrible way to end a vacation.

The show tonight was very good. It was 'World Beat' put on by the Spirit Production Cast. We enjoyed the dancers a lot. They professionally performed dances from all around the world, including a hand dance from Greece that was so fast, they were blurry! Extremely well done!

Naples, Italy tomorrow! Pompeii! Herculaneum! Mount Vesuvius! I have heard of these places all my life, but are they really real? The cruise director, Gio, said that Naples is the most densely populated city in Europe. He warned about crossing the streets, and the traffic that comes from every direction, up, down, and from every side. Could it be any worse than Istanbul? We have a tour booked with Todd and Julie, Sarah and Cue, plus Debra, whom we met back at our hotel in Venice.

Day Eight: Naples, Italy

Today began bright and early; Husband and I were up in plenty of time. Alas, I was so interested in watching the ship pull into the harbor that time got away from me. We were to meet our group in just half an hour, so no time for a leisurely sit-down VIP breakfast today. Off to the buffet. Oh-! The place was mobbed, and noisy, and there were more people looking for tables than places available to sit. Dishes and cutlery crashed, voices were raised over the din... what a start to a day!

The buffet had a nice selection, obviously trying to provide enough variety for the different nationalities onboard. I shied away from the fish soup, and baked beans. I dislike most breakfast foods; at home, my first meal of the day is usually lunch, and not until I've been awake several hours. Long day ahead, though, and I figured I'd better not tackle a new place on an empty stomach.

I quickly picked up fruit and cereal, while Husband headed for the omelet station. He loves breakfast foods, the greasier the better. I heard my name being called. Brett was just leaving, so we took his table. The food was good, but the atmosphere was draining; so much noise and commotion! Maybe tomorrow I'll make it to the VIP breakfast instead. There's something awfully nice about cream cheese flowers, prosciutto, big fresh berries, and Lobster Benedict served in a genteel quiet atmosphere first thing in the morning!

To the Tour

We had booked a tour with AP Tour Company and it was a delightful day. Our tour began at 8:30am, and ended at 4:45pm. In between, my senses were on overload. I saw things I could only imagine. This may be my favorite port so far. Our tour began with the drive out to Pompeii, again hoping to get an early start before all of the tour buses arrived. The laws governing tour guides are different in Italy and Greece, than in Turkey. In Turkey, our guides were with us all day long, by our sides in both Kusadasi and Istanbul. In both Greece and Italy, they can be either a driver or a guide, but not both. We could have opted to hire a driver and a guide separately, but we decided to just go with the driver. The tour company assured us that the drivers were knowledgeable and would keep us informed as we drove. We decided to chance it. It ended up being a very good decision! Vincente had a university degree in both economics and history, and he made a very interesting day for us, keeping us informed as he drove.

Just seven on our private tour today. The others in our bunch opted to take a public train to Pompeii and back. We had debated about that choice at home, but decided we'd be happier seeing all we could fit into a day, without worrying about sorting out local train schedules in a foreign language. Our tour driver, Vincente, met us promptly, and I liked him right away. He informed us "Today I will show you my home! this is *Napoli!* Naples is in Florida." He explained that Napoli means 'new city.'

The first thing we noticed was the castles, three of them, centuries-old, right at the port. Obviously, this area has been fought over by multiple people, multiple times. The second thing I noticed was the driving. Gio was right! Traffic in Naples was dare-devil scary.

Naples is the third largest city in Italy and is the most densely populated city in Europe. It seemed like most of those people wanted to be the same roundabout at the same time, and "take your turn" was a foreign concept. Horns blaring, mere inches between vehicles, drivers shouting, motorcycles and pedestrians darting in and out, up and over sidewalks – it's a wonder there were not more accidents! I paid attention, and was surprised that most vehicles looked quite intact. With that driving, I would have expected more scraped paint, dents, broken mirrors, etc.

Later on, midday, when we were in the very center of downtown Naples, Husband asked why all the traffic light signals were dark. Vincent shrugged, "They are off in an eight block area. The government turned them off. It does not matter. No one used them anyway." He may have been joking. I'm not sure. Every intersection seems to be a game of Bluff. The bravest vehicle gets across, while the more timid retreat and try again.

Our driver took it all in stride. He called the motor scooters "mosquitos with helmets." They were everywhere, zipping in and out of places I didn't think they'd even fit, around moving vehicles, blind corners, even up on sidewalks, dodging pedestrians and parked cars. As they darted between and around vehicles, the motor scooters would clump together at intersections, and try to cross en mass, making themselves seem larger by forming a group. Once they made it across, they'd disperse like insects, until the next intersection, where they'd repeat the process. All without any visible communication! I asked if helmets were required, since I saw very few. Surely, if they were needed anywhere, it was *here*. Our driver calmly replied, "Oh, yes, they are mandated by the law, and the fine for not wearing a helmet is very high. But we are Napolis...we take the risk. It is not easy for the policia to catch the scooters." That, I could believe.

At one point, our van was blocked by a delivery truck parked in the middle of the lane on a narrow street. Our driver patiently waited all of about four seconds, then verbally cast aspersions on the other driver's parentage. I didn't need to understand Italian to understand that. He zipped up onto the sidewalk, for TWO blocks, dropping the van over the curb, back onto the street only when a large pole blocked his path. At my gasp, he grinned. "Surely, you must do this in America, as well!" No...not usually...

I've heard of Pompeii my entire life. To think about actually seeing the place sounded about as realistic as standing on Mars, yet the day had finally come! Vincente could not enter with us; we agreed to meet back in a few hours.

Pompeii

Pompeii was a major and thriving metropolis, utterly destroyed in the course of an afternoon, although they had had warning signs that Vesuvius was waking up for a week or so ahead of time. It's the cost one pays for living in the shadow of a volcano. Our own home is located between Mount Baker and Mount Saint Helens, both active volcanoes. Do other places have annual How To Survive A Volcanic Eruption inserts in the local newspapers? Pompeii was destroyed in 79 AD; our hometown is calm, so far, except for the occasional volcanic burp. We try not to think about it.

Pompeii is a huge place and we knew we could not see it all. Debra chose to rent an audio guide while the rest of us decided to just walk around on our own. As we were in line to purchase our tickets to enter Pompeii, I overheard a man behind us talking to another couple. He was offering to be their guide. He assured them that he would show them all the highlights and that they would get a good overview of Pompeii for only €10, for a three-hour tour.

I have read that hiring a guide on site could be hit or miss. Some were just wonderful, and some were not worth the time. This man made a very good first impression. He wasn't even speaking to me, and already I liked him! The six of us made our way over to him, and promptly filled out his group. There were only eight of us.

Another good decision! Genaldo was great! He was animated and he really brought it to life, telling us all sorts of facts I know we would've missed. He was well worth the €10 we paid. Well, actually, Todd paid – – he's been extremely grateful for the tours we've arranged, and was quite certain this had been preplanned!

We had to walk up a rather steep cobblestone tunnel to get up to Pompeii proper. We were concerned about Julie and her new knee making it up the incline, but once we cleared that obstacle, Pompeii was fairly level. Walking through Pompeii was completely overwhelming to me. Again, that inner voice gasping, "I can't believe I'm really here!" over and over.

One day Pompeii was a thriving city; the next, it was buried under 70 feet of volcanic ash, completely destroyed. Yet, here we were having the opportunity to walk right through it 1935 years later! Once the excavation began, the archaeologists found it just as the people had left it, with dishes on tables, wine residue in the casks, even bread in the ovens in the public bakeries – and people encased in the pyroclastic substance from the volcano, right where they fell. Life stopped that very day as a volcano rained flaming hell from above.

We saw the famous plaster casts; people caught in death, stopped literally where they fell. We could plainly see their expressions, their togas, their belts, even a cloth held to a man's face to block the falling ash; all caught in the moment, imprinted. The early archaeologists found that the bodies of people who had died in the blast were encased in the pyroclastic flow, a shell cast of the humans long gone. They pumped the cavities where the bodies had decayed full of plaster. Once hardened, the ash and rock was swept from the outside, and there was left a detailed plaster imprint.

One plaster cast that used to be a dog was left chained, writhing as it fell and died, contorted hideously. Genaldo, our guide, said sadly, "the dog died twice; sensing the volcano was coming, and then chained by its heartless master as he fled." Our guide pointed out the plaster cast of a young woman, a slave woman. She was pregnant when she died; she fell clutching her belly below the wide belt that slaves wore. It was truly moving.

The wooden roofs in Pompeii had all burned in the volcano, but stone, marble, mosaics, tiles, and even the water pipes in the streets all endured. Once excavated, they lay as if they had been walked away from, as if the residents were soon to return. I was awed by the beautiful mosaic floors made of squares no bigger than a quarter of an inch! Even after so many centuries, the colors remained. Pompeii was pretty barren, but as we walked, Genaldo brought to life with stories, pointing out details we would have missed on our own. It was amazing.

Pompeii was remarkably advanced. One thing caught my eye; a small thing, but important. Reflectors on the streets, much like our modern road turtles! Squares of white marble embedded every few feet that could be used for navigation after dark, either by lantern or by the light of the moon. Genaldo described how the streets were laid out on a grid pattern, a design begun in ancient Roman cities. It's still common today. In fact, it is the same layout that modern cities such as New York and

Washington DC still employ. Pompeii is said to be the best-preserved example of this style.

We stood in ancient shops, storerooms, even restaurants with part of the painted menu still visible on the wall. Throughout the city, I felt a sense of awe, along with strong impressions of the people who had called this place home. Quite a lot of the city was preserved. Putting it all back together; now that was a challenge. The pieces were all there, but just crushed from 70 feet of ash from Mount Vesuvius. Archaeologists have to be very patient people!

Not all of Pompeii has been found or excavated. After two hundred years of digging, it is now estimated that approximately only 15% has been found. In fact, a house was built outside of the site for the archaeological workers, but they realized, once they began to excavate, that Pompeii goes back much further. In time, that house must be torn down to excavate under that area.

Ancient Toilets

When Pompeii was alive, a popular gathering place for sharing news, gossip, and other information was the public toilets. And I do mean *public*. Most houses had no indoor plumbing; only the upper-crust ones. There were forty seats, close enough to be almost thigh-to-thigh. The public facilities had water running constantly underneath to whisk away deposits. I guess the sound of trickling water could also speed up the process. Didn't you run the bathroom sink to encourage your toddler to Go?

The toilets were open air, covered by a wooden roof, with a pretty courtyard between the seats and the busy main street just a few feet away. The seating area had walls on two sides, quite open to breezes. Personally I could find a lot more interesting places to share information in than in a public toilet. There was a lovely public fountain in Pompeii, many shops and streets and trees under which gossip and news could've been shared, while keeping one's private behavior... well, private. My modern sensibilities cringed at the thought of doing my business almost on a busy public street!

I guess another awful job description would be Bum-Wiper Dispenser, or whatever the ancient title was called. Here's where things divided, economically speaking. While slaves, workers, and wealthy merchants, as well as ordinary townspeople of both genders, used the toilets, the...ahh... *after process* varied by socioeconomic status.

The wealthy ones were offered a sponge tied on a stick, which had been dipped in the trough to wipe their tukus. I shudder to think of how often those sponges were cleaned...they should have been discarded, in my opinion! No; they were rinsed off in that same channel by the attendants, and set aside for the next use. Poorer folks were offered a handful of leaves, since bathroom tissue had yet to be invented. Personally, I'd take the nice fresh leaves over a drippy used sponge! I'm not sure how the attendant determined rich and poor; perhaps then, like now, silver denarius was handed over upon approaching the public place.

I guess this was a better option than other contemporary towns; those that did not have a trough of running water dipped the sponge on a stick in vinegar! In drier climates or seasons of the year, when water was more precious, three small stones called pessoi were used instead of leaves or sponges. The tradition started with the ancient Greeks that three stones should be enough to finish the job; this policy was important enough to record for posterity.

Pompeii was blessed with abundant water, and used it freely. The streets were flooded daily to keep them clean. To prevent wading, the streets had big stones at the intersections for pedestrians to cross over. One or two stones for narrow streets, four at the widest crossing. Rather ingenious, I thought. The stones were spaced close enough for pedestrians to step over them easily, but far enough for chariots or cart wheels to pass through. Alongside the roads, the sidewalks were elevated to keep people dry during heavy rains, and also as the water ran down the streets. The marble streets had deep ruts from chariots' metal wheels. Chariots-- *real* Roman chariots!!

As we stopped to rest from the hot sun beating down, Genaldo asked our opinion of legalized prostitution. His view was that it was a good thing, "but the Church people have no sense." In a country of 90+% Catholics, just down the road from the Vatican, it seemed a lost cause to me. Nevertheless, it was something I had not given a lot of thought to... pensions for prostitutes? More expansion of the mind, never a bad thing.

Our guide demonstrated the acoustics in the amphitheatre. He had a voice so good that other tourists, at the far end of the amphitheatre, stopped to applaud! 2800 years ago people gathered to listen, to see and be seen, in that very theatre. The bottoms of ancient people sat on that very seat that I occupied. It was astounding to be there.

We saw the archaeologists' storage places; quiet now because it's Tourist Season here as well. Rows of ancient wine vessels, pointy at the bottoms to trap the sediment, crates of artwork, neat piles of marble slabs, and rows of clay roof tiles in such good condition, they could be sold to use today. The flasks were found with wine residue in them! Much of Pompeii's art was removed; some of it was looted, some shipped off to England. We saw a lot of it later in the day when we went to the Archaeological Museum in Naples. Pompeii was excavated before Italy was united, and the head of the Naples state put out orders when excavation began, to bring him the most beautiful artwork from Pompeii. When the government shifted---they always do---his treasures were put on public display.

After three hours of walking and hearing stories, we had covered a good bit of Pompeii. I was glad we had stumbled upon Genaldo! Eavesdropping is not always a bad thing. Although I would have been happy to stay much longer, it was time to rejoin our tour guide, waiting outside.

Husband, Tom, Sarah, and Cue were enthused about climbing Mount Vesuvius to see the caldera and the scenery below, and that was advertised as part of our day's tour. Julie and I decided months before that we would evaluate that day how much walking we felt like doing at the time. I'm secure enough to not need to kill myself, just for the bragging rights. Mount Vesuvius had a big cloud on top of it early in the morning, and so we went to Pompeii, first, hoping that the cloud cover would burn off. We checked again after our hours in Pompeii, and it was still socked in. The mountain is seven miles away and plainly visible all day! That thing is huge. There's no benefit to climbing to the top of the mountain to see the inside of a cloud. We are from Seattle. We can do that at home. Off we went on to Herculaneum, planning to check the volcano again later on.

Herculaneum

I was startled when I saw Herculaneum for the first time. It's an obviously ancient city, gob smack dab in the middle of the modern city! Blocky apartment buildings with laundry flapping out their windows, perched on the very edge of Herculaneum, which sits in a deep pit. Startling contrast! It was apparent that the modern buildings were constructed before the ancient ruins were found, and equally obvious that the ancient city extends much farther than excavated parts. Imagine living on top of 2800-year-old ruins!

Our guide shrugged, and said it's very common. Just last month, Vincente explained, where a new train station construction began down by the port an ancient Roman cemetery was uncovered, along with two beautifully preserved boats, over 1500 years old. Roman coins are very common and can be found almost anywhere one digs deep enough; last week a big cache of gold coins was found, buried by some gladiator who never made it back to reclaim them. They had not been valued yet, but Vincente's eyes were round as he told about the find. Just months before our visit, the most emotional part of our entire trip was uncovered. I'll tell about that in a bit.

I was interested in the archaeologists' work, as Herculaneum is also an active archaeological dig. Herculaneum was destroyed by Mount Vesuvius at the same time as Pompeii, but it was different. Herculaneum was buried under ash, not the pyroclastic flow that took out Pompeii. This caused the damage to be very different. The searing heat preserved things like thick wooden beams and houses, which are still there and still visible, but they were instantly turned into carbon-based charcoal by the volcano. Public bakery, public baths, gymnasium, pillars, columns, roads, frescoes on walls, statures – the degree of preservation here was astonishing! Pompeii was much more barren; Herculaneum was not as stripped. I walked the streets. I stepped into buildings. I ran my hand over ancient carved stones. I could feel the stories in the history under my hand.

Again Vincente could not enter the site, and we decided to wander on our own this time. We explored for well over two hours, marveling over the baths, the art, the architecture. Husband made his way down to look at the ancient swimming pool. I was tired by now from all the walking and I decided to wait at the top of a very steep walkway. I was very content to just sit there and absorb the feeling of Herculaneum. I watched Husband walk down a treacherous path and wander around the bottom, admiring a statue. He disappeared around the corner and then he came back into view, frantically motioning me to come down to where he was. I shook my head; no, I'm happy right here. He waved more urgently.

Oh, well. Very carefully, I made my way down, hanging onto the wobbly railing as I traversed the steep marble stones, thinking about how inconvenient a twisted ankle would be just now. I admired the statues, the mosaics in the flooring, and then Husband led me around the corner, turned me back to face the arch I had just walked over ---and tears flooded my eyes instantly.

A puzzling thing about Herculaneum is that there were no victims found as they were at Pompeii. Historians thought that all the residents had made it out, taken to the sea, or fled inland at the volcano's first rumblings. Suddenly, just a few feet in front of me, there was the answer.

Skeletons! Over three hundred, I read later, in groups, large groups, with two smaller groups a few paces from the others, tangled together as they died. They did not die alone. They died with family and neighbors, arms clearly around one another. These terrified people desperately tried to out run the fiery hell that rained down from the volcano, fleeing to the only place of safety they could find. The coastline was moved over a mile by the eruption of Vesuvius; this was no small event.

As we stood there, I could clearly envision these people, terrified residents of Herculaneum, fleeing to the river. When they realized that the boats would not get them far enough, or perhaps there were no boats, or maybe the water was on fire, they retreated, taking refuge in the arched brick boat houses right there on the docks. They huddled together with their arms around one another as their world ended 2800 years ago.

 Just a few months before our trip, the boat houses had been opened for the first time since the volcano erupted. The skeletons were plainly visible, crouched together, heaped as they lay, protected only by a low chain fence. They boat houses were so newly excavated, the skeletons had not yet been examined. To be able to see them so clearly, so near, to think of those panicked people so long ago, fleeing for their lives, really touched me. I won't soon forget them.

And again, I looked at it from an American viewpoint. In America, had such a find been found, the area would've been promptly blocked off from view. The skeletons would have been marked, counted, categorized, numbered, secured, gathered, labeled, and packed up in crates to be hauled away to the back recesses of some obscure museum, not where ordinary humans could see them. After study and reassembly, if people were ever to see them again, the bones would be displayed under glass, not left out in the elements. To have these authentic skeletons just a few feet from me was the most moving thing I saw on the whole trip

.

Pizza

Mount Vesuvius was still under cloud cover when we left Herculaneum, although the area we were in was bright and sunny. And *hot*—did I mention hot? Our group decided to have lunch, then reassess the weather. Pizza was invented in Naples, and so we asked Vincente to take us somewhere good. Oh, yes, it was! Authentic, local, and I think were the only non-Italians in the place.

We could see the brick oven in the back. At over 700° a pizza could be done in only three to five minutes. Flour, salt, water, and yeast are the only ingredients in a proper pizza crust. Hand tossing incorporates air to create the light, chewy texture. The most traditional and popular pizza is the Margarita, named after Princess Margaret. It has the colors of the Italian flag, red tomato, white mozzarella, and green basil. Husband opted for that one. Mine had fresh buffalo mozzarella and prosciutto-- oh Yum. If it's possible to overdose on prosciutto, I'm well on my way. It may have been the most delicious pizza I've ever had in my life. Vincente had abandoned us, once we were seated, promising to wait outside. In my limited Italian, combined with some pantomime, I tried to ask how big the pizzas were... should our group plan on sharing or get individual ones? The waiter assured us "one, one," but each pizza was the size of a turkey platter. I made a dent in mine.

Archaeological Museum

Mount Vesuvius was really being uncooperative today, and a light rain had begun to fall. Obviously, the climb was out. We decided to give it up and go to the Archaeological Museum, instead. It's small, dusty, far from a classy structure, but the treasures inside made the few dusty sneezes a trade-off. This is where much of the artwork from Pompeii was displayed, after it was stripped from the city. Pompeii was quite barren and this is why. This was not like sterile American museums – the artwork was right there for visitors to examine and admire. How could ripples of fabric, fringes, even hair, be carved of stone? There were busts, frescoes, statues, flasks, sculptures, paintings, and friezes. I couldn't take it all in, but I dearly loved trying.

Those sculptures were of actual Pompeii residents! Many wealthy residents of Pompeii commissioned a statue or bust or fresco of themselves. This art has endured, like formal portraits, family photos, a Who's Who of Pompeii. All had such lifelike detail, it seemed like they would speak.

There was a 3-D model of Pompeii on the wall at the Museum. We were surprised – we had walked for over three hours at Pompeii, and yet we only saw a small section of the city! Astonishing that so much has been excavated. I liked seeing both Pompeii and Herculaneum, and soaking in the differences. Pompeii was huge, and further along in recovery, but fairly barren. There was a rawness in Herculaneum. I saw partially dug up stairways and walls sticking up in the fields, and I'm certain that that rise over there holds many more treasures. And the skeletons~!

On the way back to the ship, we asked our guide to stop for gelato. We were hot and dusty, and this is the place, after all. He smiled, "I know a good place." Yes, he did. Again, I think our group was among the first Americans to stop here; no tourist trap, this! We all chose different flavors, and all insisted our choice was the best. I love being in authentic places and tasting local foods. I'm after the experience wherever we travel.

I cannot believe the things I'm seeing on this trip. How will I ever remember it all? People talk about life-changing trips. This is one for me. I'm never going to forget this; the giant grain mills at Pompeii's bakery, the skeletons, the stone walkways worn by over 2000 years of humans coming and going about their lives. Again, as on every day so far, we have been thrilled with the guide we chose and the tour we booked from home. Not bragging, mind you, but I am certain beyond any doubt that we are seeing more and experiencing more than other passengers on the same cruise.

Wrap Up the Day

Back to the ship; we were met on the pier with live music, icy washcloths, and frozen fruit skewers, just the thing after a warm and busy day! Our group split off at the elevators, agreeing the day had been delightful. Four of us ended up having a light dinner at the Blue Lagoon, still full from the fabulous pizza hours before. A burger for The Cruise Addict and some wonton soup for me made a good quick dinner. It felt good to *just sit*. I can't believe how much we have walked on this trip!

A messenger delivered a plate of artfully arranged cheeses and herbed baguettes to our cabin, compliments of the concierge. He's been great about finding us a couple of times a day, and inquiring what he might do to make our cruise more special. Tickets? Dinner reservations, spa appointments, anything? I guess we're pretty low maintenance, but I do like the attention!

Tomorrow we will visit Rome, and the Vatican. Husband is very anxious to be in Rome, certain it's going to be the highlight of the whole cruise for him. I'm not as excited as I should be. Part of it, I recognize, is my knowledge of history. I guess I know too much. Rome is of course, Catholic; the Vatican, even more so. Catholics' history has not been nice over the centuries. They were less overtly scary than some other religions, perhaps, but harsh and corrupt over the generations, with graft, oppression, slavery, killing anyone who disagreed – look at Galileo for instance, or Michelangelo. The pompous overdressed priests and popes put themselves way up above the people who supported them, while they were themselves know- it- all self-righteous evildoers. Just my opinion, of course.

I was raised Catholic, and as a child, I had many questions. Even at that advanced and modern age, say the 1960s and 70s, I was sharply told 'it's a mystery' or 'asking is a sin; if you need to know, the priest will tell you' when I had legitimate questions. I think that's why I raised my children to always question, to be curious and informed, to seek out answers for themselves, and use the resources all around them. Literacy was discouraged by the Catholic Church across the ages. That way, the priest and the popes and the bishops and cardinals could retain power over the little people. They lived like royalty while surrounded by poverty, and that makes me sick. I just don't have a good feeling about the Catholic Church, although certainly as an entity, not as individuals. We will go to Rome and to the Vatican. I will focus on the artwork and try not to let what I know about history get in my way. I may never be here again; I intend to enjoy the good parts!

Another reason I am not thrilled is a story that Sarah told. She and Cue and Kim came early and spent three days in Rome. Sarah said that they stood in a line six hours long to get into the Vatican Museum! She said there was no place to sit and the hygiene of the crowd left much to be desired. Actually, she said, it smelled like "an overcrowded seventh grade boys' locker room at the end of a day's worth of PE classes on a hot spring day." Not my favorite aroma. We have purchased skip the line advance tickets. I hope it helps—we don't have six hours to waste. On to Rome!

Day Nine: Rome, Italy

Oh, what a trip this is! And for the record, I was wrong about not liking Rome; go ahead and say "I told you so." Today I saw art treasures that have colored my whole life thus far, and I saw it all with my own eyes. It was really too much to absorb. We met our driver at 8 AM after another hasty breakfast of a banana and a croissant. It seems both The Cruise Addict and I are more interested in hanging over the railing watching the ship arrive and the first impression of the port than in showing up early enough for a leisurely VIP breakfast. I must admit, the buffet is way more convenient, although the atmosphere there does leave a great deal to be desired.

Today's private tour included Husband, Tom, Julie, Clint, Mary, Melissa, and Cade, who took Brett's place at the last minute. When Cade was added to the cruise just days before we left America, his family contacted each tour company to see about adding him. In Rome, the company's van held only six people; that was fine, until Cade added on. He made seven. We could have taken two vans, but that would have been considerable extra expense. Instead, Brett decided to take a train into Rome and do a walking tour on his own. Actually, I think he decided his son would be safer in a group, rather than on *his* own. The others in our group flew into Rome a few days early, before they went to Venice. They had already spent three days seeing the main sites in Rome. Today, their plan was just to explore the port of Citivecchia, and then get back on the ship early and call it a spa day.

Citivecchia's first impression was industrial areas, mixed with the ancient, including neon signs right near three very old forts. Rome is about an hour and fifteen minutes from Citivecchia. Our tour headed to Rome, first thing; our hopes were high, after avoiding crowds in the other ports so far! We enjoyed the countryside, and our guide's stories as we drove. Traffic was light, until we neared the city, when it reached new levels of craziness. I thought Naples was bad! Well, it was, but Rome was worse. The speedy little motorcycles reminded me of Road Runner cartoons.

And walking---whoa! To cross a street, you look left, look right, look left again; all clear. Step into the street and suddenly eight speeding motorcycles are coming at you from every direction; left, right, up, down, across the sidewalks – truly insane!

We quickly found the trick to crossing any street in Rome; follow a local. Pick any confident, local-looking pedestrian, watch them carefully, and go when they go. If you match their stride, just a couple of paces behind (so as not to appear as obvious) you could get across the street, less dead than on your own. Catching the rhythm of the traffic cannot be learned in a day just by tourists passing through. We quickly determined that this is the only safe method to cross the semi controlled chaos that is Italian traffic.

I heard a different rationale for why Italians don't wear motorcycle helmets. A man explained---with a straight face—that only Bad People Doing Bad Things would have a need to cover their heads and faces. "If they were on their way to murder, or rob someone, of course they would prefer to cover their faces, but an honest man wishes his face to be seen. A good person has nothing to hide." I guess I see his point, but a helmet is also a good deterrent to brain matter splattered on pavement!

Saint Paul's Basilica

We stopped first at Saint Paul's Basilica outside of Rome. Oh, the art was *stunning*. It's a massive structure with gold mosaics, intimidating pillars, and an atmosphere of over-the-top opulence. Paul the apostle was beheaded on that very spot, and so they built a basilica to honor him. I don't get it---a bad thing occurred, so they built a church on top of the spot. We saw this over and over! Paul's sarcophagus is still visible. People were praying at it.

It seemed disrespectful to me. In America we speak of "laying the dead to rest." Having one's body parts divided up, labeled as relics, and put on display here and there seemed disrespectful and rather crass. Apparently I'm the only one who thinks so, because there were people fervently praying at the sarcophagus, three steps below the floor level. Saint Paul's Basilica is a working church, although it is centuries old. A small mass was taking place in a smaller room off the main nave. It was truly amazing and I was overwhelmed.

I saw Todd solemnly drop a euro in a collection box, then light a candle for his friend who had died a couple of days ago. Todd smiled at me, and commented, "Wrong religion, but it can't hurt, right?" I assured him that Ron, wherever he was, would smile at the gesture. Warm thoughts cannot be categorized by creed.

Our group availed itself of the restrooms, which were hard to find, and cost a whole euro. And as we made our way back to the van, I happened to be first. Oh, good; an opportunity to admire the wares of that vendor right over there! As I headed for the van, holding three bright scarves that wanted to come home with me, our driver pulled me aside.

He said quietly, "You are Italian. I see you try to hide it, but I can tell. It is true, yes?"

I explained that, yes, my mother's family came from Italy, but they are from *northern* Italy. We think of Italians as being Mediterranean-colored people, but my mom's people have a Swiss influence. They have light hair, blue eyes, and very fair skin. I have dark hair, brown eyes, and olive skin. I guess I do look Italian, but actually, I look more like my father's Syrian relatives, not at all like my Italian kin. The driver was not convinced. "I knew it," he nodded sagely. "I could tell." Wonder what made him think I was hiding anything? I didn't even have a motorcycle helmet on!

Seven Hills of Rome

Once our group gathered, we drove to Palatine Hill, one of the Seven Hills of Rome, where the rich and famous of their day lived. It's a place I recalled from many history classes long ago. Well, not *that* long ago. I've only heard of the famous Claudius aqueducts, and there they were, right above our heads, centuries later. That degree of engineering had to have been inspired, to bring fresh water from the springs in the mountains to the people in the city so many centuries ago. How many areas in the modern world lack fresh water, even today? And it still works---many of Rome's fountains are still fed by the aqueducts!

I've been to Las Vegas, and I must say, those designers took some serious liberties with Caesar's Palace---this was the real thing! My heart was amazed as we walked through the ruins of other Emperors' palaces. We walked where the mad Emperor Nero lived! We saw the very hill where he sat, watching the destruction of Rome below him. So much rich history here—the Senate arches, Nero's gate, the house of Claudius, ruins of fountains and castles from long ago. As I admired Nero's gate, again I thought about the people who had lived there, the feet that walked along these same paths, kicking these same stones across so many generations. I felt myself expanding, and wondering why so many history teachers make the subject so painfully dry, when it is really full of life.

The Circus Maximus is near the Coliseum, up from the Roman Forum. I had heard that the Coliseum was under renovation. It had exterior scaffolding, but less than expected. We could *see* it, but finding the right path to it took rather a long time with some backtracking down dead-end paths. Italian rules applied; our guide had dropped us off again, unable to walk with us. We only had ninety minutes total. I wanted another hour at least!

Coliseum or Colosseo

At last, we made our way to the Coliseum. Actually, it's called the "Colosseo," because there is only one. The "-um" ending makes it plural in the Latin form, but Americans are like that. We're not good with "aquaria" or even "ravioli," for that matter. Regardless, the long lines and massive crowds heading to the Coliseum were daunting, completely overwhelming.

I found a guard and asked where to go, with our advance tickets in my hand. She said briskly, "those are vouchers, not tickets" and said we would have to exchange them over there, indicating the very longest line. I pleaded, "But we are short on time!" She barked, "Well, then come back tomorrow." I explained that we were on a ship, leaving tonight. Her stern face suddenly softened. She said, "Then you must see the Colosseo! You'd better come this way." She opened up a gated area and shoved me gently. We hurried past about 3000 people, just us!

We entered the giant structure, and I felt a rush of history, like a breeze, flow over me. I could imagine ancient scenes as I looked at the crumbling structure. I could almost hear the voices of people there, shouting, cheering. I longed for more time, but we were ready overdue for meeting our driver. We lingered for about twenty five minutes. I knew our guide would wait; after all, we are paying him.

As we made our way back to our meeting point, we passed many aggressive costumed gladiators. Our guide had warned us about them. They charge 20 euros to pose for a photo—with your own camera! Furthermore, they were poorly dressed, with sports team shirts plainly visible under their plastic chest plates. For that much money, I expect some authenticity. They are aggressive, but not very creative.

I thought about the traffic zinging past. Buses, cars, trucks, bikes, the omnipresent motorcycles---do local people even *see* the massive Coliseum anymore? Or has it just become the background scenery to them? I know I'm guilty of that at home; many tourists come to our area to see things that I don't even think about anymore. Travel is important! So is cultivating the art of being where you are.

Back on the Road

Our guide, after a mild scolding consisting of "late! No lunch for you!" drove us next to the Altare della Patria, the national monument built in honor of Victor Emmanuel, the first king of a unified Italy. It's an imposing building that is dubbed "the wedding cake building." I thought it looked more like a typewriter, but I guess that's just giving away my age. Its sprawling steps were a draw for many, many people lying in the sunshine. I enjoy leisurely people watching, but no time today.

Today was so packed that it was almost more overwhelming than pleasurable! and it wasn't even lunchtime yet. Rome itself seemed frantic – with lots of graffiti, I mean tagging, trash in the streets, and bars on the windows. I thought about the people who live in those tightly packed buildings with their laundry flapping out of the windows and wondered what kind of lives they had. Our guide, when asked about real estate prices ---one never knows!—shrugged. "No one lives here; the best places are out of the city." For a place where "no one" lives, it sure felt crowded to me!

I felt rushed in Rome. Our group agreed we needed more time to this explore the city. I guess we will have to come back. The tradition in Rome is that if you throw a coin into the Trevi fountain, you will surely someday return to Rome. Hey, it worked in Hawaii, except there, it's a flower lei in the ocean, not a coin in a fountain. Hawaiians are less mercenary.

The Trevi fountain is being renovated, completely covered in plastic and scaffolding, so we skipped it. Our guide solemnly assured us that the tradition works in any fountain in Italy, not just the Trevi. It's just the most famous, the site of many movies. He made sure to take us to a couple of Piazza with fountains and even offered to make change for us if we didn't have any euro coins to throw into the fountain. The Trevi fountain, when it is open, gathers coins of every single nation on earth, the equivalent of approximately €1.4 million per year, and all of it is given to local charities in Rome. A wish combined with a good deed; I like it!

Torre Argentina is the site of an ongoing and extensive archaeological dig, taking place there right in the middle of the city. It's important because that's where the Senate met, and also where Julius Caesar was murdered. The assassination took place at the base of some steps, near the Curia of Pompeii. The poor man was stabbed thirty-two times, one by each of the Senators, so as to spread the blame. Corruption in politics goes back a long ways.

We stepped at Navona Piazza. To walk around the giant fountain and sculpture in the center of the square was breathtaking. And once again I appreciated the designated historic district, laws in Italy that that ban vehicle traffic from the squares and from certain other areas. Our van let us off a block from the sites and squares, much closer than the big tour buses were permitted to go. It was nice to be able to walk around and admire the sculptured fountains without feeling like I was about to be run over by those little motor scooters, which are everywhere else.

I was amazed to see ancient art again unprotected, out in the elements, touchable, accessible. As I admired the sculpture, the Fountain of the Four Rivers, at Navano Fountain, I noticed a jagged toenail on a sculpted foot. A marble toe, quite perfect in every way, with a nail, and a broken toenail, as if the barefoot man had stubbed it as he walked the dusty streets centuries ago, then leaped up to be part of the fountain. That lifelike aspect, the attention to detail, is astonishing!

We had told our guides in every port, as we arranged tours from home, that we did not wish to have long, leisurely lunch breaks. After all, we've never been to these places before and we wanted to see as much as possible. We can eat anywhere. Our lunch break in Rome netted sandwiches at a sort of a fast food place, like a deli with premade wares. I opted for a banana, and another water bottle. At home, I rarely use water bottles. Since I landed in Europe, it seems I always have one close at hand. I just can't get over seeing meats, cheeses, eggs, and cooked items left unrefrigerated. I don't have time for food poisoning on this trip! A banana is always a safe choice, and they come pre-sealed.

The Pantheon

The glorious Pantheon -- is it even a real place? I think the beautiful structure showed up in every history and art history class I've even sat in. But where is it? As he wove down a little narrow street, more of an alley, hardly wide enough for our van, the driver said he would meet us back here in an hour. I was surprised when he stopped between two nondescript buildings. I didn't recognize the Pantheon, until we walked around the front. Oh, wow! I had fallen into another postcard! The giant fountain in front, the arching façade---yes, I knew this place!

This ancient Roman monument was originally designed to honor the gods of the seven planets; the name means "honor all gods." This building could pass all modern building codes, but it really is ancient. How old, is blurred by history. Legend says Agrippa built the first Pantheon in 27 BC, on the very spot where Romulus was taken to heaven, once he established Rome. It burned in the great fire of 80 AD, was rebuilt by Emperor Domitian, and burned again in 110 AD after being struck by lightning. The fact that the Pantheon managed to survive assorted barbarian raids when all the rest of Roman monuments were ruined is a mystery. It was hastily converted into a church in 609AD; that made it less of a target.

The Pantheon's open design made it seem even more spacious. The architecture was way ahead of its time. The material is still unknown, although you can bet many scientists have tried to identify it. It is similar to modern concrete, which had not been discovered until centuries after the Pantheon was built. I'm very impressed with this engineering; again, remember the builders had no laser levels or power tools, or computers on which to design all this!

The perfectly symmetrical dome is self-supporting, with a thirty foot wide open eye, or oculus, in the center. There are no interior supports at all; the massive dome is supported by its own enormous weight. It is still the largest dome of its kind in the world.

The eye is open in the center of the dome, open to the elements and weather. That, plus the door, is the only source of natural light. I'm from Washington, thus chronically light-deprived, and very sensitive to lighting. I was surprised at how bright and comfortable it felt inside. I expect the Pantheon would be less pleasant on a rainy gloomy day. I saw drains in the ancient flooring. I could imagine that on a blustery rainy day, it could be quite different. We happened to be there a sunshiny day.

I was amazed at the artwork, even beyond the architecture of the pantheon itself. The sculptures set into the walls were each exquisite. How do artists make ruffles, curls, even fabric folds out of *marble?* I just can't get over this!

The Pantheon has a spirit of its own, even as crowded as it was. I wish I had more time there, but I had to waste fifteen minutes trying to find Husband in the crowd. I had been using his floppy hat as a landmark all day. Sigh; he respectfully removed it in the Pantheon and we were separated.

Spanish Steps

Once our group had reassembled, we found the van and made our way next to the Spanish steps. Spanish? We are nowhere near Spain! We learned the square at the bottom of the irregular steps was the base of the Spanish Embassy to the Vatican long ago. Names stick, you know. The area was crowded on this sunny day, and hundreds of people sprawled on the steps.

Interestingly, we saw many pickpockets; very fast, but not all that sneaky. One more blatant enterprise involved fresh roses. A man would approach a woman tourist, force roses into her hands, and then loudly demand money. I was also interested in the little 'selfie sticks' for sale on the street. They were everywhere! They are extendable poles on which one can perch a camera, then hold it up and take a selfie, while holding one's arm low enough to be out of the frame. It's a way to look as though you had a friend to take your photo. Not a terrible idea, if you overlook the narcissist aspect...until I saw at least three camera thefts in under five minutes! The tourist would set the camera at the end of the pole, extend it, smile---and whoosh! the camera was snatched from its little perch and *gone,* that fast! As people watching places go, the Spanish Steps was interesting, but a little unnerving, having to be on alert to that degree!

The Vatican

In every shop and corner kiosk, many postcards are for sale---they're everywhere, not just here. I like postcards; they are a photo that you already know turned out well, and a cheap reminder of the historic buildings everywhere. Not so here; almost all were of the Pope. Kissing babies, waving, greeting crowds, close-ups of his face, in every postcard rack in Rome, totally dominating the options! There were even 3-D postcards that looked like he was making the sign of the cross when the card was shifted. The current Pope is known for his simple lifestyle. The people we spoke to were respectful of the Pope, but admitted they were baffled by his untypical desire for modest living. "He will not even use the Pope Mobile! He refused to live in the elegant Papal apartments! Instead he sleeps in a cell with a narrow bed and a table with a lamp, like a common monk!"

As we slowly drove towards the Vatican Museum, our guide pointed out Mussolini's balcony and embassies representing Spain, France, Brazil and the USA, among others. It's hard to conceive that this is a *country*. It's smaller than my hometown, by a big margin. And speaking of conceiving, as I learned in a recent trivia game on a cruise ship, the Vatican is the only country with zero birthrate.

We crossed the border into the Vatican next, effortlessly. I am used to crossing the US-Canadian border, and it's a serious pain. Here, we drove across borders without even slowing down. The Vatican is a free standing foreign country compete with its own currency, 758 passport holders, and a post office reputed to be much more reliable that Italy's.

Our tour guide had advised us to purchase online tickets for 3 PM for the Vatican Museum, ahead of time. That process was so complicated, it came with an online video to walk us through the buying! As we approached the Museo, we saw Saint Peter's square, with the Pope's balcony. It looked surprisingly small, considering the weight of history it bears. The Swiss guards were on duty, in their beautiful colorful uniforms, designed centuries ago by Michelangelo. As our driver hunted for a parking spot, we saw many little shops, boutique-sized, but not selling the latest fashions---they were clerical outfitters! I never considered where those fancy robes and such that the Catholic clergy wear came from. Now I know.

Vatican Museum

I know the Vatican has incredible, irreplaceable art work. It's a free-standing country so they can do what they want, but I was startled by the stiff security getting into the Vatican Museum. It was worse than any airport. A country this small has meager military might; apparently, intimidation is their weapon of choice.

Our main goal at the Vatican was to see the Sistine Chapel. Near the entrance, we saw signs pointing in different directions, in Italian. One was the long route, through the entire Museum, the other a more direct route, right to the Sistine Chapel. We'd miss a lot of the art that way, but being short on time, we had to prioritize. We opted for the shorter route. There were encouraging signs all along the path, assuring us we were on the shorter route to the chapel, but I think we walked almost three hours inside the Vatican to get to the Sistine Chapel---how long was the longer route??

Whoever designed that 4.7 mile route through the Vatican Museum had a serious mean streak. The route led up, down, around; up 21 steps, then down 18, around a corner, back up 11 more, sloping ramps and stairs for no apparent reason, and at that, we sidestepped many smaller galleries off the main route through the Vatican Museum. The art along the way was incredible, but the senses can only take in so much.

Sarah had warned us that their visit here the previous week was tiring. She was right! She told us there was no place to stop, or sit, but I think we were there on a less crowded day than they were. It was still quite very crowded, and I see what she meant about hygiene. Perhaps calling the pervasive odor 'a seventh-grade boys' locker room' was charitable. It was so hot, with infrequent breezes coming in through some of the windows along the route.

We saw astonishing art; gilded ceilings, mosaics, tapestries, paintings, sculptures, stained glass. Even so I think we missed a lot of it, just concentrating on making our way to the Sistine Chapel and trying to stay more or less together as a group without being trampled in the pressing crowd. The coved ceilings' paintings and frescoes were my favorite. I do love gold, in any form or place.

The artwork as we walked to the Sistine Chapel was stunning. Each piece was worthy of study, but I could feel my senses going on overload. I flat out cannot absorb that much beauty and history at that speed!

The Sistine Chapel

The Sistine Chapel at last! It was much larger than I had expected, with wall-to-wall people in it. Michelangelo's painting on the ceiling was amazing, and still vivid, after so many centuries! No wonder so many people have tried to copy his style over the centuries. Any corner I looked at was breathtaking, and it was huge. It was brighter and more bold than the pictures I've ever seen. It was really too much to take in, but I did love trying. I would have loved to be able to lie on the floor, all alone, with a pair of binoculars, free to admire this great work on the arching ceiling.

The atmosphere in the Sistine Chapel was not restful, certainly not worshipful. Uniformed guards pushed people and shouted, "No photo! Move to the right!" over and over. Every few moments, a hiss came over the loudspeakers, and a deep voice intoned *"Silencio!"* which I didn't think added to the reverent spirit of the chapel much at all.

I thought about the history that took place in that very room, including the conclaves that result in a new pope when the previous one dies. Campaigning, corruption, repeated voting, even conspiracy to the point where hourly scans are made to check for listening devices as the process takes place--- not unlike a political election, with flashy dressers. Popes and peasants have worshipped in this room for centuries, awed by the art, and I joined them.

Finding our way back out of the Vatican Museum was also a challenge. We saw exit signs, enough to make us feel hopeful, but it was at least forty minutes walking out to the exit. Up, down, around, upstairs, downstairs, only to go back upstairs twenty feet later... who designed this place? We finally saw daylight, in the form of an enormous ramp made of steps and slopes, at least five stories long, with the exit at the bottom. Julie had a knee replacement not long ago, and while she'd been a trooper, she balked at that long ramp, sure she'd never make it. I looked around and spotted an elevator tucked back in the corner. She and Todd took it; being a good (and exhausted) friend, I joined them. It was a very elegant elevator; wood paneled with seats inside, a wrought iron door, and the first elevator attendant I've ever seen in my life.

I also saw another restroom attendant today; we just don't see those at home. This was a grim woman in a uniform, with a rag. She bustled out of a stall in the ladies room, which enclosed a toilet that was, incidentally, knee-high and had no seat. She told me firmly, "Is clean. One euro." As I came out, she told me, "Wash. Use soapa." She went in where I came from and then reappeared moments later and told the waiting woman, "Is clean. One euro." All day --? What a job.

After stopping for more pastries, our group was quiet on the ride back to Citivecchia, thoroughly tired out. We had a peaceful trip back to the ship with our driver cursing other drivers all the way. Really, "A pox on your dead ugly relatives!" was pretty creative! He made the day fun. We made a good choice with this tour, too.

Wrap Up The Day

I was beyond overwhelmed by the art and history that I saw today. It really was too much to take in. The art in the Vatican Museum was astonishing, with not enough time to stop and appreciate any one piece of artwork. It was hot, crowded and not very pleasant. People say this visit is once-in-a-lifetime. That's likely true for me; once is probably enough for me.

It was too much too fast – maybe someday I'll return to Rome so I can see everything more leisurely, but I can tell you I will not rent a car. My heart stopped several times throughout the day and I wasn't even the one driving.

We were so tired when we reached the ship, but also hungry. NCL greeted us, as they had in every port, with chilled towels and fresh fruit on the pier, a party atmosphere. Melissa, Cade, Husband, and I went to the main dining room for a leisurely dinner. Even after so much time together, we still found plenty of things to talk about. It's been an amazing day---and I doubt anyone saw more of Rome in a day than our group!

The main show tonight was more jugglers, so we opted for the Latin Fiesta with Star Trio band in the Galaxy of the Stars lounge instead, and then headed back to our cabin. This group has talent! Even though dinner was very good, we still found room for the elegant little shortbread tarts we found waiting in our cabin, compliments of the hotel director. This VIP stuff could go to my head. I really am having a marvelous time, complete with a lot of jaw-dropping marveling along the way!

Tomorrow the Spirit will port at Livorno, Italy. Our last formal tour is tomorrow, to Pisa, Florence, then up into Tuscany. This tour will include just be me, The Cruise Addict, Todd and Julie; the rest have other plans. All along, I've been very, very pleased with each of our private tours. We did a good job researching, and each company has exceeded my expectations. I'm not that hard to please, but these tours have been great! I hope it goes as smoothly tomorrow. The next day we will be in Toulon, France, and then the cruise will end the following day in Barcelona. It's almost over.

I may never return to Europe, but it's been a fabulous trip. We've had an amazing overview of the cities. I am pretty sure that we've seen more and done more than anyone else on the ship, certainly much more than we could have on the ship's shore excursions. At home, I admit I was stressed out about all the research and planning of the tours. Think about it---since Husband and I did most of the tour planning, we had the power to totally ruin the vacation of ten of our friends, as well as our own! It was a risk, choosing tours sight unseen online, trusting reviews and their emailed responses. It was worth the occasional sleepless night. Every tour has been great, and everyone who has gone with us has been cooperative and even appreciative. We have good friends!

Day Ten: Florence/ Pisa, Italy

First Impressions

This is the tour guide that I've looking forward to the most, although the cities are less exotic than some of the other we visited. If it's possible to 'connect' with someone from six thousand miles away, here we are. We are booked with Sunflower Tours today. Months ago at home, I narrowed down the tour companies in this port, and emailed each, as I did for the other ports. I compared prices, and what was offered, where they would take us; I evaluated the tours in every way I could think of. In the process of this research, I read hundreds of online reviews, I made a chart, and a spreadsheet of which tours would be best for each city. I really put a lot of work into this! I weighed them in a very analytical way.

Not this time. For this tour out of the port of Livorno, I admit that I decided on pure emotion. I emailed Sunflower Tours, along with the few others I was considering, describing what we had in mind, and asking if they could take us around Florence and Pisa. Most replied in a typical businesslike fashion, answering my questions and agreeing to my requests. Sunflower Tours was different.

Giovanni's reply email began "Bon Giorno!" and concluded with "ciao, Giovanni." I take pride in being logical and reasonable, but that struck a chord. It's amazing, looking back, that from my family room computer in America, I could find one man, a semi-retired Tuscan, who drives a single car far far away in Italy, and we hit it off on immediately. This really was one of our best days of the whole trip! Giovanni was funny, informative, and seemed genuinely interested in showing us his home region.

Giovanni had worked as a purser on cruise ships, and was full of stories. He lamented never having married or had a family. "I missed that window while at sea." My thoughts turned to the many cruise ship crew members we have met over the years. Some had relationships on the ships, including partners assigned to the same ship, so they could be together after a workday. It's pretty common to be attracted to people you encounter often, after all. A cruise ship is just a small city. Other mentioned families far away at home, and sighed over the long contracts, with no days off. Imagine, only seeing your young children once a year? We have talked to others who spoke of "the one who got away," assuring us they could have had a long term marriage, but for the long days at sea.

I had not considered those in Giovanni's boat, so to speak. If he was at sea for a decade, of course it would have been very difficult to form or maintain a land-based relationship. My heart went out to this elderly man, all alone at the end of his life. He has a job that allows him to meet new –and potentially interesting—travelers most days. That's good, but not as fulfilling as a stable family waiting at home at the end of a day.

At home, I had wondered about the name of the company: Sunflower Tours. I don't think of sunflowers when I think of Tuscany; grapes and olives and rolling hills come to mind. It was made clear as we passed many acres of fields with neat rows of tall sunflowers with their heads tied together. Giovanni explained that they were grown for sunflower oil, and it was almost harvest time. The seed heads were drying a few more days in the sun before being harvested and pressed into cooking oil. Interesting! I never associated sunflowers with Italy before.

Now I will probably never see a sunflower without remembering our one beautiful day in Tuscany.

Today was our smallest tour, with just Todd and Julie, Husband and myself. The others decided to take a train into Pisa, hoping to be able to find an opportunity to climb the Leaning Tower. They're a lot more athletic than we four! We planned a more leisurely day, with museums, and an overview of the area, with much less walking than previous days.

A fleet of buses, really big ones, loaded up on the pier next to the ship. I was grateful not to be among the hordes of tourists. Anywhere they went, they brought along their own crowds and lines to stand in. We were much more nimble. NCL offers a shore excursion in Livorno, a private car for two people that goes anywhere the travelers wish to go. It's pretty much what we had; except there were four of us, and that one takes only two. The NCL excursion cost $2600 per person for six hours. Our tour cost €400 for all four of us, for seven hours, and we had a fabulous day.

Pisa and the Leaning Tower

First, on to Pisa, driving a very straight road which Giovanni told us was an ancient Roman byway that stretches through Rome, Naples, Pisa, and on into France and Spain; I think we call it the Appian Way. I must research that when we get back home. We passed rolling farmland with neat rows of sunflowers, corn, and even bamboo. It was a relaxing drive, if one could ignore the life-peril that is driving on Italian roads! Even as we passed through small towns, we had several close calls. Giovanni calmly explained that the stop signs are optional. Oddly, I believed him.

We passed a giant US Army base on the right, with obviously American vehicles and equipment. That startled us! What was *that* doing there, in the Italian countryside? We asked, and our guide told us it has been there since World War II. Giovanni explained it had been quiet for decades, but it is gearing up now as the unrest in Ukraine and Russia heats up. I asked about it in more detail.

Giovanni fervently insisted that the Italians are "most grateful for America's wealth and economic support since The Great War." He listed some economic boons, such as schools, roads, and other infrastructure. He repeatedly assured us the Italians are very grateful to let Americans have a base there, as well as to share half of the Galilei airport, nearby. I don't think Americans would tolerate any country setting up a base in Ohio, but for some reason, it works in Italy.

At last, we reached the walled city of Pisa, the place of postcards! Both the historic site and the city itself were bigger than we expected. We beat the crowds, for which I was grateful. They streamed in as we were leaving the Basilica area. Again, a private tour is the way to go!

The Leaning Tower of Pisa really does lean! Four percent, Giovanni said. It was taller than I had envisioned, and dramatic. It was recently renovated, with stronger supports built in, to prevent it from eventually falling over. Husband wondered aloud, "As long as they were renovating it, why didn't they *straighten* it?" Of course, that defeats the whole purpose; he can be very black and white.

The bell tower looked crisp and clean and fresh against the bright blue sky. We posed as if pushing the tower up; the same photo shot about seven million other people have on their cameras. Oh, well, we don't *always* have to avoid the crowds!

The baptistery building was beautiful, almost delicate in architecture, with a lacy marble façade. Lacy and marble; not words often used together, but that was the effect. In the Middle Ages, people could not enter the church proper unless they were baptized, and so the buildings were separate. We had seen that in other places on this journey, as well.

Overlooking Florence

After exploring Pisa, the five of us drove towards Florence, back on the old Roman road. Giovanni stopped several times to show us interesting things. There is a beautiful park overlooking Florence, Piazzale Michelangelo on the Arcetri hillside. It was designed to show replicas of the sculpture's works, but morphed from a museum into a restaurant. We planned to see the Galleria dell'Accademia later in the day, where The David is housed, but we took time to admire the bronze replica of The David at this park as well. Good thing; our plans changed as the day progressed.

Today, the big parking lot atop Piazzale Michelangelo happened to be hosting a gelato festival--- bonus! I was interested in the semi-truck that had floor-to-ceiling glass on one whole side. Inside were eight or ten people busily making gelato, moving very fast, then running the metal tins of the finished gelato to various stands for sale. One can never have too much gelato!

The overlook of Florence city from that vantage point was breathtaking. Giovanni pointed out tall spired churches, the city wall, old museums, even a huge synagogue in the Jewish ghetto section, all mixed in with modern apartment buildings and offices. The Arno River snaked through Florence, spanned by arching bridges. Throughout the day, Giovanni informed us of the history and the culture of the area. He really made it come alive.

The Arno River was in the way during World War II, and so the Germans blew up the bridges along the way to slow the Allies' progress. Giovanni pointed out the new bridges built to replace the old ones. Those war movies? That happened right here!

Angels of the Mud

I like the story about the thousand-year-old National Library in Florence that Giovanni related. It's on the banks of the Arno River. Forty-nine years ago, the river flooded severely, and muddy water rushed into the first two stories. Residents left their homes and ran to save the ancient books and paintings stored there. The Mayor drew his weapon and announced that anyone who came to the National Museum to save merely old paintings and books would be shot on the spot. He insisted that saving the city itself was more important than a bunch of old art and books.

A flood of young people came from the cities nearby, from the universities, overwhelming the Mayor. They formed a brigade and quickly passed out the ancient books and paintings and sculptures. They stayed to wash the mud from the eyes of the statues. They saved the treasures, and the townspeople were forever grateful. The young people were dubbed "Angelo de Fango," *Angels of the Mud.* Next year, they will return on the 50th anniversary of their efforts for a grand celebration. Giovanni said with a derisive snort, "and the Mayor, we no longer speak his name." It seems the Italians love their art more than life itself, and forgiveness is not up for discussion.

Santa Croce Basilica

This huge baroque Basilica was built in 325 AD. I was again jaw-dropped stunned. Even after all the incredible art I've seen on this trip, the glittering gold mosaics, the ornate altars, the worn graves in the floors, the Chapel of the Holy Relics, took my breath away. Amazingly, it's still going strong today. Besides tourists, I saw a mass going on, people praying, touching history as it reached the present.

I wandered, and came upon another fascinating sight: a full-sized, exact replica of the Shroud of Turin! It is stretched out on the wall at eye level and well-lit, providing a close -up view of the famous relic up close. I shuddered at a gory statue of Jesus nearby; entirely too lifelike for me.

The Florence Leather School is on site, dating back to 1294. That's 482 years before our country was even formed, and it's been in constant use the whole time. 1292 was a tough period, just after yet another war. As usual, the youngest, most innocent victims are the most affected. Many children had been left as war orphans. The school's aim was to teach these children the professional craft of working leather so that they would be able to earn a living in the future. Those skills carried down generations.

Dante is buried in the basilica! His ornate gravestone is marked simply 'Poeta." Appropriate, I thought. Michelangelo is entombed there, with a suitably over-the-top sculpture gracing his sarcophagus. Machiavelli and Rossini also have tombs there, right by the leather school entrance.

Most surprising was Galileo's grave right there in the wall inside the church. I knew that he'd been born in nearby Pisa, but I thought he had been excommunicated for heresy. Wild ideas he had, about space and time and art and anatomy and medicine, ideas that shook the hierarchy. How did he end up buried right inside the main church? I guess there was some forgiveness, after a few centuries. I could imagine Galileo in his grave, muttering, "I told you so."

As we walked slowly around admiring the artwork, Julie commented on a massive painting. It was probably four feet wide and eight feet tall, above an altar. She commented on how the colors were so vivid at the bottom of the painting, yet so dark and muted at the top. What had the artist been thinking? I pointed out the tall candles on the altar. Julie was horrified at the idea of candles, with their accompanying soot and wax particles, being allowed to burn so close to an ancient painting. Don't these people value what they have? Perhaps not. Perhaps they are overwhelmed with the art and take it for granted.

As we walked slowly around inside the Basilica admiring the awesome ceiling and the stained glass, the bells rang out in the bell tower overhead! It just added to the experience. I've always had a fondness for bell towers. And stained glass; this was a happy stop.

I needed a banji, a restroom, and so I wandered away across the grassy courtyard. There was a line, as usual, but this one was automated, the first I'd seen. I had developed the habit of carrying a couple of half euro coins in my pocket. Good thing – this one had a coin operated machine (exact change only). It opened the turnstile that led into the restrooms, both male and female. The machine was too big to climb over or under, requiring exactly half euro to enter. Woe to him or her who did not have exact change! The line was quite long, and I felt sorry for the poor woman going up and down the line, waving her 5 euro note, begging for change! I wished I could have helped her, but I only had one half euro coin (set aside after a postcard purchase) and I had a need, which is why I found myself in line in the first place. The toilet and sink were both very, very small, very low to the ground and very square. I wonder why Italian loos don't have seats. I also wonder why churches and basilicas have a fee for using the toilet. One would think in a place of worship they could make an exception, especially since it cost six euro get into the place! One would be mistaken.

As I left the restroom, I ducked into an archway on the left, instead of going back out in the courtyard to meet our group. I found myself alone in a sort of underground catacomb, completely covered in marble. It was lined, floor, walls, even the ceiling, with graves, statues, etchings. I couldn't step anywhere in the giant structure without walking on a grave in the floor. As I walked along I read some of the dates. Some were so old and so worn I could not make them out. The most modern one I found was 1403 A.D., 373 years before our country was even born! I was so far from home and so delighted to be there. I dragged Husband and our friends back through the tunnel. They were duly awed.

The Duomo

Next stop was at the Duomo and the Duomo Museum. The sculptures there were just awesome. Several of them seemed about to speak. I really am amazed at the quality and detail of the ancient artwork! It seems that, as society has advanced, modern art has fallen a long way from this quality and consistency. Where are the great artists today? As I admired the delicate carvings and brush strokes, I thought about that art gallery show at home, the one displaying canvasses with paint flung on by an elephant's trunk. That's not art.

We had lunch on San Croce square. Giovanni had scouted out a very authentic trattoria for us. Again, I think we were the only non-locals in the place. Lunch was delicious, although our plates were served ten minutes apart. I had handmade pasta with a creamy sauce. Husband had pizza. Todd and Julie shared a fish dish. We detoured to a gelatoria for dessert; last chance for gelato in Italy. Mango and plum, yum!

When I travel, besides trying local foods, I also like to seek local items as souvenirs that are not souvenirs at all. I knew that Florence was known for marbled paper and I wanted some. While the others lingered over their lunch, I asked Giovanni where I could acquire such an item. He nodded, and led me to a tiny place around a couple of corners, and down an alley. "Stationery store," he smiled. "I think you will find some fine paper here." He turned to walk out.

I panicked. Wait-! Don't leave me! I'm in a foreign country. I have no sense of direction to speak of. I can't speak the language, and I'm pretty sure an American had never been in this particular store before. I called, "Giovanni, wait!"

He immediately turned around, heard my problem, and introduced me to the proprietor. Her English was about as good as my Italian, but with Giovanni interpreting, I was able to buy some beautiful marbled paper quite quickly. It seemed to me that the proprietor was saying a lot more than our guide was translating, though. On the way back to the group, Giovanni told me a story. The paper had been made by a 79-year-old man who had devoted his life to preserving the art of marbling paper. Imagine spending your life making sheets of beautiful unique patterns of marbled paper? Not a bad life, really.

We drove to the Old Bridge in Florence. I wondered why it wasn't destroyed, too, during the war? Fisherman and butchers used to be there for centuries, but now it's been taken over by high-end fashion and jewelry shops. Crowds were intense here, waves and waves of people teeming over the sidewalks. The shops here in Florence, and in most of Italy, are open from 9:30 AM to 1:30 PM and then again from 4 PM to 8 PM. At this time of day, most were closed. It seems silly to me to take a nap in the middle of the day in a country with such a wobbly economy when there are swarms of tourists nearby, ready to open their purses. I am not in charge.

Tuscany Awaits

The four of us voted to skip the Academia. Even with our reserved tickets, it would have taken at least two hours to get in. We are still exhausted from walking so much the last few days. I know in Florence, we are obligated to see the statue of David; it is what visitors *do*. We had already seen a perfectly good replica of the David back at the viewpoint when we arrived in the city. We took a vote, and decided that was good enough this time. We were all fatigued, both physically and with regards to art appreciation. Once our decision was made, Giovanni offered to drive us up in the countryside, away from the frenzied city atmosphere. Oh, yes, this was the Tuscany I had imagined!

I felt like we'd fallen into a beautiful tabletop book! Rolling hills with rows of Chianti grapes growing, ready for harvest. Olive trees, with their dull gray leaves and shiny green olives criss-crossed the hillsides, far off into the distance. The only signs of humans were the narrow dusty road, and a few villas perched on the hillsides. It was gorgeous! We happily stopped for pictures, knowing that even the bad ones would look like a postcard. Julie jokingly pointed to a couple of villas as we drove and sighed, "I could happily live there." I think she was joking. I'm not sure.

It was time to head back towards the ship. We had taken the main highway from Livorno in the morning. On the way back, Giovanni leisurely drove through small towns, avoiding the main roads. It was gorgeous. People waved at us. We waved back. We saw children and families and schools, and it felt alive. I found Rome and Florence a little too hectic for my taste, but I loved being in the countryside. Giovanni was wonderful, telling us stories and relating more history as we drove.

When we reached the ship, we paid our driver, as on every previous day. There were two couples; we each chipped in our 200 euros, plus a tip. Giovanni quickly counted it and gave back €55 to Todd in change. Todd made direct eye contact with Giovanni. He cupped both of his hands over the old Italian's hand. He said, "No, it is for you, Giovanni. Grazia!" Giovanni looked startled. As it dawned on him that the pile of money in his hand was for him, his face lit up. It was a big tip and Italians don't expect tips at all. I think in this economy that money meant a lot to Giovanni. He repeatedly thanked Tom, saying "you are a good man, a generous man!" Did I imagine Todd being choked up as he turned away? And he's right; Todd is a good man, an absolute character. We very much enjoyed being with him and Julie today.

Wrap Up the Day

This was our last organized tour of the trip. I must say all of our efforts and prayers paid off handsomely. Each tour was so good; I would not have changed a thing. Well, perhaps the Vatican... I wonder how far we walked up and down and through and past? Where's a pedometer when you need one? It's a good thing we took the route in the beginning that indicated the shorter, most direct route. Had we taken the longer route, we might still be there.

Tomorrow we will be in Toulon, in the South of France. It's a lazy day, the last day of the cruise. The Maritime Museum is reputed to be worthwhile, as is a small touristy train. We may go sunning on a beach, too. I'd be content to simply wander, getting a feel for the place. The organized part of the cruise is over. It'll be just us two tomorrow, The Cruise Addict and me. What a trip! I cannot believe the places we've seen.

Every night we've had a treat in our cabin before dinner, and twice, a couple of times, part of the VIP perks. Each has arrived with a little card, compliments of somebody-- the Captain, events coordinator, hotel director, cruise director, concierge, a staff member we met on another ship who remembered us, etc. Tonight's was garlicky baguette slices with olive tapenade, and fancy cheeses. Mmmmm. I have enjoyed the VIP status on this cruise; the breakfasts away from the zoo that is the buffet, elegant quiet lunches on days when we had time to linger, being greeted by name by senior staff all over the ship. I still don't know why we had VIP status, but it really has made the cruise special. You don't think they know I'm writing a book, do you?

My feet are no longer on speaking terms with me. I'm grateful for my soft, light walking shoes; it could have been worse. By the time we reach home, we will have been in ten new countries and will have covered over 16,000 miles. It's okay to be tired!

Elements was the show in the theatre that night. The very high-energy contemporary dance show seemed to have almost every entertainer that we had seen the whole week in it. It was very entertaining, well worth the watching. We actually debated watching it again at the later showing, but we were both tired. We happily spent about 45 minutes on the very back of the ship instead, watching the wake in the moonlight... very good for the soul.

My face ached from yawning. I tumbled into bed, only to be wakened less than an hour later! Husband had gone to the chocolate buffet and was nice enough to bring some chocolate pastries back to share with me. Of course he had to wake me up first. He complained that I was not as appreciative as he would've liked. I think he's lucky I didn't whack him with a pillow. We have been married a very long time!

Day Eleven: Toulon, France

The south of France! It seemed like pretty much every other passenger we had talked to all week long had planned to zoom through Toulon on their way to Marseille or Monte Carlo, or other places. We decided to take it easy and just enjoy the port city itself.

Toulon is a pretty port with hundreds of colorful sailboats in the marina, little shops all around, and bright, brilliant sunshine sparkling on the water. It's more populated than I was expecting. Toulon feels laid-back and calm. I like it! The narrow side streets are lined with apartments all around, with French balconies. I know they are French because we are in France, and all of those balconies were festooned with laundry drying in the breeze. All across Europe, we've seen a lot of laundry on a lot of French balconies, flapping in the breeze, in every country since Sweden. Maybe dryers are not used here.

I was startled first thing this morning to pull back the cabin's curtains and see what looked like the entire Navy of France right there in the harbor! Again with my American viewpoint, I was surprised to see warships, battleships, and destroyers, just floating around, apparently unsecured. In America, even the cruise ships are patrolled by Coast Guard or Harbor Patrol; these looked deserted. I guess they know what they're doing.

After a relaxed, elegant breakfast of fruit, more prosciutto, and tasty waffles with berries in the VIP restaurant, The Cruise Addict and I made our way off the ship. Toulon's an easy port; the ship docked nearly downtown. After perusing the little shops in the terminal, we made our way out and found Le Petit train, which translates into 'the little train.' I didn't need French skills for that one! We decided to take it to get a good overview of the area. It was advertised as being forty-five minutes long and cost seven euros each. It was a little open sided tram, ideal for this sunny day.

As we reached the ticket seller, he stopped, looked at us, and asked "where are you from?" Ignoring the line forming behind us, he launched into telling us about his first trip to America, next month. He was going to fly to Pennsylvania and then he planned to drive to Virginia. He asked if we thought he would be safe, going so far from home, was the gun situation as bad as he had heard, and how was the driving in America? Funny---he had the same concerns I had from my home.

He has a daughter in University, he explained. "She has a young man, and she thinks she has found love with him. She is only 19 years old. She has no judgment. She needs her Papa, and so I go." I understood—hasn't every parent of a young adult checked out a potential mate for their kid? Parents are the same, worldwide. Everywhere we've gone, everyone we met has had a story about their life, the state of their country. It seems to me that every one of them has known someone who knows someone who's been to America. I believe firmly in the power of story. I've enjoyed the glimpses into people's lives on this journey.

Le Petit Train

Le Petit Train had narration in both French and English. My Turkish and Greek language ability is about as good as my Martian, but a lot of French words are either familiar or easily guessed, so I did just fine. I could even make out most signs.

The Petit Train said Toulon gets 207 days of sunshine per year. My kind of place! The disembodied voice told about the French Navy as we drove past the homeport. The voice said 90% of the Navy was either destroyed or scuttled in one day, right in that beautiful, calm harbor. The narrator solemnly intoned, "Thus, the government had kept a promise to the French people, that no matter how severe the war, the French Navy would never fall into the hands of another country," and so it was scuttled by French command.

Husband, a history buff, leaned over and whispered that yes, the fleet may have been scuttled. However, it was scuttled with the help of the British Navy's torpedoes during a battle that day! In other words, the cheerful Petit Train in the bright sunshine lied. Ah, well, best foot forward!

There's still an important military presence in Toulon. The main project is making submarines even more silent; invisible, almost. Even I know that there can never be a submarine that's undetectable, regardless of how quiet the engines are made to run. Marine animals are a giveaway, every time! The moaning whales, crunching parrotfish, snapping clams, octopi, all of them fall silent and go into defense mode when any unfamiliar craft or creature comes past. Even if the submarines are undetectable to humans, there's no way to get the sea residents to go on as though nothing happened.

The Petit train rode along the shore, past the ugly military-issue apartments hastily constructed in the 1960's. This part of Toulon felt scrappy, modern, rebuilt with speed, not beauty, in mind. We saw a pretty park. It had strolling people, families, children at play, and a large playground, the first playground I've seen since we came to Europe. There was a carousel with bright animals: lion, tiger, giraffe, beautiful horses... and two army tanks, complete with a gun turret out the front! Never seen one of those in America, either.

As the train left the beach area, suddenly horns and sirens blared. The road was abruptly blocked by motorcycle police right in front of us. As the police officer in the motorcycle veered right in front of us, the little train stopped. The uniformed police officer walked over to the driver of the train, kissed her thoroughly on both cheeks, and then went back and sat on his motorcycle, without a word being spoken. Indeed, we're not in Kansas anymore.

Runners! Some sort of a foot race. Many people ran in front of us, I guessed 1200 people or so. Most wore matching race-issued T-shirts, but others were plainly cross-dressing. Wigs flying in the breeze and balloons stuffed under blouses, elaborate hats with ribbons flying as they ran, added to the atmosphere! It was very funny to see them stream by. Good thing I enjoyed it, because we were forced to stop for about twenty minutes before the ride resumed.

Maritime Museum

We toured the Maritime Museum next. Husband had looking forward to that; he loves ships and history. It had a discount for ship passengers, but it wasn't expensive either way. I noticed that they greeted the people in front of us at the desk in French, but they greeted us in English. Before we even spoke, they handed us head phones and said, "Americans. To listen, press the number and then press play." I guess I really can't disguise my nationality. The Maritime Museum had many interesting things on display. Each of the artifacts and displays had a number; the audio phone enabled us to listen to the ones we were interested in. It was interesting to see the war's influence in such a calm and pleasant place. There hasn't been a war on American soil, to speak of, since the Civil War, yet the people of this pleasant city lived it very personally.

We leisurely made our way down the harbor side, stopping in several little shops. Everyone seemed very friendly. Even the crossing guards look happy here! They wear neon vests, and carry a sort of ping-pong paddle, red on one side, green on the other to indicate when to go, or stop. Pedestrians probably have a longer life expectancy here than ones we encountered in Greece and Italy.

I dearly love markets! Husband and I walked to the open-air market. Clothing, vegetables, fruits, trinkets, and cheeses was arranged for sale in little kiosks, stretching on for blocks. The cheeses were big wheels, at least thirty to fifty pounds, each. We don't see that at home! Today happens to be Sunday. The Cathedral Sainte Marie de la Seds was right beside the market and midday mass had just let out. Priests and congregants lingered in the sidewalks along with tourists and market goers. I admired the priests with their elegant robes and flowing, embroidered capes; I seldom dress that elegantly, even on special occasions! The Cathedral was gorgeous.

As we walked, we had some treats. I had a frozen peach drink that tasted more peachy than a perfectly ripe summer peach. The server practiced her English, which was only slightly better than my French. We shared smiles; good enough. Husband had more gelato, although we were no longer in Italy. To redeem himself, he found a patisserie and bought an innocuous looking éclair.

A French Éclair!

Oh, the éclair! Let's just say it's a good thing they don't sell them anywhere near my house, or I would eat five a day, and five more at night. It was the most fabulous, perfect example of the art of pastry that one could even imagine! The shell was crisp, with a not- too- sweet sour cream glaze on top, and a perfectly smooth icy cold cream filling. I like to bake. I've taken several pastry classes. I know how to make éclairs and petit chou. Never have I even encountered such a fabulously intense example of what a French éclair ought to be. It was so good that I decided then and there that I will probably never eat another éclair in my life. What would be the point? It couldn't possibly measure up!

We had missed lunch, and although I was perfectly content with the éclair, Husband was starting to mutter. He lingered as we passed Le Tacos Toulon, but I quickly vetoed that. I told him to just find a snack; I was not hungry.

Today was the day that we had decided to try and find Wi-Fi again to communicate with our kids back in the states. No news is good news, but I had not contacted anyone since Mykonos. We came upon Clint and Mary, who were also seeking a Wi-Fi spot. As we walked we found a pizza place – *in France* – with a group of crew members from the ship with their noses intent on their electronic devices. Good sign – that's how they communicate with their faraway families, so we knew we were in the right spot.

As I set up my tablet and got online at an outdoor table, Husband and Clint went into the restaurant. Of course, if we were going to use their free Wi-Fi, we should purchase something. Soon, however, *cheeseburgers* arrived! They came with pomme frite, which looked a lot like french fries to me, except they had a big blob of greasy mayonnaise on top of them. I guess that makes sense. Mayonnaise is French, right? I was disgusted... Who eats *cheeseburgers* in France?! Is it worse than Le Tacos Toulon?

We made our way back to the ship after emailing our kids. I may have posted something about The Cruise Addict ordering a cheeseburger in France, on Facebook, just in passing. Before we even left the little open air restaurant, I had many comments from friends and family who know my Husband too well!

We had talked about going back to the beach we passed on the train. It's a topless beach, but that's easily ignored. Sigh. The Le Petit Train had stopped running, and there were no taxis to be had; it was siesta time, 1pm. I'm in favor of a nap as much as the next guy, but to close for three hours when there are an extra 2200 tourists in port, willing to part with their euros... I can't say that this makes any sense to me in any country.

As we sailed out of Toulon, I think we passed the whole French Navy. It looked deserted to me. I'm not a violent person, but it seems to me if you wanted to invade France, this would be the time and the place to do it, while no one is paying attention, and the whole city is basking in the sunshine.

Wrap Up the Day

We had dinner tonight in Cagney's steakhouse with Brett and Melissa. That's the specialty steak house on the Spirit. The appetizer and soup and salad were so good and so filling that by the time my dinner came, I almost didn't have room to eat it. I was, however, very disappointed in my dessert. Something odd about a human stomach; no matter how full you are from eating your dinner, there is always room for dessert. I ordered the raspberry crème brûlée. I've had raspberry crème brûlée on NCL before and it's been very good. Raspberries at the bottom of the dish, pot au crème on top of it, and then the crisp brulee'd sugar on top of that; it's usually excellent. This version was just sad. The only raspberry in the whole dessert was one little raspberry sitting on the whipped cream. The custard was dry and the sugar crust was not even thick enough to be crunchy. Oh well, I didn't need those extra calories.

During dinner, Ryan, the concierge, came to us to greet us. He must somehow keep track of where VIP types are dining; he had appeared at nearly every dinner! He greeted us by name, as he had the rest of the week, and then asked if we needed anything, and could he help us with tomorrow at all. Brett raised an eyebrow, so we ended up explaining about the VIP status. Brett and Melissa laughed and told us we are very good for not taking advantage of Ryan ---we could've easily had him running ragged all week. Not my style... I have to live with myself, you know!

Bye, France; bye, last port of the cruise. We must pack tonight. We will have priority VIP disembarkation in Barcelona tomorrow. Our group of friends will split up again. Some of us are going home through Frankfurt, others through Copenhagen or Amsterdam, but I think all of us are staying at least one to three days in Barcelona. It's really hard to get off the ship, and head directly to an airplane, especially in a place I've never been to before. I won't have it. The Cruise Addict and I have planned about 40 hours in Barcelona; not enough, but we have another cruise in only ten days and we need to be home at some point.

Day 12, Disembarkation Day: Barcelona, Spain

We had our last VIP elegant breakfast of Crab Cakes Benedict, lobster brioche, and more prosciutto. I love prosciutto and I've eaten it almost every day on this cruise. Then I spent the rest of the day sucking water bottles dry in port. The preserved meat is so salty and so delicious! As we left the ship, the senior officers called to us and wished us well. I've enjoyed being greeted by name all over the trip, as if I was an important person. I'm still puzzled about the unexpected VIP status. The entire cruise, officers made a great effort to check on us, to stop and chat for a minute whenever we've encountered them. I've had no reason to complain, but I certainly had a lot of opportunities had I wanted to speak to someone who could fix something. It's been an incredible trip and the staff and crew on the NCL Spirit are among the best.

We're in Spain! Also, Catalunya. Catalunian is a strong independent undercurrent, a tangible pride here. It's almost visible. It seems that we missed a major secession rally just yesterday. Half a million Barcelonans and Catalunians turned out to protest, to march there and to let their opinion be known of their desire to secede from Spain. Most of the protest evidence was gone when we arrived, but there were still a lot of bright Catalunian banners and flags hanging from the balconies. We saw fliers on all the street posts, and in windows, signs calling people to the rally. We heard that it was a very calm, organized rally. Being an American, I'm all in favor of letting your government know how you feel, in a nonviolent manner, of course.

Disembarking was easy. We took a taxi to the Hotel Jazz. The Hotel Jazz is a five star hotel, with great reviews, and our first impression was delight. It's located right off of Los Ramblas, a really good location. Since it was only midmorning, we assumed it was too early to check in. We hoped the hotel would keep our luggage until we returned later, after some exploring. The smiling desk clerk asked our names and said, "Oh, I see that you've been upgraded to our best suite." What? This whole trip has been full of serendipity and wonderful treats, and I'm loving it. We went ahead and checked in.

It was a beautiful suite! Three rooms, spacious, very modern, with a big bathroom. This seemed a treat after the cabin-sized one on the ship. Best of all, the suite was on a corner, the fourth floor, which they say is the third; Europe counts from zero floor, not the first floor. Our suite has four French balconies! Ideal for people watching, later on.

People *walk* here! We watched an endless stream of people walking, walking, walking. Most are very casually dressed, while others look like magazine models. Our balconies afforded us a view of both residents and tourists mixed, most of them carrying shopping bags. We quickly dropped off our luggage, washed our faces, and headed out to explore. I'm in *Spain!*

Hop On Hop Off

We booked a Hop On Hop Off tour at home. It was highly rated, but I guess I wasn't the only one who read that. It was hopelessly inefficient. The lines were very long. We waited 40 minutes to catch a bus! At that point, we were afraid to get off because we might not catch another one back, and so we stayed on for the whole circuit. We were exhausted and half cooked after two hours on the open upper deck of the bus in the sunshine. It did give a good overview of the city, but I would not recommend this tour.

One of the most moving landmarks we saw was the Columbus monument. It's at the waterfront end of Los Ramblas. He stands high, maybe 200 feet up in the air, holding a map, pointing out to sea. It is as if he is saying, "I'm going afar and the world will never be the same because of it." Okay, the statue is actually pointing to Africa, not North America, but let's not mess with the story, shall we? I'm American; I know where Columbus' passion led. We have been in the Spice Islands, including three separate islands that lay claim to the explorer's first landing in the New World. I've even toured replicas of *The Nina, the Pinta,* and *the Santa Maria*, none of which were ocean- worthy, in my opinion. Tiny little ships, barely big enough for a lake! The courage of these early explorers has always touched my soul. I enjoy finding circles in life. I stand, as an American, at one side of the circle. Barcelona closes that link.

Los Ramblas

We rested a little in our elegant suite after the bus ride, then headed out in search of lunch. We aimed for Los Ramblas on the way. There were high-end shops, elegant boutiques, open air flower markets every ten feet, street performers, and interesting people all around. Walking in the sunshine was relaxing.

Our taxi driver who brought us from the ship to the hotel had warned us not to eat along Los Ramblas. He said the food was expensive and not very good. "It is meant for tourists, not you." Far be it from me to act like a tourist, even when I am 6000 miles from home. We detoured down a side street. It was just a few feet wide, barely enough for a car to fit. Different, but definitely charming in its own way. The buildings towered 6-8 stories above us, like an urban canyon. Obviously we were the only nonlocals for many blocks; we received several puzzled glances, and a few smiles.

French balconies at every window had laundry drying in the breeze; what is it with the laundry? Narrow balconies were on most of the buildings, wide enough just for one small chair, at most. The fancy wrought iron railings reminded me of New Orleans. The side streets had a different atmosphere, calmer, more local. The high-end boutiques and expensive stores and shops on Los Ramblas were replaced by cheap electronic stores with barred windows. There was a lot of graffiti, including "Indepencion!" and "Libertad!" This needed no translation. It felt like a genuine slice of Barcelona, not the upscale for-show section just a few blocks ago.

We lost track of time in our wandering. Suddenly, it was 3 o'clock and we were quite hungry. Husband was uneasy. At home, he admitted to a fear of tapas. Yes, I said tapas. Those are little plates with a small quantity of flavorful food. The word 'tapas' refers to the little lids that people put on top, as they wander through the streets, snacking and socializing. I know my husband is not real courageous, culinarily speaking; he tends to go for the familiar foods, recognizable things. However, being afraid of tapas is a weird thing that I simply could not countenance. Double goal: lunch *and* tapas.

We found a place to eat, with ordinary working people in it; the best kind! My Spanish isn't very good-- I have maybe 40 words – but I do speak Food, and with some pantomime, three plates of tapas and a big water jug appeared on our table. We had a prawn omelet, grilled chicken with chimichurri sauce and little roasted potatoes, and a plate of buttafucco, the spicy local sausage, which the cabbie had recommended. Husband and I happily shared it. He didn't flinch when the bill came, plainly listing 'three tapas.'

We ventured into Saint Joseph's market, the Bouqueria, which, again, is not where tourists go. I was enthralled! The colorful foods, some I did not recognize, all displayed like photographs, were so enticing! There were rows of local Iberico hams, so authentic, they still had the hooves on them. I hoped I misread the price, but I didn't. I thought it said €116 per kilo! a little bit out of my household budget! Sausages of all shapes and sizes and colors hung above the colorful stalls, most covered in tasty white mold. Cut and ground meats were below, including heaps labeled "100% Bovine." Oh, dear, what was the other ground meat made of? Perhaps it was just as well my limited Spanish failed me. Multi colored fruit juices in covered clear plastic cups were popular, I noticed, throughout the market. They are not big on refrigeration here, either. We did not buy anything, knowing that we could not take it home on the plane tomorrow, but I took lots of pictures and I was happy being in Saint Joseph's market.

At last, Los Ramblas! We had cut through it earlier, but now we had time for getting into the spirit of the place. This area is known for people watching, and I loved it. The atmosphere in Barcelona feels laid-back, relaxed, and people smile a lot here, more than we have seen elsewhere. We came upon another gelato stop. Well, gelato is not Spanish, but we were hot and thirsty and it sounded good. The flavors were delicious, as expected – I may swear off ice cream forever and seek gelato henceforth! Plus, the presentation was stunning. The man made little delicate scoops into the cone, forming a gelato rose. Husband's even had pink cherry sauce tips on each petal! These unexpected works of art were melting too fast for us to admire for long. We did take photos of each.

We stepped out of the cool gelato shop back onto Los Ramblas, us and thousands of people walking, walking. Suddenly a familiar shout rang out. It was Clint and Mary, right there in front of us! What were the chances of us finding them in this busy place? I doubt we could have found them, had we been trying! They were happy to see us. We spent a few moments agreeing the cruise had been marvelous, complete with lots of marveling. Clint and Mary mentioned that they were concerned about getting home, because their airline is scheduled to have an eight hour pilot strike in Frankfurt, the city where their homebound flight is scheduled for a connection. We four parted with warm hugs. I saw them make a beeline for the gelato shop.

Back at the hotel later that evening, I found the internet center. I had struggled to communicate with home the whole trip. Finding Wi-Fi on days when I had my tablet with me was hard, and I found the auto correct on the thing a needless annoyance. I hate it when electronic devices think they are smarter than I, and try to guess my intentions. I found myself writing ridiculous things such as 'we had dinner last night with a fungus leader', 'we explored the righteous moneybags today' and 'the marbles and bully mollusks are smelly!' And even after that, I'm not sure my messages actually reached home. I don't do well with electronic devices. I firmly believe they have personalities, and they don't like me very well, as a rule.

We opted not to use the internet services on the ship, for several reasons. It's glacially slow, very expensive, and crowded every time we passed it. At last, in the hotel, a full-size computer! Oh, with a keyboard in Spanish... Well, how hard could it be? I know where the keys on a keyboard are, after all, right? The extra keys made it a challenge. Many had squiggly symbols over numbers. Some keys had three or four symbols each. I never did find the exclamation point. Nearly every word I found was redlined for misspelling, but at least it did not auto correct!

I like Barcelona. I even felt safe crossing busy streets. Drivers here are so courteous, it startled me. I even saw several politely wave mid- block jaywalkers across! Very different than Naples, where drivers were so crazy that even crossing at a traffic light in a crowd felt like attempted mass suicide.

Is It Time To Panic Yet?

We had a fabulous laid-back, relaxing time in Barcelona. As darkness fell, that all came to a screeching halt. Back at the elegant hotel, I kicked off my shoes and flung open the French balcony doors to continue people watching while Husband printed out our boarding passes for our flights tomorrow. The plan is, we fly to Copenhagen, have a two hour layover, during which we must change airlines and then fly to Iceland, change planes and then on to Seattle. We had three separate flights on two airlines for two people. The plan sounded very workable when he booked it months ago at home, and we saved a few hundred dollars each by not booking it directly.

It took a while for Husband to get the boarding passes all printed out. The hotel has only one printer, requiring each boarding pass to be individually emailed to the desk, and several had to be sent twice, with Husband going up and down three stories each time to print and verify. I thought he was making good progress, there in the background, while I people-watched from the balconies, until he let out a shout.

As he printed out our boarding passes, Husband noticed in the fine print that, while we had a two hour layover in Denmark, the luggage check-in closes just fifteen minutes after our flight was to land. Uh, oh---how could we possibly deplane, find our way who knows how far through an unfamiliar foreign airport, locate our luggage, go through Security, and check our bags in, all in under fifteen minutes? And that's assuming the flight would be on time!   There was no way.

 Husband and I pulled every string we had.   I got online and began frantically hunting for an earlier flight, a train, even a bus—anything that would get us to Copenhagen in time to catch the connecting flight. Meanwhile, Husband was calling Travelocity for help. We had booked the flights through them. It took seven phone calls. We were on hold for two hours total, with numerous turnovers and great frustration, to learn that the only earlier flight was leaving in 40 minutes. The hotel is 30 minutes from the airport. The flight only had one seat. Not an option. If we are going to have An Adventure, it's better to do it together.

I figure it'll work out. If we can check our luggage, perhaps we can go home later, or catch another flight through a different city. There's only one flight a day directly to Iceland, but if we are stuck in Denmark; well, that would be all right. I've never been to Denmark before. Worse things could happen. It may require buying new plane tickets or maybe the travel insurance would help, once their business hours open. We've done all we can do, including ruining our only evening in Barcelona while trying to sort this out. We prayed. It's out of our hands.

People are hardly ever lost and gone forever. We would either get home, or we'll have a great story to tell. Turns out we got both.

Leaving Barcelona, Heading Home?

The day started out with another small serendipity; it's a day for counting our blessings and this was number one. Frankly, we needed one, after checking out of the hotel and being told that we had a €160 phone charge. That's more than the five star hotel price we paid. I will dispute that with Travelocity, if we make it home, because we were on hold with them for over two hours, in between hanging up on us repeatedly, and they were frankly no help.

We planned to cross the street and walk down a block to catch a taxi. There is a built in surcharge for picking up passengers on hotel property in Spain. As we crossed the street, a cab pulled around, backed up half a block on the one-way street and greeted us. "To the airport? May I take you?" Small blessing; we will take it.

We found when we reached the airport in Barcelona, a couple of things. The first thing was all of the signs were in Spanish. I guess we have slowly become reliant on the clip art signs that are all over North America. All of the Help Desk people only spoke Spanish, and if we're not discussing a menu, our Spanish is not that great.

We finally made it to the right airline line, after a couple of fumbles, only to find out that our flight reservations were somehow canceled by Travelocity during last night's marathon phone calls. We were able to get on the plane, only because the gate agent took mercy on us! She was on a phone call, apparently pleading our case, or a good ten minutes. We ended up three rows apart on the plane. I heard Husband chatting in Swedish most of the flight; seems the two women next to him spoke Danish, and there was enough of an overlap for them to communicate. Later, I found out he was telling them our troubles.

Once we were on the flight to Copenhagen, it was an easy flight and really pretty. There are mountains and glaciers below. I need to come back to Europe to explore a little bit more, focusing on mountains and glaciers and Nature. However, the pretty scenery did not really take my mind off the fact that Barcelona's laid-back vibe that I enjoyed so much was more pervasive than I would've liked.

Copenhagen, at High Speed

When we started out, we only had fifteen minutes in Copenhagen to get our luggage checked in, had all gone smoothly. All didn't go smoothly. This plane from Barcelona to Copenhagen departed *twenty-eight minutes late!* We were five minutes past the posted boarding time when the Captain and the crew leisurely made their way on, stopping to chat. I'm not in control here and so I really tried not to panic, but of course I reserve the right to have a full feathered come- apart later on, as needed.

Copenhagen's airport is enormous, with a modern design, everyone we encountered spoke English, and it is full of kind people. At that speed, sadly, that's the only impression I have. We landed 36 minutes late, way past the time the airline website insisted that luggage check in would be closed. All we could do was to do our best, and keep praying.

We certainly had to do our part, but very obviously God cleared the way for us, starting with the women seated by Husband on the flight. They wished him well, told him which terminal to head through, and then met up again at luggage claim to tell us which way was shorter. We ran into them a few minutes later; they shouted "take the escalator! Much faster!" Another bit of serendipity was that our suitcases were the third and fourth to appear on the luggage carousel off the plane at baggage claim, and that never happens. We grabbed them and ran, cheered on by two kind Danish women.

The line at the check-in desk had thirty-six people in it. Yes, I rapidly counted, and my heart sunk. There was nothing we could do about it; obviously, we would miss the only flight to Iceland that day. We joined the end of the line, hoping that if we could not check our luggage onto the flight that was going to leave very soon, maybe the agent would help us find another flight, another connecting city, some other way to get home.

Suddenly an airline worker in a uniform hurried to open up another lane. Ignoring the three dozen people in front of us, he motioned Husband and me to the front of the new line, without saying a word. We had been running full-bore from the time the plane landed, down the terminal, to the baggage claim. We had grabbed our suitcases and ran all the way to the luggage check-in area. With our bright red faces, maybe we looked desperate.

The agent checked the computer, and his smile faded fast. And then he brightened. "Wait, I have an idea! The baggage has already gone to your plane, but I will declare yours oversized and overweight and then you will have a *small* chance. You must hurry!" He quickly tagged our suitcases Odd Size and Heavy – they are neither – and shouted good luck to us. "Go that way! Godspeed!" Yes, that was the kind of speed we'd need to make this flight!

Husband and I took off running across the terminal to the Oversize Baggage ramp. My back hurt. My backpack felt like a sack of rocks. I wish I could've just chucked it all into the suitcase and not had a carry on at all. My backpack had all of my papers and brochures and maps and notebooks and electronics that a writer needs, plus things to pass the time on the long long flight home. I needed all that with me!

At last, we found the Oversize Luggage ramp. A friendly man looked startled. He beamed, "Oh, there you are. I was waiting for you. Next time you must stay longer in Denmark; we would love to host you both." I was puzzled. He was *waiting?* Why would he be waiting *for us?* The uniformed man took our suitcases. "You must run," and pointed, "Security is up there. All the best to you—now RUN."

Again we were off, running through the airport like crazy people. We took the Up escalator three steps at a time. Oh, no---my heart sunk yet again. The electronic sign at the top of the escalator said Security Wait: Nine Minutes. Our plane was to leave in eleven minutes, by this time, and we had no idea where the gate even was.

Oh, *Not* the South Koreans!

At the top of the escalator, we found ourselves behind a large group of bewildered looking South Korean tourists.

I hate to be judgmental. I really do. But in our travels over the years, both domestic and foreign, we've encountered the same group of South Korean tourists over and over. I'm pretty sure it's the same group. There's maybe twenty of them. They move together, en masse, like a giant well-dressed amoeba, and they are lost. They are *always* lost. They wave maps and brochures and plenty of papers, but apparently it doesn't help. They wander aimlessly, loudly consulting one another, blocking doors and entrances, tourist sites, and in this case, the Airport Security line. There were two Security lines, one for everybody, blocked of course by the unmoving South Korean tourists, and then there was the Danish equivalent of a Fast Pass line, which was closed. We were doomed.

Just as we reached the end of the line, a Security agent hurried up, rushing as though he was way behind schedule. Ignoring the South Koreans and other travelers, he motioned Husband and me to the exclusive line, turning on lights as he went. "You mustn't miss your plane." He smiled as he barely glanced at either our passport or boarding passes. He quickly scanned our boarding passes; that at least would notify the airline that we were indeed in the airport, somewhere, and on our way. The agent almost pushed us through the metal detector. I reached for the zipper on my backpack to take out my laptop, but the agent barked at me "No, no, don't bother, you haven't time. Just *go!*"

Even in my frantic state, I could not help but compare that Security scan to TSA. Had we shown up in an American airline airport, red-faced and sweating, visibly anxious and obviously running, it would have triggered extra scrutiny, certainly none of the compassion we felt in Denmark.

Only One Flight Per Day

Wait – are we really going to make the flight? did we have a chance? Oh, no, our flight was waiting at from the farthest gate in the terminal. Why is my gate always the farthest one? Who are the lucky people booked at the closer gates? This one was the very last one. It looked like a very long terminal to me. I was already tired from running. Somewhere along the route Husband had reached back to carry my backpack, but as we went through Security, he just took his own and ran on ahead, leaving me with the extra 18 pounds. I simply could not keep up. I ran as fast as I could, but I am an out of shape overweight grandmother with a fat and interesting medical chart and I just couldn't catch up.

We were still five and seven gates away from our destination – I could see Husband ahead of me – when I heard our names on the terminal's public address system, calling us by name: "please make your way to gate B 40." Not exactly a novel idea...we were trying to do just that! I know that meant the plane doors were closing. I needed an extra burst of speed, but I don't have a reserve tank of stamina. I continued to run as fast as I could, which frankly wasn't very fast.

I considered jettisoning my backpack; just how badly did I want the contents? Suddenly a rolling baggage cart flung itself right in front of me, perhaps from a gate. I did not see a person push it, but it was just what I needed and I was very grateful for this blessing. I chucked my heavy backpack into it and continued to run as I pushed the cart. I saw my Husband turned into Gate B 40. I hoped he could forestall the plane a few seconds more.

As my legs continued to run, aching, burning, my brain slowed down. I thought about options. Let's see; there was only this one flight per day. Husband could probably make the plane, and I would not. Would he go without me? This would be a minor problem, because I would be alone in Denmark, a foreign country, and I knew that both passports were in his backpack, not mine. On the bright side, I would be able to rest, to stop running, and wash my red sweaty face. Not a terrible trade off.

As I neared the gate, I heard a gate agent berating Husband. "Where have you been? What took you so long? Don't ever do that again!" I rushed up, just seconds behind him. The gate agent smiled at me, and pleasantly said, "Oh, I am so glad to see you. You have made it. Please relax now," as he waved us down the jet way. Husband flung a reproachful glare at the agent, who winked at me as he closed the door.

Amazingly, we made our way onto the plane, hearts pounding, dripping in sweat. Husband apologized profusely to the passengers as we made our way down the aisle. They'd obviously been delayed just for us. I didn't have enough breath, but I'm pretty sure the passengers could tell by looking at us that we had done our best to hurry.

On a flight that's not totally full, right before the plane backs off from the gate, passengers scramble to move to better seats. Our assigned seats were taken by passengers who'd moved around after the Go time. No problem! The plane was not full, and Husband and I quickly sat down in the two first available seats. They turned out to be aisle seats, which I prefer, one row apart, with no one at all in the middle seats... pretty much ideal.

I glanced back at Husband. He flopped into his seat and promptly reached up to turn on his air vent, aiming it at his sweating face. Without a word, his seatmate reached up, turned *his* air vent on, and also the one for the empty middle seat, and aimed both at my husband. We were on our way to Iceland!

There is simply no way we could have made that flight without divine help. From the cabbie who stopped, the gate agent who fought for us to get on a plane when our reservations had been cancelled, the airline agents in Copenhagen who helped us, the Danish women who shouted directions and encouragement, the Security agent *and* the airline agent who both opened a new line for us, even the plane waiting for us twenty-one minutes past departure time... too many coincidences to be coincidence!

I cannot believe we made the second flight. It was in flight about twenty minutes before my heart stopped thundering. I really am out of shape – maybe I should fix that. On the other hand, even with a fat, interesting medical chart, I was healthy enough to tromp all over Europe. I'm just not so good with sprinting through airports.

It was a four hour flight from Barcelona to Iceland, quite uneventful. For the first hour, I was content just to sit and breathe. I ached and I was so tired. Perhaps I overdid, suddenly running a marathon to catch the flight. The second hour, I read for a while. In the third hour, my seat companion, by the window, began to speak.

Icelandic Perspective

Turns out she was an Icelandic travel agent, as well as a tour guide. She gave me her business card. One never knows. I admired her business card and noticed that, had her name been just two letters longer, she would've needed to continue on the next line! I did not attempt pronouncing it. I remembered that in Iceland, children are named according to their gender and their parentage. By merely looking at a name, you can tell who's whose child. They are the either the daughter of somebody, or the son of somebody, and it indicates that right in the name. Thus, a brother and a sister would have different surnames, maybe "Joan Hanson*dotter*," and "John Hanson*son*." I held her genealogy on her business card!

The volcano that gummed up air traffic for weeks four years ago, Bardarbunga, came into our view. From that distance, it looked about five inches tall, and ominous. It was wreathed in steam, and belching dark ash. The volcano had been on the news all week, expected to erupt at any time. My seat mate insisted I change seats with her to see it better out her window. She politely asked, "how long is your layover in Reykjavik?" She mused, "oh...four hours...you just might make it out before it erupts." Okay, that was more imminent than I expected! Really, though, being stranded in such a beautiful place would not have been a hardship. As she spoke, I made up my mind to return to Iceland for longer than a layover in the airport.

The travel agent talked about Iceland in glowing terms. I was anxious to plan a trip here, after listening to her! Untouched Nature, waterfalls, glaciers, hot springs, hiking, golfing... quite a fascinating description! I don't even golf, and yet she had me convinced this would be the place to play.

Suddenly, her face crumpled. She sighed wistfully, "I wish I had been born in America. Oh, *how* I wish I had been born in America! In Iceland, you see, everyone knows everyone and their grandparents, and they gossip like a small town. There is no opportunity, no way to get ahead or to make one's own way. In America, the country is so large. One could go anywhere and be anyone; their choice, and no one to hold them back. Do you know how envious I am?"

Americans complain; we are very good at it, and sometimes we have cause. And yet she's right. America is a vast and varied land with unlimited opportunities. Across this whole trip, I noticed that in every place we went, people wanted to go to America. They all knew someone from their family, from their neighborhood, their nephew, perhaps, who had gone to America and taken advantage of the opportunities we take for granted. Sure, we have it rough; taxes are high, employment is low, the government is out of whack, yet people can thrive if they are willing to work and be flexible. We could do better!

We had a leisurely four-hour layover in Iceland. It was time to find lunch; thick sandwiches and juice. I opted to avoid the dried fish chips, which were in little bags right next to the potato chips. We did buy some rather fabulous Icelandic chocolate.

Finding our gate took quite a while. The Departures board listed numbers for other flights, but ours was the only lettered gate. We hunted end to end for Gate A! We found gates 1 through 31, but there seem to be no Gate A. Did it exist? Finally we found a friendly looking store clerk and asked where Gate A might be located. Oh, of course--- it was through the electronics store, out the other side, and down a hall, by itself. We never would have found it on our own.

The same procedure for boarding took place as on the trip over to Europe: onto a bus, up the stairs, onto the plane. Wonder how disabled passengers make it? Hard to climb stairs in a wheelchair! Again, the differences stood out to me---the Americans With Disabilities Act's effects are such a part of our everyday life in America, that when I encounter a hazard, I'm startled. And yet, it works for them.

The flight from Iceland to Seattle was long and rather boring. My legs were still aching from galloping through Copenhagen's airport. I had hoped I could sleep, but apparently the time zones don't allow night to settle in, going this direction. When we flew from Seattle to Iceland, we experienced a glorious six hour sunset. Now we had an extra few hours in the middle of the afternoon with bright sunshine. It'll still be 4:45 PM, daylight, when we land. We are missing night in Europe!

I had plenty of time to think over the cruise, the tours, the whole trip, on the long wakeful flight towards home.

I'm very grateful for the calm, goodhearted people who were placed in our way to help us today, and for the little things that are not little at all, right down to Husband packing the last minute things in the hotel room so quickly that I couldn't locate my makeup first thing this morning. As sweaty as my face was, it would've dripped off anyway. That's not a look I aspire to! I was glad he had not swept up the little Jet Zone jet lag tablets, which I dutifully chewed on the flight over to Europe. I can see where it'll take a long time for my body clock to reset at home. Sigh...we have another cruise in just ten days! Good thing it's only four time zones away. It's rough, I tell you, living with a Cruise Addict.

What We Learned

…and might have done differently: Some Final Thoughts on a Marvelous Journey

When I return from any trip, I always evaluate what we might have done differently, what we could have done better. I think the only things I wish we could have done differently—well, the flight home was a bit of a challenge – were minor. I would have enjoyed another day in Barcelona, and we could have happily spent another week in Sweden. That's it; I wanted more time at both ends of the cruise. We will happily go back to Sweden another time, and will take advantage of Iceland Air's free layover so will have a few days in Iceland on our way. It would be fun to take a train across Europe some time, to be able to see the places we missed, more leisurely.

I've seen European Union flags, as well as the flags of Sweden, Iceland, Denmark, France, Italy, Greece, Spain, and Turkey, all countries that we had visited, plus the Catalunian Independence flag flying, as people struggle to make their way, as people always have done. I wonder if this experience will change the way that I follow the news, day to day, at home. Greece and Turkey worry about their governments falling. Greece and Italy worry about the economy, taxes, unemployment, young people fleeing their homes, never to return. Turkey worries about the flood of refugees, and war on its very doorstep. Iceland expects a volcanic eruption any day. Italy *should*; Mount Vesuvius is very much alive, yet the people live in its shadow, as carefree as the people of Pompeii in 79 AD.

I feel expanded, broader somehow, connected to places I've heard of my whole life. I think travel does that; forces people to remember that the world is bigger than *my* town, *my* job, *my* way of life. It certainly has expanded my outlook! I will never hear of these countries again without thinking about the people we met. The tour guides who enriched our experience in so many ways, the ordinary people that we've encountered along our way, are no longer generic people, but real people with emotions and interests.

I was concerned about the language barrier, but we found it was only an issue in Italy and Spain, where we could not communicate much at all, once we were off the beaten tourist path. Even then, a smile and some pantomime worked pretty well. Denmark, Sweden, Turkey, Greece, and France all require students to have at least a couple of years of rudimentary English in school. While we were not always able to get our point across, at least we were not met with totally blank stares there! We found that most signs and menus have English subtitles, at least in the major areas. I was most comfortable in Sweden, where every sign, every menu, every placard was in both English and Swedish. In France, it seemed most people we met were anxious to practice their English on *us!*

The Barcelona airport was the most confusing place on the whole trip. Every sign was in Spanish —reasonable; it's their country, after all--- but I realized how dependent I have become on those little symbols everywhere! When they were none available, we ended up guessing. That was tough, considering we were already a little stressed.

We learned a few very basic words in each language. Please, thank you, toilet, yes, no...it made a difference! I found it surprisingly tricky not to mix them up, likely because we were in a new country almost every day. "Grazi" and "Gracias" were both met with a smile in Italy, but "Merci" just didn't go over in Turkey.

I definitely believe private tours were the way to go. As we zipped around in our cars all over Europe, we kept passing giant buses full of bedraggled tourists from our ship. We saw them in groups, wearing stickers on their chests like kindergartners. We saw crowds, even hordes, approaching, often as we were already leaving a particular site. We had arrived well before the busses, and were already on to the next locale when they arrived, due to our skilled drivers.

Our guides were out to make our time in their city as personal as could be. They were also very agreeable---if we asked to pull over to take a photo, or to stop at that fountain over there, the van stopped. Try doing that on a massive bus! We asked them to do what we wanted, plus show us what they thought we must not overlook, and we ended up having a fabulous trip. I think the fact that our group was relaxed and interested in them made a big difference; had we coldly ignored them, or treated them like part of the vehicle, the guides would not have tried to open up to us. Once they knew we really wanted their perspective, they were genuinely anxious to engage with us, to tell us about their hometowns. They were also very interested in America and in our viewpoints and in comparing it to their own homes. Over and over again, I was reminded that people are people are people, all over the world.

All the research we did on private tours paid off handsomely! Not only did we have a rich experience, we also saved significant money. By searching out private tours, we typically saved an average of 30% to 60% over the comparable tours offered by the cruise lines in each port. However, I know we saw more things, and we certainly had an easier time of it, being in a small air-conditioned van with our friends and a private guide, as opposed to being stuffed onto a crowded bus. It was nice to be able to ask the driver his opinion on what we should see, instead of going with a come-hell-or-high- water schedule. Who knows a place better, after all, than someone who actually calls it home?

Having our own private tour gave us flexibility in what we wanted to see and where we wanted to go. Being able to personalize our days meant a lot to me. For example, in Florence, when we were simply flagged out from all the other museums, our guide took us up into the countryside in Tuscany. When I wanted to buy marbled paper, our driver walked me right to a small stationary shop, where he knew the proprietor personally. We were able to dictate how long we would stop for lunch and what kind of food we wanted to have; in every case, our guides knew the restaurants well enough to recommend them.

Husband and I had a private tour in every port, except for Toulon and Mykonos. We spent only **$894 total** ---for both of us--on tours, and that included most entrance fees to museums and historic sites. We could have easily spent that much money in one day, had we taken the ship's excursions!

Of course, we did not have time on this itinerary to be able to explore every port city in great depth. There was a lot more to see, but if I think about it, there is a lot more to see in my hometown, too. Now that we've had a brief glimpse of what Europe is like, and found a cheaper way to get there, we will definitely go back. I would like more time in Barcelona. I would like to go to Copenhagen, beyond the airport, and England, Scotland, Wales, perhaps; definitely more time in Scandinavia. Europe is no longer a daunting place to me. I was uneasy very few times. Actually I felt safer in a lot of places than I do in my home country at times.

It was a delightful cruise with calm seas the whole time, remarkably! I think we had two foot waves, once. The Cruise Director kept commenting, "this isn't normal! There are usually at least two pretty rough days." The weather was ideal, sunny and warm, but not melt-your-body hot. We encountered two well timed, violent, fast-moving rainstorms; once when we were eating lunch in Turkey, another while we were in a museum, both done and gone before we exited. That's my kind of rain. We live in Seattle, where it rains nine months out of the year, and drips off the cedar trees the other three months. My opinion has always been, if you're going to rain, *rain* already, and then stop it. Had I been in charge of the weather, I could not have planned a string of more perfect days on this trip.

This is been our longest cruise, our most expensive, and it's been the best by far. My one regret: I should've taken a pedometer with me. We covered some turf! Looking back, I'm pretty sure we saw more, and did more, than anyone else on this cruise. It was all due to the advanced planning. When I travel, I have a great fear of missing something wonderful. Imagine how bad I would feel to go home from a glorious vacation and learn that there was a wonderful thing *right there* and I missed it. I know there was more to see, but with the time we had, we saw an astonishing amount and variety! We had a taste of the history, art, culture, food, society long ago as well as current.

The Amazing Race

One of my favorite TV shows is *The Amazing Race.* The premise of the program shows teams of two, having different adventures and tasks to complete, while racing to various places all around the world. As we traveled, I was startled to see some places that I remember from the program-- the boat turned youth hostel in Stockholm Harbor, the Altare della Patria (famous typewriter building) in Rome, the Vatican museum, the Spanish Steps, the Turkish bathhouse in Istanbul, along with the Grand Bazaar and a few others... one task even had them enter the Sultan Ahmet Mosque. The idea behind *The Amazing Race* is to get people to see that the world is a grand and glorious place with a lot of variety. Through it all, the teams that do best are the ones who engage local advice and ask for directions. They remind us that most people are basically good, interesting, and even willing to help.

I was reminded of that on this trip. Our tour guides were all professional and they were all open to telling us about their family, their home, their education, military service, likes and dislikes, making each city we visited come alive. Far far away in my home, at my own computer, we somehow found these people. Without exception, every one of them turned out to be wonderful. They really enriched our trip.

I have been awed by incredible art on this trip. Standing there looking at it with my own brown eyes, I did not believe I was seeing that, over and over again. I was profoundly moved by the skeletons of people from twenty centuries ago, amazed by ancient sculptures, architecture, buildings that still stand, huge grandiose basilicas, still in daily use.

For whatever reason, stones and feet stood out to me on this trip. Cobblestones and marble paths, worn down by millions of feet. Think of it; centuries ago, long-forgotten workers laid the stones. As time passed and styles changed, many feet crossed that place. Bare feet, Roman sandals, fancy leather boots, soldiers' shoes, laced sandals, worn shoes on the feet of travelers from many nations, medieval footwear, on to flip-flops and modern athletic footwear, even the preposterous high heels I saw in some sites, across the centuries, on the same byways, scuffing the same stones.

Think about what the stone walls could say if they would speak! The people that they've seen walking by; families across generations, government leaders, warriors, people whose names were destined to go down in history, slaves in shackles, societies in crushing poverty, others in great wealth, rulers and leaders bedecked in jewels and gold, peasants in rags. The battle of religions as Christians, Catholics, Muslims, and smaller groups jostled back and forth for the same territory, conquerors, warriors, ordinary residents trying to take care of their family as families take care of their children all across the generations and all across the world—to walk where they walked was astonishing.

I was startled over and over how familiar so many things were. I recognized a lot of the art and was delighted to be able to see it in person. I remembered stories of the history that I learned long ago in classes that I thought I'd forgotten. I think, as Americans, we tend to not be very much in tune with history. We are busy rushing forward, and often do not value the past. To be with people who literally trip over ancient ruins daily, and worship in centuries-old cathedrals in their day-to-day lives... they have a have a different outlook, a different viewpoint. They have not erased the shadows of their ancestors. Surely that must affect their future. It was really good to interact with them, to get to know some of the people on a personal basis, even if it was very brief. I'm going to remember this trip and the people we met for very long time.

A cruise vacation only gives a taste of an area. To me, the taste of Europe, the places we visited, the experiences we enjoyed, were *delicious*.

PART THREE

This is the nuts-and -bolts section. I'll detail some of the itineraries, cruise lines, and tours and how to book your own. The one part I'll add to the story itself is that we made it home safely, and our luggage missed the flight. It was deposited on our doorstep the following day.

Potential Cruise Itineraries:

Let's look at several possible cruise itineraries that we considered:

Celebrity Cruise Line goes to: Marseille, France, Villefranche (Nice), France, Florence / Pisa (Livorno),Italy, Rome (Civitavecchia), Italy,Naples (Salerno), Italy,Kotor, Montenegro, Venice, Italy , Dubrovnik, Croatia, and ends in Barcelona, Spain

Princess has two interesting itineraries on the *Ocean Princess*

Ports: Rome (Civitavecchia), Italy, Salerno, Italy, Nazareth/Galilee (Haifa), Israel, Jerusalem/Bethlehem (Ashdod), Israel, Santorini, Greece, Rhodes, Greece, Kusadasi, Turkey(for Ephesus), Patmos, Greece, and Athens (Piraeus), Greece

OR

London (Southampton), England, Barcelona, Spain, Corsica (Ajaccio), France, Rome (Civitavecchia), Italy, Florence/Pisa (Livorno), Italy, Genoa, Italy (for Milan), Monte Carlo, Monaco, Gibraltar, to London (Southampton), England

These sound great, but the rest of the group wants to go somewhere totally exotic. They wanted to factor Turkey into the **discussion.**

Royal Caribbean had a couple of possible itineraries on the *Splendor of the Seas*, seven nights each, both round trip out of Venice:

Venice, Italy; Dubrovnik, Croatia; Corfu, Greece; Santorini, Greece; Kusadasi (Ephesus), Turkey; Piraeus (Athens), Greece; Katakolon, Greece; Venice, Italy

and one that goes to:

Venice, Italy; Kotor, Montenegro; Piraeus (Athens), Greece; Corfu, Greece; Dubrovnik, Croatia; Venice, Italy.

None of the group was excited about Croatia, however, and the NCL Spirit seemed to go a lot more places in just a few more days. After all, once we committed to go that far, we decided to make the most of the trip, and seven days just seemed too short. We opted for a twelve day cruise.

We booked a Grand Mediterranean cruise on The Norwegian Spirit, **Norwegian Cruise lines**. It began in Venice, and went to Athens, Greece, Kusdasi, and Istanbul, both in Turkey, Mykonos, Greece, Florence and Pisa, Italy, Rome, Italy, Tulon, France, and ended in Barcelona, Spain.

Shore Excursions Versus Private Tours

Websites and Comparisons

As I related throughout this book, I am a firm believer in booking private excursions! This cruise would have not been nearly as fantastic without them! In a bit, I'll go over the tours we chose and compare them to the ones offered by the cruise line. I'll also tell you my personal criteria in going this route. First, let's review other alternatives.

Yes, you do have other options. You can take your chances once you step off the ship. You can hope to catch a taxi willing to take you to a site...but all you get is a taxi driver, who may or may not speak your language, who may or may not know anything about what to see in the area, and you don't have a confirmed price ahead of time. The driver may be very willing to take you to one or two sites, but odds are, they'll balk at running you from place to place all day. That makes your experience more limited, even before you begin. You also might worry about the return trip to the ship. Will he wait for you (and do you want to pay for him to do so)? Can you hope another taxi will come by right when you want it to?

You can take public transportation; it is cheaper than any tour. I heard the train to Pompeii was easy, but it took so much time that's all they had time to see all day. We were uneasy relying on figuring out timetables and schedules of a bus or train system in foreign cities, in a foreign language. Also, public transportation is almost never a direct route, so you must factor in the time wasted at all the stops before you reach your destination. Keep an eye on your watch, too; if you miss the last train back to the ship, you have a problem!

You can wing it. We met a couple as we neared Citivecchia, and asked "So, what's your plan for the day?" They mused, "Oh, we don't know... just see what's around, I guess. What is there to do in Rome, anyway?" They did not even know that Rome was over an hour away! In some places, "just get off the ship and see what looks good" works pretty well. For example, in Juneau, Alaska, there are numerous kiosks right off the pier, selling excursions to dog sled camps, glacier tours, and wildlife watching tours. Juneau is pretty small; whatever you choose to do there will be fun. But to be that close to Europe's history and not even bother to learn anything about what to do...well, that is flabbergasting to me.

You can stay on the ship. Personally, I don't understand why anyone would pay that much to take a cruise to a place, then opt to completely miss it, but I have met people who love port days for the simple reason that they have the ship pretty much to themselves when the other passengers go exploring. I don't get it.

You could rent a car in a port, and drive yourself. This obviously comes with no skilled guide, and you don't know the best routes, either. You may find traffic confusing, as in Naples, where I found myself wondering why every single vehicle did not show damage. Those roundabouts can be scary, especially in the larger cities; even worse in places where they drive on The Wrong Side of the road. . You don't know shortcuts, or the prettiest drive, and face it---without a local driver, you're going to miss a lot. Add in the risk of fines or citations for not understanding local laws...this is not even a close option for me.

In this section, I'll go over my thought process as I decided which tours to book in each city. First, let me list the pros and cons:

Advantages of Private Tours

First, Control. I *like* control, and flexibility, and personal attention.

On a ship shore excursion, there is a set itinerary, and it is not flexible, not one whit. In Ephesus, we were not interested in the House of Mary, which is a standard stop on ship-sponsored shore excursions. We substituted the Terraced houses, and had a marvelous experience. In Florence, when we tired before hitting the last two museums, our guide asked "May I show you the real Tuscany?" and drove us up into the hills lined with vineyards and olive groves, and through tiny towns, untouched by tourists. Loved it!

Some of the ship's tours included lunch, but passengers have no choice of food or venue, or time spent there. We told our guides what we desired---usually, local food in a non-tourist place that won't take too long, please. In every case, they were able to recommend a few options, and knew the owners personally! In Athens, our guide asked if we cared to see the Changing of the Guard at the Presidential Palace. Oh, yes! He took to a side entrance, with the same ceremony, but no crowd at all. Had we been on our own, we would have missed that. Had we been on a ship's excursion, I would have been lost in a crowd.

Also in Athens, after meeting our group, and seeing that we were really interested in the history of the place, our guide decided to change the order of his tour, going first to the Acropolis, and to the Museum later, instead of the other way around, as he usually did. That enabled us to get to the site so early, we pretty much had the ancient complex to ourselves. As we were leaving, thousands of tourists were flowing off hundreds of busses, teeming up the walkways. We had a much different experience! In several cities, our guides asked "what else can I do to make your day perfect?" then did it, including gelato and baklava stops and a quick trip to a pharmacy for aspirin. Try *that* on a bus. We were not disappointed once.

Efficient use of time. Because I had clearly specified our desires in emails to the tour companies from home, they knew our group's goal was to see as much as possible in the short time we had in each city. With just us and our friends, every stop was the right length of time. We never had to wait for the slow moving crowd to get off the bus for a brief photo stop, or wait while they blocked our way to and from any place. On a bus, the group is the crowd. Our group was small enough to zip in and out, allowing us to see more and go to more places. Think about it; even a 'comfort stop' takes a long time with 60 people in line to use a single restroom!

Private tours go where the big tour busses cannot go. Motor coaches are not allowed in the Historic Districts; they must park in lots up to 45 minutes walking distance from sites. That means you'd be tired before you even reached the place you wish to see! The vans we hired were able to take us right to the site's entrances, saving us long walks back to the 'motor coach parking lot" outside of the Historic Districts. You may not feel safe in the areas where busses drop off and pick up passengers. With my (lack of) sense of direction, I would worry about getting lost.

Fluffy descriptions: Read any tour description carefully! Be aware of words such as "brief stop" "photo opportunity," "drive by," and "look at" in tour descriptions. That's not the same as actually seeing the place! A photo op may consist of a ten minute stop outside a site, some of which will be spent fuming at the slow moving passengers in front of you, only to find your view of what you want to see is blocked by fifty-seven of your new best friends. A 'motor coach' sounds classy, but it is just a bus, with no guarantee of comfort level, air conditioning, etc.

Personal service. In each tour, we were able to engage the guide and driver in actual conversation, including who they are and how they lived. Each quickly learned that we were genuinely interested, and told stories and details the larger groups would never hear. No canned script for us! We came away with an intimate insight into the places were visited that few people get.

Cost: Our total cost for the two of us was under $900, for *all* of the tours, TOTAL, including tickets into the museums and historic sites. You can't beat that! The ship's shore excursions tend to be significantly higher. This is especially true for a group. A bus transfer to Rome for $69 may not *sound* high, but when you multiply that by your spouse and kids and buddies, suddenly, that is a wad of cash for just a bus ride! For the same cost (or probably much less) you could book a private van, fill it with your group, and have a personally guided tour, seeing more, doing more, and with lot less aggravation along the way. The tours in cars or vans offered by the cruise lines have shocking price tags--- who'd pay $2499 per person for a car for 6 hours?!

Safety. On this trip, we ventured several light years past our comfort zones. It was our first trip to Europe, after all! Having a local guide who also spoke fluent English went a long way in easing our minds. We could ask questions—and we did, all day long. Each tour company was licensed with the country's government. We had a contract with each, with the price clearly stated. We had read enough reviews to feel secure. When our guides were not right beside us, we had a clear meeting point and time, and mobile phone numbers to the van as well as the parent company in case of any problems.

Tours will reserve times for museums and sites, and often **prepurchase tickets** for you, or at least tell you how and what time to book online. The lines at just about every site to buy tickets were enormous, including a wait of over four hours to get into the Vatican! With our tickets in hand, we breezed right in, skipping the lines altogether, over and over.

You won't miss the ship. Some people fear private tours, because they are certain they will miss the ship. This is silly, if you think about it. These companies rely heavily on reviews by past customers. If they get a reputation for missing a ship—even once—they could easily be out of business. These companies are very conscious of time, including what time ships come and go into their home cities. In every case, our tours picked us up soon after the ship docked, and brought us back 45-70 minutes before sailaway. If you are really nervous, you could book a half-day tour, ensuring you'd be back at the ship with hours to spare. Of course, you'd miss a lot with this option; there would not be time to venture into Rome or Florence at all.

If Something Dire was to happen to make you miss the ship while on a private tour, such as Mount Vesuvius waking up, most likely it would affect other passengers as well. In this case, yes, you would have no guarantee the ship would wait for you, and if it sailed, you would be responsible to get yourself to the next port, after notifying the cruise line of your dilemma. We see the benefits to a private tour so far outweighing this very very rare occurrence that we barely factor it into our planning. In a worst case scenario, however, it's not that bad. The next port is not that far away. A quick plane or train ride is not a terrible thing, nor a serious expense. Plus, your travel insurance would come into play here.

Some passengers swear by ship excursions solely for the cruise lines' guarantee that, if they are on a ship's tour, they will get back to the ship. They do not read the fine print. Yes, you'll get back to the ship, but no one said how or when. Ports are like choreography; each ship has a designated arrival and departure time. In Athens, our captain was visibly furious when a container ship cut him off, thus delaying our arrival by twenty minutes...and racking up a huge late arrival fee. Ships pay enormous charges for their time in port. They are not going to risk fines and excessive costs by staying longer than their reserved time in a berth to wait for a few passengers on a random bus! Passengers on a ship's excursion may be sent to meet the ship in the next port by plane, bus, or train, at the cruise line's expense. That's another thing; to avoid this, ship's excursions tend to be considerably shorter than the time the ship is in port. Fine, if you want time by the pool; not so good, if you have never been there before and long to see as much as you can!

Disadvantages of Private Tours

It takes planning. You must do the work at home, long before the ship sails into port. The best tours fill up months in advance. Our wonderful tour in Florence consisted of one man, with one car, who did one tour each day a ship was in port. How good are your chances of snagging Giovani, last minute? We read reviews and data on multiple websites and tour books for each company we considered. We compared attitude, offerings, and prices, and in all but one case, went with the more logical choice. In Florence, I admit it was purely emotional---I liked the warmth in Giovanni's emailed response. Face it; in choosing a dentist, I would go with Dr Smiley over Dr Payne any time.

On a ship's excursions, **thinking is not required.** They give you a sticker, you show up, and spend the day being herded from place to place, on and off the motor coach. Decisions such as lunch, where to go next, to spend extra time at a site or to cut it short, to stop at that glorious fountain, to spend time shopping or see another church, are out of your hands. This makes me a little crazy; some people prefer it.

Cost: All but one of the private tours we booked required a written agreement, with payment made at the end of the tour, preferably in cash. The tour company in Turkey requested 50% deposit, which we negotiated to 25%, then the remainder on the first of the two-day tours. This is reasonable, especially considering they prepurchased most of the tickets for museums and historic sites. Some people may not want to carry cash on them in foreign cities. If you book a shore excursion through the cruise line, the price is rolled into your onboard account. Some might find that painless...unless they look at the numbers.

Criteria in Choosing Tours:

I'm really not a demanding consumer, but this was meant to be a once-in-a-lifetime trip, so it was essential that everything go the best possible way! Our criteria in choosing a tour company in each port was pretty basic. They had to be English speaking, but local. They had to be knowledgeable, not prone to wandering aimlessly around ports, wondering what to do. In that vein, they had to have a good itinerary, listing main sites we wished to see. Yet, they also had to be flexible, taking into account our groups' needs and desires. Many promised long leisurely wine-soaked lunch breaks with glorious scenery. Not for us---we were there to see and do as much as we possibly could! A couple of companies we considered seemed set in stone; not our style.

Our goals: see as much as possible in our limited time, focusing on history and culture, while avoiding time wasters such as long lunches, excessive shopping, art galleries and aimless driving. We needed to find tour companies that would meet those goals. Some came close, but we went with the ones that seemed happy to meet our needs. After all, they work for us, since we were paying them!

Price was a consideration; we did not gravitate towards the top of the line companies, nor did we spend much time scraping the bottom of the barrel. Several companies quoted prices even higher than the cruise line's! We did not want a stretch limousine, or a rattle trap car with no brakes. Each company described their vehicle. Air conditioned vans that fit our whole group were just fine for our needs.

Websites, reviews, and descriptions were very important. It's really all we had to go on. A few websites with pretty pictures but minimal description were quickly discarded. Ones that required every bit of information about us, including mother in law's shoe size, before even answering basic questions, were also out. We looked for websites with detailed descriptions and an air of confidence in their product. After all, we were entrusting ourselves to them! Several we came upon looked just a little shady, almost covert in their descriptions, as if we were to hand over a lot of money and take our chances. I'm not that trusting.

Reviews by past customers were very important. Having read thousands of reviews on tours, cruises, as well as many other products, I know that they must often be taken with a grain ---or a bucket—of salt. Still, they can be a valuable resource if you read them very carefully. Comments like "the guide walked so fast, we lost four people who had to catch a taxi back to the ship" or "we could not understand the guide; she mumbled and described everything as Just The Best" or " they changed the plans without notifying us"...those are bright red flags! Reviews that include comments such as "our driver was courteous and really knew his stuff," "our guide kept up a running commentary on the city as we drove, and answered our many questions" and " the tour company took us to extra places, once we expressed interest in them"---make note of those!

You'll also want to heavily weigh your group's dynamic as you plan any tour. Are you adventuresome, or interested in only paintings? Do you have children along, or older folks with limited mobility? Are you interested in nature, history, architecture, food, wine, local crafts, meeting local residents? Would you prefer a guided tour, or one that drops you off and meets back hours later? Are you interested in local culture, perhaps a visit to a resident's home, or are you happier in the main tourist sites? Do you need help buying tickets, or are you a do-it-yourself-type? Each traveler has different style. You'll be much happier if you identify yours early on in the planning stages!

Comparing Tours:

Some people have marveled that we could actually book a private tour from 6000 miles away, without going through the cruise line. Let me assure you, it's not hard! Technology frequently annoys me, such as when an unfinished email sends itself, or the auto correct on my tablet begins making up stories. But in this day and age, the internet is a terrific resource for finding tours in faraway places, and it's surprisingly easy!

We considered booking the same company in every port, specifically cruisingexcursions.com, which was recommended by our travel agent. In our reading, we found they were less flexible than other tour companies, and more interested in following a set schedule. Also, the price they quoted for our group for all ports was significantly higher than individual tours. There's also the risk of us not enjoying the first day, and being stuck the other days; unlikely, though. On top of all that, there were twelve in our group, but not all twelve wanted to take a tour in every port.

For each port, we did an internet search for "shore excursions" plus the port's name. Calling it a 'shore excursion' instead of "tour" or "day tour" automatically eliminated tours that picked up at hotels or the airports, or ones that extended over multiple days. These cater especially to cruise passengers, factoring their time and dates into the schedule.

Next we read the companies' websites' tour descriptions very thoroughly. On to reading past customers' reviews, both on their site and elsewhere. Tripadvisor.com, cruisecritic.com, and viatour.com are good starting points. Read the ones on the companies' own websites, too, keeping that bucket of salt handy.

The next step was to email each company, using the contact information on their websites. We declined to give our home phone numbers, just to avoid needless calls; we preferred email. If you feel better calling, go right ahead. Don't forget to factor in the difference in time zones; another reason email appealed to us. In the emails, we listed our date and time in that specific port, the high points we desired to see, our goals with regard to quick lunches, and seeing as much as possible, plus the number of people interested in going on the tour (this varied, right up until just days before we left, and all were accommodating).

The time in responding also was a factor, although a minor one. Several companies took days to reply. That suggested they were too big, too busy, or perhaps too impersonal for our needs. A couple sent instant auto-replies, something like "your email is important, and we will respond in due time." I'm not big on being on hold; just get back to me in a reasonable time, please. Of course we allowed for the time zones; when I wrote an email at 5pm, it was the middle of the night in Europe!

When each company responded, we weighed their comments. Did they seem friendly, flexible, or set in concrete? What amenities did it include? Tickets to sites, air conditioning, vehicle description? Were there any cost add-ons, not mentioned in the listed price? What impression did they give? Personal, or businesslike? How was their English (purely subjective; knowing our own language skills did not include *their* language!), and did they seem genuinely interested in meeting our wishes? Did they make any suggestions we had not considered?

There may have been another email or two, clarifying and/or asking questions. Then we agreed to book the tour, or thanked them for considering us.

An agreement was made, and a confirmation letter sent, like an electronic handshake, and there we were. Not a difficult process; you can do this!

I'm including these brief descriptions of ship's shore excursions just as a point of reference. They are representative of tours offered at the time of this particular cruise. If you have read this far, you will quickly see that our private tours covered many more sites---and we had more fun, too! Note that these prices are *per person*. Our private tours were *per vehicle*, divided by the number of passengers. Much less money!

Watch for key words: "photo stop, drive by, overview, view" means you will have no time to explore the places. "On your own" mean you get dropped off, with no guide, and a meeting place later on for the ride back to the ship. "Transfer" is just a bus ride, with no points of interest. And look carefully at the prices! The "private touring car" options are astronomical, for what is essentially a taxi!

Shore excursions on Norwegian Cruise Line   FOR COMPARISON ONLY

Splendor Of Florence & Michelangelo's David

$ 229/pp   estimated time: 9 hours

Coach to Basilica of Santa Croce, up-close look at the David, carved by Michelangelo. Main attractions in Florence are centrally located, ideally suited for a self-walking tour. Stop at the Piazza Michelangelo for an overview of the city. Visit the Galleria Dell'Accademia where you may see Michelangelo's famous Statue of David. Next drive by Piazza del Duomo in front of the Cathedral of Santa Maria del Fiore. Continue on to the Piazza della Signoria, the Basilica of Santa Croce and then walk to the Ponte Vecchio for a photo opportunity. Free time to explore further on your own or shop before returning to Livorno.

Florence & Pisa On Your Own

$ 119/pp   estimated time: 10 hours

Motorcoach transfer to Florence and Pisa, with an English speaking escort. Arriving in Pisa, walk 15 minutes to the famous Miracle Square to take pictures of the Leaning Tower. Continue to Florence, where you will be dropped off at a central location, and have approximately 3 1/2 hours to explore the city at your leisure.

Best Of Athens

estimated time: 8hours

Introduction to Athens' highlights. With your guide, walk up the uneven footpath heading to the Acropolis. Sights include the Propylaea, Temple of Apteros Niki, Erectheum and the Architectural Triumph of the Parthenon. As the drive progresses, see Constitution Square, the Tomb of the Unknown Soldier, Royal Palace, Hadrian's Gate and the Old Olympic Stadium. Lunch on your own. Drive along the scenic coastal road through some of Athens' most beautiful suburbs.

Private Touring Car (limited 2 Guests) Half Day

$ 399/pp   estimated time: 4 hours

Maximize your time, explore the places that really interest you. Discover at your own pace with the convenience of a private vehicle, driver and English speaking guide at your disposal. You set your pace and itinerary. Set itinerary 48 hours in advance.

Classical Istanbul

$ 149/pp Estimated time: 8 hours

This tour is designed to cover the major highlights of Istanbul and maximize your time in this classical city. Walk to the Hippodrome to see what was once the location for political struggles in the capital city of the Byzantine Empire. Visit the Hagai Sophia, a masterpiece of Byzantine architecture and considered as the 8th wonder of the world by most art historians. (closed on Monday) Walk through Topkapi Palace, once the residence of the Ottoman Sultans. Other stops in your itinerary are a historical mosque and the Grand Bazaar. Explore the exotic atmosphere for a brief period of time. Also visit the modern section for a presentation of carpets, leather or jewelry, followed by time for shopping.

Rome & The Vatican

$ 249/pp estimated time: 9.5 hours

A quick pace and substantial amount of walking is required. Orientation drive through the Eternal City, passing Piazza Venezia, the Roman Forum, the Arch of Constantine and the famed Coliseum. After lunch, visit the Vatican Museum and the Sistine Chapel. See Piazza San Pietro, that faces the largest church in the world, St. Peter's. Rejoin your motorcoach for the return to Civitavecchia.

Set your Own Rome

$ 2499/pp estimated time: 9 hours

Private Touring Van

This touring option allows you complete freedom to maximize your time and explore the places that really interest you. Discover at your own pace with the convenience of a private vehicle, and English speaking guide at your disposal. You set your pace and itinerary; itinerary required in writing 48 hours in advance. Just tell us where you want to go!

Magnificent Ephesus

$59/pp   estimated time: 3.5 hours

Visit Ephesus, dedicated to the goddess Artemis. Discover an impressive amphitheatre, the Library of Celsus, the Temple of Hadrian, Scholastica Baths, the Lower Agora, State Agora and Odeon. Return to Kusadasi for refreshment and a presentation of carpets, leather or jewelry.

Best Of Ephesus

$ 119/pp estimated time: 6 hours

Combine the most relevant sites of historical and religious values with a typical Turkish lunch. Drive to the House of the Virgin Mary. Explore the ancient site of Ephesus as you pass by the Magnesia Gate. See the Odeon, the Fountain of Trajan, the steam baths of Scholastica and the Library of Celsus. Stop for an interactive show and a traditional Turkish lunch at Ephesus Park.

Back in Kusadasi, stop for a brief carpet presentation and refreshment as well as time for shopping.

ATHENS   Private Touring Car (- 2 Guests)

$ 1199/pp estimated time: 8 hours

Complete freedom to explore the places that really interest you. Convenience of a private vehicle, driver and English speaking guide at your disposal. You set your pace and itinerary, just tell us where you want to go! In Greek ports, vehicles might be taxis.

The Acropolis & Archaeological Museum

$ 159/pp estimated time: 7.5 hours

Visit the Acropolis and see the highlights of Athens. Admire the Propylaea, the temple of Apteros Niki, the Erectheum, and stand in awe in front of the Parthenon. Lunch in the Plaka, followed by some free time to explore this interesting district. Visit the National Archaeological Museum.

MYKONOS ON FOOT   *(this is essentially a walk, an <u>expensive</u> walk.)*

$ 69/pp estimated time: 2.5 hours

Both the lifestyle and history of the island are showcased during this walking tour. You'll visit the Mykonos Archaeological

Museum. Continue your walk through narrow winding streets, discovering the town's deliberately confusing layout, designed to fool attacking pirates. Enjoy ouzo with traditional mezedes before returning to your ship.

Scenic Views Of Mykonos

(much of the town center is off limits to vehicles, but very walkable. Note the wording; "pass by" and "photo stop")

$ 69/pp   estimated time: 3 hours

You'll pass by Ornos Beach, one of the most cosmopolitan beaches on the island. You'll make a short photo stop at the beach of Kalafatis; experience one of the island's beautiful beaches and enjoy the breathtaking view. Head to the center of the island to visit the village of Ano Mera and the Monastery Panayia Tourliani.

Toulon Walking Tour   *(do people pay $20 an hour for a walk?)*

$ 39/pp   estimated time: 2 hours

Interesting walking tour starts alongside the main pier of the traditional fishing harbor. Admire the facade of the 17th century City Hall, the old quarter of Toulon and Cathedral Sainte Marie de la Seds, founded in the 5th century. See shady Provencal squares with moss-covered fountains. All the sites are within walking distance. Take some free time to stroll around the streets and the morning market.

NAPLES   Private Touring Car (- 2 Guests) Full Day

(this is essentially what we booked, except   many times the price, with room for just two people, and you'd have to do your own planning)

$ 1299/pp   estimated time: 8 hours

This option allows complete freedom to discover at your own pace with the convenience of a private vehicle, driver and English speaking guide at your disposal. You set your pace and itinerary, just tell us where you want to go!

Mount Vesuvius & Pompeii

$ 149/pp   Estimated time: 6 hours

For the adventurous, this is the perfect tour to correlate the disastrous eruption of Vesuvius and the destruction of the city of Pompeii. Learn how prior to the eruption of Vesuvius, Pompeii was a thriving city, teeming with rich people and ordinary slaves. See their homes and places of work during the Roman Empire. Hike up to the volcano's crater and see the rivers of lava where crevices still exude fumes and heat.

Ruins Of Herculaneum

$ 89/pp   Estimated time: 3½ hours

See the houses, shops, and baths, of the ancient city, offering a unique vision of their lives long ago. En route, visit a cameo factory nearby to see how the famous jewelry is made and then have some time to browse the store.

Tours Research

For each port, we read reviews and followed links, and narrowed the search down to a handful of companies.

Athens, Greece 7am-5pm

We considered:

   http://www.greektaxi.gr/shore-excursions/private-tours/

   http://www.kensingtontours.com/Travel/Tours/Greece

   http://www.shoreexcursionsgroup.com/Athens-Shore-Excursions-

   http://www.privategreecetours.com/

   https://www.pktravelgreece.com/

and ultimately booked with **https://www.pktravelgreece.com/**. PK Travel is a small and personable family-owned company, run by two brothers. This tour was one of the best! Dimitrius made the place come alive. He was skilled at dodging crowds and finding the balance between showing us everything without overwhelming us. We were very happy with this choice.

Kusadasi, Turkey 7am-2pm

Our main goal here was touring Ephesus. We booked a two-port tour with the same company as in Istanbul.

We considered:

Luxury Turkey   http://www.luxuryturkeytour.com/

http://www.kusadasi.net/info/kusadasi_shore_excursions.htm

Ephesus Shuttle   http://www.ephesusshuttle.com/

We decided to book *two* tours with **http://www.ekoltravel.com/,** both in Istanbul and Kusadasi. The price was very good, about $120 per person for two full days, including all entrance fees and a guide who was right with us both days. I felt much safer with a guided tour! Eklo was good about skipping the House of Mary and adding in the Terraced House instead, and even picked up the cost difference.

Istanbul, Turkey 9am-7pm

We briefly considered not booking a tour here, just using public transport to get from the ship to the main area, since so many of the major sites are just a few blocks apart. We quickly regained our senses---being alone in a very foreign place with no guide was too much adventure!

We considered:

http://www.shoreexcursionsgroup.com/Istanbul-Shore-Excursions-s/

http://www.istanbultours.com/

http://www.ekoltravel.com/

and decided to book with Eklo Tours, the same company we hired in Kusadasi. The per-person price for both ports was surprisingly low, and even included all entrance fees. In both cities, the tour had a guide and a driver. That allowed us to have the guide's full attention.

Mykonos 1-9pm

We opted to not book a tour in this port. It's a small place, after all! Husband and I did hire a risky local driver to take us to the high points of the island, at the spur of the moment. That became one of our best memories. Sometimes serenity befalls you, if you leave room for it.

Naples: 8am-7pm

Pompeii and Herculaneum were our main goals here. We also hoped to climb to the caldera on the top of Mount Vesuvius, and visit the Archaeological Museum in in Naples,; neither of which were offered by the cruise line.

We considered:

http://www.aptours.it/

http://www.naplesportshoreexcursion.com/

http://www.getyourguide.com/naples-1162/shared-tour-pompeii-sorrento-positano-t42152/

We chose to book a tour with **http://www.aptours.it/.** They had the best selection of tours for the price, and we were able to easily customize one to fit our desires. Italian law forbids being both a guide and a driver; we could have hired both, but found our driver to be well versed in the area, as well as the history. We easily hired a walking guide in Pompeii, and were fine on our own in Herculaneum. We appreciated the driver's flexibility as the volcano remained under heavy cloud cover all day.

Rome

Our group opted to book a private tour, due to the distance from the port and amount of things we wished to see. Priorities: Sistine Chapel, Spanish Steps, Pantheon, Roman Forum and Coliseum. Trevi Fountain was closed due to major reconstruction when we were there.

We considered:

http://www.romecabs.com/

http://www.citywonders.com/en/italy/rome/rome-tours

http://www.cruisingexcursions.com/groups.php

shareashoreexcusrioninitaly.com

https://www.romedrivingtours.com/shore-excursions/

www.romeshuttlelimousine.com.

Rome's tours had the widest price range. We chose to go with romecabs.com. With the port being over an hour from Rome, this was the best use of our time. Our guide dropped us off at each doorstep, and was waiting as we returned. At each point of interest, he gave us a good overview.

Livorno (Pisa, Florence) 8am – 7pm

We decided a private tour would be best, due to the distance from Livorno to Florence and Pisa.

Many people told us "Florence is not to be missed!" and "Skip Pisa if you have to---it's small and not much there to see. " With our tour, we had plenty of time for both places, plus a leisurely jaunt into the Tuscan countryside, and a good tour of the surrounding areas. Pisa is just three blocks long. We considered the following companies:

http://www.sunflower-tours.com/

http://tours-italy.com/florence-tours/shore-excursions/

http://www.papillonservice.com/

http://www.getyourguide.com/livorno-l427/pisa-and-florence-day-tour-from-livorno-port-t42150/

We ultimately chose Sunflower Tours. Our guide was so full of stories and history and obvious love for the area---Giovanni made the day wonderful! We were actually sad at the end of the day, as if we were leaving a friend behind.

Toulon(Provence) 9am- 5pm

The town is small; our group decided to have a day on our own, with no tour booked. Most ship passengers seemed to be using Toulon as a jumping off point to cities inland. By this time of the port-intensive cruise, The Cruise Addict and I were happy to have a more laidback day!

The Debate about Travel Insurance:

Our thoughts on whether or not to buy travel insurance for any cruise is based on the following criteria: how far are we going, how long we will be gone, how far in advance did we book the cruise, and the cost of the trip, all told.

For example, when we go on one day cruises between Seattle and Vancouver, the cost is about $29-$49 per night, and we never buy cruise insurance. It just isn't worth it for us because in an emergency we can afford to get home, and a full-blown crisis in a 24 hour cruise is pretty unlikely. By the way, if you are wondering why on earth anyone would take a one day cruise, think of it this way: it's a good way to check out a ship, and a cheap get-away! Where else can you get four meals, lodging, and entertainment for less than the cost of a Holiday Inn?

Sometimes we travel somewhere a little more foreign, distant, or where I don't really trust the medical facilities. It would be very expensive to be airlifted home, then we consider cruise insurance. For a trip as long as our first journey to Europe, being gone about three weeks total, and with as much expense and that distance... It's not up for discussion. Of course we bought trip insurance!

But what kind to buy? There are many cruise lines that offer their own travel insurance, but we thought that a third-party was the best way to go because it would be more comprehensive. For example, if we buy an insurance policy from a cruise line, directly, it covers the cruise exclusively. If we buy a third-party one, airfare and hotels, before and after the cruise, as well as other incidentals, would also be covered. If we had a sick family member, or missed a sailing, or even had a delay caused by a volcano, we'd be covered.

There are quite a few highly-recommended, reputable insurance providers. Common ones used are Access America, InsureMyTrip.com, and Travel Guard, to name a few good ones. Our travel agent (who's become a family friend at this point; we actually went on a cruise with him just ten days after this Mediterranean cruise) recommended we go with Travel Guard insurance. We found them to be inexpensive, easy to work with, and they cover pretty much anything we could possibly need.

Bottom Line: would we take another Grand Mediterranean Cruise? In a New York Minute! Right this very day, thousands of people are enjoying exploring the treasures of the Mediterranean ports. Don't let caution hold you back!

HAPPY CRUISING!

If you have enjoyed or learned anything from reading this book, please take a minute to leave a 5-star review. Positive reviews mean more than you can know! You can even be anonymous if you wish. Thanks!

Other Books By Deb Graham:

Tips From The Cruise Addict's Wife

Whether you are an experienced cruiser, or in the dreaming-about-it stage, you'll enjoy **_Tips From The Cruise Addict's Wife_**. Besides being crammed with more tips and hints than you'll find anywhere else, including how to save money, be the smartest passenger on any ship, and plan a great vacation, this acclaimed book is loaded with tips and stories that will have you laughing aloud.

How To Write Your Story record your personal history in 30 minutes a day

. No one can tell your life's story as clearly or as accurately as you can! Now's the time, before it's too late. In only thirty short minutes a day, you can begin to tell your own personal history, drawn from your own memories, using these easy prompts.

How To Complain...and get what you deserve

A customer's guide to complaining effectively in this day and age when customers feel like the low man on the totem pole.

Kid Food On A Stick

From breakfast to midnight snack, kids love food on a stick. This book contains recipes easy enough for a child, yet fancy enough for a party, all on a stick!

Quick and Clever Kids' Crafts

Loaded with easy, classy crafts for children and adults. A must for parents, teachers, scout leaders and anyone else who'd rather see a creative child than a bored one

Awesome Science Experiments for Kids

Simple, oh-wow! science experiments; a fun teaching tool for adults to share with kids, one on one or in group settings

Savory Mug Cooking

Easy-yet-impressive lunch recipes made with fresh ingredients, cooked right in your favorite mug! Expensive Take Out lunches—not anymore!

Uncommon Household Tips

Use ordinary items in extraordinary ways! Dozens of new uses for twenty ordinary household items you don't think twice about. From using golf tees to hang your hammer to dental floss for scrapbooking, you'll be inspired to look around the house before you run back to the store.

Printed in Great Britain
by Amazon.co.uk, Ltd.,
Marston Gate.